Key to symbols used in this book

Organisation Network

Ethernet Network

Terminal

Communications Link

The Internet

Bridge

Firewall

Router

Switch

Wireless link

Multistation Access Unit (MAU)

Repeater

Wireless Bridge

FDDI Concer

Mainframe/Mini Computer System

ATM Cellplex

Server

Tablet PC

PC

Personal Digital Assistant (PDA)

Laptop computer

Wireless Access Point

Light weight Wireless Access Point (LWAPP)

Wireless LAN Controller (WLC)

Multiplexor

MPLS/RSM

Ethernet Hub

Symbols courtesy of Cisco Networking Academy

5

Computer Networks

Philip J Irving

Lexden Publishing Ltd
www.lexden-publishing.co.uk

Dedication

As always, this book is dedicated to the special people in my life who made this all possible: Elizabeth, Victoria Rose, Philip, Margaret, Frank, Ena, Pat and Keith. Thanks for your help and support. Special thanks to Dave Nelson and Dave Ho for their keen eye and willingness to help and to Jane Lewis from Cisco particularly for the use of diagrams and images.

Third Edition published in 2010 by Lexden Publishing Ltd.

Second Edition published in 2005 by Lexden Publishing Ltd.

Reprinted 2006

Reprinted 2008

First Edition published in 2003 by Crucial, a division of Learning Matters Ltd.

British Library Cataloguing in Publication Data

A CIP record for this book is available from the British Library.

ISBN: 978 190499554 8 1

Printed by Lightning Source.

Lexden Publishing Ltd
Tel: 01206 533164
Email: info@lexden-publishing.co.uk
www.lexden-publishing.co.uk

Contents

Contents

Also from Lexden Publishing:

Title	Author	ISBN
Computer Systems Architecture	R Newman, E Gaura, D Hibbs	978-1-904995-09-8
Databases	R Warrender	978-1-903337-08-0
JavaScript: Creating Dynamic Web Pages	E Gandy, S Stobart	978-1-904995-07-4
Multimedia Computing	D Cunliffe, G Elliott	978-1-904995-19-7
User Interface Design	J Le Peuple, R Scane	978-1-904995-43-2
Visual Programming	D Leigh	978-1-903337-11-0
Get On Up With Java	R Picking	978-1-904995-18-0

These books are written for students studying degree programmes, HND courses and foundation degrees in Computing and Information Technology.

Visit our website at www.lexden-publishing.co.uk for further information.

Introduction
Computer Networks

Networking is a strange subject to study – it moves at such a rapid pace that it seems that just as you become familiar with the technology, it becomes outdated and is replaced. If we compare the development of Ethernet performance over the last 10 years to the development of cars, a car that could reach a speed of 100 mph in 1992 would, be capable of travelling at 100,000 mph in 2009. As is usual for the computing market, the price would also fall dramatically. In terms of cost, if a car cost £20,000 in 1994, the improved model would retail in 2009 for about £40.

Networking is the fastest growing area of computing and, despite efforts, there is still a large skills shortage. Results of a Cisco-commissioned IDC survey in 2005 (their most recent) showed that there was a shortfall of over 55,000 full-time networking staff across Europe with an estimate of 173,000 skilled individuals needed, which was expected to rise to 288,000 by 2008. The survey shows an even greater skills shortage of specialised network professionals (VoIP, CCNP, wireless, security, etc.). More recent surveys confirm this: "...the skill with the widest gap in proficiency is security/firewalls/data privacy" (*Comp-Tia Skills Gap in the World 2008*).

Which courses does the book cover?

This book has been designed for students studying general networking and will be useful to any course that covers computer networking. Networking is a huge subject and as a student studying general networking, depth of coverage is neither what you need nor want. Instead, this book provides a solid overview of general networking, explaining the concepts and providing you with enough information to study successfully at least six possible courses:

- EDEXCEL Computer Networking module;
- General Degree networking module;
- General Foundation Degree networking module;
- General "HND level" networking module;
- General Masters degree networking module;
- Basic introduction to Computer Networking a preparation for, or to accompany, professional courses such as Cisco CCNA or Microsoft MCSA courses.

This book is intended to provide you with sufficient theory to aid your understanding and, where possible, with some practical skills. For example, *Chapter 7* gives you the basic practical skills to analyse and design small computer networks; and *Chapter 9* walks you through a typical installation.

Learning outcomes

Almost all UK courses of study in networking are aligned with the **Quality Assurance Agency (QAA)** code of practice, which requires learning outcomes to be specified for each module of a programme and the programme overall. This book is aligned with this practice and, at the beginning of each chapter you will find details of the learning outcomes addressed. Overall, the book covers the following learning outcomes:

- To understand network principles, applications and VoIP definitions of a computer network, including remote access, email, cost/benefits, intranets, extranets and the Internet.

- To understand networking resources, including facilities provided, hardware, software, security, constraints, performance and licensing.

- To understand and be able to undertake the design and evaluation of computer networks, including the ISO 7 layer model, topologies, communication devices, popular technologies (including wireless), the TCP/IP model, capacity planning and network design.

- To be able to undertake simple management of computer networks – management of users, groups, workgroups, security implications and responsibilities. Elements of good practice concerning computer viruses, monitoring, estimating resource usage and connection to the outside world.

- To understand the basic principles involved in setting up a computer network including the basic steps of installation.

- To understand the need for network security and be able to evaluate network security; devise, implement and monitor security policies.

- To understand Wireless networking technology and be able to design and implement a **Small Office Home Office (SOHO)** wireless network.

Using learning outcomes to plan your study

Learning outcomes are intended to be assessed directly, and you must demonstrate competence in all of them. Be careful here – if you pass one out of two assignments with 100% and decide to skip the second, you will most probably fail as you haven't demonstrated competence in all learning outcomes. **The bottom line is: don't miss an assessment**.

There are two possible ways you can be assessed: either by an assignment/practical or by a time-constrained exam or test (TCT) . Your assignment usually comes first, and you can use the content of the assignment to cross off the learning outcomes it covers – in some institutions the learning outcomes covered are printed on the front of the assignment. Not every learning outcome is assessed twice, you will therefore have a fairly good idea what is going to be covered in the exam/TCT.

Networking has both practical and theoretical elements to it. Most institutions do not have the resources to allow students to set up a computer network or to 'play' with the equipment. As such, practical assessments are likely to be limited to designing a computer network, to producing a user guide on the installation of a networked operating system or to undertaking a capacity planning exercise. The theoretical aspects lend themselves to being covered in the exam/TCT.

What's in the book

In a nutshell, this book covers the basics you would need to know if studying a general computer networking module as part of any further or higher education course of study. If you are studying a specialist course (for example networked computing), you will still find it a useful study guide but will certainly require more depth in certain areas, which should be apparent from the lectures you attend.

Tips and tricks

The main tips and tricks associated with studying computer networking are as follows:

- Get used to memorising and drawing diagrams – they help you understand, explain and demonstrate your understanding to the examiner.

- Try to learn a phrase or saying that will help you remember sequences or theories (this book offers a number of suggestions).

- Try to think of an everyday example of the item you are studying (this book offers a number of suggestions).

- Ensure you understand the key concepts before you move on.

- Maintain a log book of acronyms and their meaning. Try to commit these to memory (*see Glossary*).

- Ask questions when you are unsure – your tutors will appreciate this as it shows your commitment.

Textbooks

Rather than specify textbooks for further study at the beginning of the book, recommended further reading is provided on a chapter-by-chapter basis. A general tip would be to avoid the large computer networking books if you are only studying the subjects at an introductory level – they are likely to confuse rather than help you.

Additional materials and resources

An additional chapter, *Revision*, is available to download from the publisher's website. This chapter offers advice on tackling assignment questions, marking schemes and sample multiple-choice questions.

To obtain this chapter and view other resources please visit: **www.lexden-publishing.co.uk/it/computernetworks**

Chapter 1
Introduction to networks

Chapter summary

This chapter provides an introduction to computer networks and networking. When studying computer networking, it is important to understand that it has evolved and will continue to evolve. As new technologies become available, the uses to which these technologies are being put (and can be put) will also evolve. A computer network can be categorised according to the geographical area it covers, as well as by the type of access it provides to the outside world.

Learning outcomes

After studying this chapter, you should aim to test your achievement of the following outcomes. You should be able to:

Outcome 1: Evolution of networks

Understand the way in which computer networks have evolved and the principal stages of this evolution. Question 1 at the end of this chapter will test your ability to do this.

Outcome 2: Two main types of networked computing

Understand the two main categories of computer networking and be able to describe the differences. Question 2 at the end of this chapter will test your ability to do this.

Outcome 3: Network categories

Understand and be able to explain what is meant by the terms LAN, WAN, MAN, PAN, VAN and VLAN. Question 3 at the end of this chapter will test your ability to do this.

Outcome 4: Intranets/Extranets/Internet

Understand and be able to describe what is meant by the terms intranet, Internet, extranet and VPN. Question 4 at the end of this chapter will test your ability to do this.

Outcome 5: Voice over IP

Understand and be able to explain what is meant by the term VoIP. Question 5 at the end of this chapter will test your ability to do this.

Outcome 6: Grid/Cluster Computing

Understand and be able to explain what is meant by the terms Grid computing and Cluster computing. Question 6 at the end of this chapter will test your ability to do this.

Outcome 7: Benefits of Networking

Understand and be able to explain the changes that networking is making to our world – it is important to discuss the negative as well as the positive aspects. Question 7 at the end of this chapter will test your ability to do this.

How will you be assessed on this?

Assessors want you to demonstrate your knowledge; they don't want you to regurgitate the contents of a book. By understanding networks and their evolution you will be better placed to demonstrate your knowledge. The subject matter of this chapter could be assessed on its own or it could be embedded with the answer to other networking questions.

Section 1: The evolution of computer networks

Computer networks have been evolving for almost half a century. Organisations have become critically dependent upon the services provided by these networks during this time, and today there are few organisations that could survive without them. This section traces the milestones in the evolution of computer networks.

What are computer networks?

There are many definitions of computer networks but they all have one thing in common: a computer network facilitates the exchange (and processing) of data (and information) between two or more interconnected devices (or points/nodes).

Early computer systems

The earliest computer systems usually comprised a mainframe computer that had little or no interaction with other machines (see *Figure 1.1*). The cost of this equipment was huge and so the time spent working on them had to be maximised to justify the cost involved. However, the processing power of these machines was extremely limited (probably not more than the equivalent of a contemporary mid-range digital watch). Programmers produced punched cards or paper tape containing code, whilst data-input clerks produced punch cards (or paper tape) of the data to be input into the machine. These cards were then taken to the 'machine room', where the computer was housed, the cards fed in, processed and the results printed out.

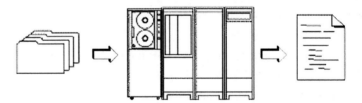

Figure 1.1: Early computer systems
(diagram courtesy of Prof. J. Tait, University of Sunderland)

These early computer systems had enormous benefits for the large organisations that owned them. Routine systems, such as payroll, sales and purchase order processing, were amongst the first systems to be computerised. However, the benefits they brought, although huge in terms of reducing staff costs and time savings, were limited because the programs and data had to be fed into the computer, as there was no interactive computing – everything had to be fed in via punched cards (or paper tape).

The code , used by these earlier programmers, was in a format that could not be read by other people. It was put on to punched cards or paper tape and fed into the machine for compilation or execution. Compilation and logic errors were then printed, and the programmers had to work 'offline' on these error messages, amending the punched cards and often rekeying the batch. Therefore it was not long before the demand for more interaction with the computer grew. Today, editing and recompiling code are done 'online', as a result of the development of networks, so a modern programmer's (or Software Engineer's/Developer's) time is used more efficiently than that of early programmers.

> **KEY CONCEPT**
>
> In early systems, all the equipment was in one room and was controlled totally by the computer operators. There was no connectivity outside the computer room.

Local interactive terminals

As computer systems developed, their processing power increased and they were given secondary storage (tapes, disks). This phase of development was important for the growth of networks. Although early computers had a main console, terminals were now attached to computer systems for the first time. Often in the form of a teletype (a combined printer and typewriter), these terminals enabled users to interact with the computer. The terminals were connected directly to the computer and were in the same area of the building as the mainframe computer (see *Figure 1.2*). These links were nearly always made using serial lines (RS232), which meant a limited distance (typically a maximum of 15 m or 50 ft) and limited speed, but nonetheless, they heralded the first computer network. Interactive computing was born, and programmers could now edit, compile and execute their code online.

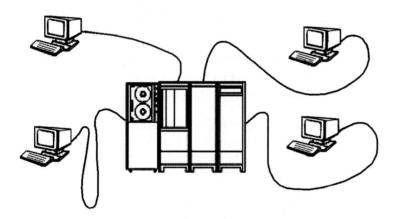

**Figure 1.2: Local interactive terminals
(diagram courtesy of Prof. J. Tait, University of Sunderland)**

Interactive computing also signalled another advance of the operating system. Previously, operating systems could typically only support one user and one task (single user, single tasking). Now the operating system could support multiple users and multiple tasks (multi-user, multitasking).

> **KEY CONCEPT**
>
> Local users could now edit and control the running of their own programs.

Remote access

As the concept of interactive computing became more widely known, people in other buildings and at other sites also wanted to gain access to the computers. A method was developed to support this – terminals were connected via modems (modulator/demodulators) and telephone lines (see *Figure 1.3*). These connections allowed the use of normal dial-up telephone lines as simple (but unfortunately slow and unreliable), long-distance computer connections.

Just as they are today, modems were used to connect the terminals and remote computer systems to a telephone line, carrying the data over a line designed to carry voice traffic. Hence, the modem carried out a digital-to-analogue conversion. The speed of these modems was about 300 **bits per second (bps)**, compared with today's typical speeds of 56,000 bps. However, the volume of data transmitted was not great, as these devices worked only in characters.

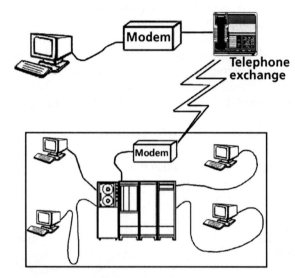

Figure 1.3: Remote modem connections
(diagram courtesy of Prof. J. Tait, University of Sunderland)

The telephone lines, provided by telecomms companies (such as British Telecom), were normal telephone lines in almost every sense – they passed through normal telephone exchanges and could be dialled up. Programmers and users no longer needed to work in the same building as the computer, and so many large organisations used this technology to provide terminals in their branch offices. For example, electricity companies provided terminals at their local branches and local authorities installed terminals in their libraries for automated library systems.

Leased lines

By the middle to late 1970s, many larger organisations had more than one computer and their staff needed regular access to data and computing facilities at sites other than their base. The scale of communication, as well as the required speed and reliability, meant that modem connection through the ordinary, switched telephone network could no longer support their needs. This led to the adoption of permanently connected long-distance lines between two end points terminating in an organisation's own premises (usually provided by telephone companies). Such lines could span the country or even the world. These connections are known as leased lines (see *Figure 1.4*) and are still offered by most communication service providers today, although, in practice, they rarely offer the fixed wire copper connection of previous years. Leased line networks were the first real wide area networks and were the forerunners of packet switched networks and **Asynchronous Transfer Mode (ATM)** networks.

Leased lines were analogue and, as such, still required modems. However, the modems and the links used were high quality and high speed, delivering up to 14,400 bps. The links were secure and costs were based on line rental rather than call costs. Usually, their capacity was far in excess of the capacity needed by a single terminal and, to utilise the line to its fullest extent, multiplexors were developed and added to either end of the link. The purpose of a multiplexor is to share the line capacity amongst a number of terminals. In *Figure 1.5* there are two terminals connected to a multiplexor. As the multiplexor is a simple **Time Division Multiplexor (TDM)**, it will share the time slot (e.g. 1 second) between the two terminals in short bursts. Therefore each terminal will get half the time slot, in this instance, half a second each. The multiplexors at each end of the line are synchronised with each other, ensuring that the correct data is passed down the correct time slot. In practice, eight terminals would be typically linked through a multiplexor. This arrangement was common up until the mid-1990s.

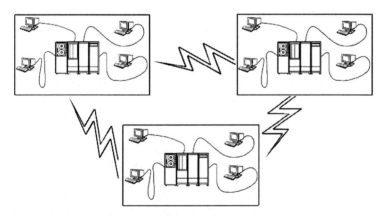

Figure 1.4: Leased line networks
(diagram courtesy of Prof. J. Tait, University of Sunderland)

Leased lines continued to extend the benefits that were being were offered to organisations by networks. Heralding the first, real **Wide Area Network (WAN)**, they allowed more access from remote locations (such as local offices) through the sharing of a private line. Utility companies and local authorities deployed such systems to give local offices access to the centrally-held information. It is important to note, however, that such access cannot be considered client/server (*see Section 2*) as the users are using dumb terminals (terminals with no computing power) – simply a monitor and a keyboard.

> **KEY CONCEPT**
>
> Leased lines provided remote users with high-security, high-speed dedicated links, which increased the opportunities for remote access to the computer system.

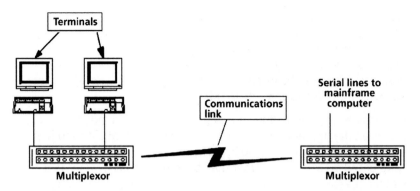

Figure 1.5: Leased line arrangement using multiplexors

Local area networks

By the late 1970s, many organisations (large and small) had more than one computer. This trend accelerated rapidly in the early 1980s with the availability of powerful (for that time) stand-alone personal computers (PCs) – a trend that continues to the present day (although now PCs are almost always networked). The method of access at this time meant that users needed one terminal per system, but demand grew for PCs to be able to access many systems (including other PCs) and to transfer files. This led to the need for a system that was capable of transferring data at high speed between different sorts of computers, typically located close together at the same site or in the same building.

This need was answered by the development of high-speed **Local Area Networks** (**LANs**), such as Ethernet and Token Ring. The mid-1980s saw the introduction of these in many organisations, but they were used more widely in the 1990s. These technologies bridge the gap between high-speed computer-room networks (parallel interfaces, etc.) and low-speed serial interfaces (e.g. RS-232) (*see the earlier section 'Local interactive terminals'*). They allowed multiple devices to be connected via a shared transmission medium (see *Figure 1.6*). Since their inception, a number of LAN technologies has been developed and, in the early days, there were a number of standards for LANs, including Arcnet (for the BBC micros) and the Cambridge Ring. As often happens, the market is dominated by a small number of technologies, primarily **Ethernet** and **Token Ring** (these will be discussed in detail in *Chapters 3* and *5*). The benefits of networks were further extended by LANs by allowing the interconnection of multiple computing facilities (such as PCs, mainframes and mini-computers) through a high-speed link.

KEY CONCEPT

LANs provided easy-to-establish, high-speed connectivity between any connected devices, but with limited distances.

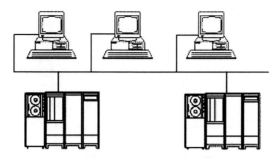

**Figure 1.6: Local area networks
(diagram courtesy of Prof. J. Tait, University of Sunderland)**

Quick test

Briefly outline the major stages in the evolution of networks.

Section 2: Types of networked computing

The main purpose of computer networking is to provide an organisation with services. Initially, this was for interactive computing but, with the introduction of PCs, the network has evolved to allow communication between PCs and also to provide services such as shared printing, shared disk access, etc. Networks typically provide these services to a client from either a dedicated server (known as **client/server computing** or **networking**) or from a peer computer (known as **peer-to-peer networking**). Networks constructed with a server are often said to have a client/server architecture, and those with a community of equals are often said to have a peer-to-peer architecture. Understanding these architectures is fundamental to the study of networking.

Introduction

All networked computing facilities can be grouped into two architectures:

- peer-to-peer networking;
- client/server networking.

Both architectures are intended for different uses and require **Networked Operating Systems** (**NOS**) support (now built into Microsoft Windows).

Client/server computing

This is the traditional model of networked computing (see *Figure 1.7*). Here clients make requests of a server (the diagrams shows a single-server system) and the server then carries out the request and provides a response to the client. This model has been in operation for many years and we have all probably encountered it at some point. It is 'full blown' networking architecture and is supported by all network operating system vendors, such as Novell and Microsoft in Windows versions since NT and 2000. It is also supported by all versions of UNIX.

KEY CONCEPT

The fundamental difference between the two architectures is that client/server architectures require a dedicated server whereas, with peer-to-peer networks, there is no separate server and the work of the server is shared between the connected computers. Comparing *Figures 1.7* and *1.8* (*see below*) you will notice that *Figure 1.8* does not have a server. However, the physical connections to the media are still the same.

KEY CONCEPT

With client/server network architectures, there is (at least one) server that is a dedicated machine providing services to the client. This machine may be unusable other than through one of its client computers.

13

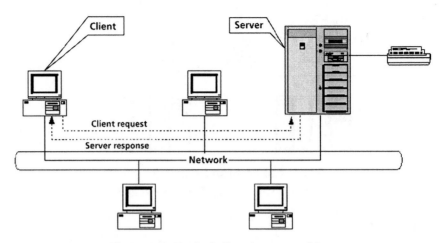

Figure 1.7: Typical client/server architecture

Key to this architecture is that there is (at least) one serving computer (the server) which provides all the client machines with the facilities they need – usually file and printer sharing. Although these services now might seem trivial, they revolutionised computing. Without a network, sharing files was a real problem requiring users to share a floppy disk. As can be imagined, many problems arise from sharing a floppy disk, the most obvious being the inconvenience of having physically to take the disk to the other user. Other problems include the compatibility and reliability of floppy disks and their limited capacity. In some cases, sharing a floppy disk is impossible – consider a gig or cinema booking system with multiple users trying to access the same file: could they really operate by sharing a floppy disk?

Specialist devices (such as colour laser printers or plotters) can be expensive and might not be used very often. By attaching such devices to a server, their facilities are made available to all network users, giving everyone access with minimal inconvenience.

As the client/server architecture and its supporting **Network Operating System** (commonly called a **NOS**) have developed, other facilities have been added. For example, users can now be allocated to groups and security can be increased through the allocation of rights to those groups, granting access to specific files or devices. Files can also be accessed simultaneously by many users (although locking controls need to be in place to stop two users updating the same record at the same time). Printers have queues, which allow a client machine to send its entire print job to the server for processing – thus freeing up the client machine's own processing capacity. Some NOSs work on different types of computers, allowing the machines to 'talk' to each other. An example of this is Novell Netware, which was available for Mac and PC platforms. Email facilities also require a central server.

Client/server computing has undoubtedly revolutionised computing and provides benefits which are desired by almost all organisations. The advantages far outweigh the disadvantages. The principal disadvantage is cost – with client/server computing, there is a need to purchase a central serving machine that should be fast and have huge storage capacity. Such machines are not cheap and this sometimes puts them out of the reach of smaller businesses – enter the alternative approach of peer-to-peer networking!

One other disadvantage of client/server computing is the reliance upon one central system for the provision of services. If something happens to that machine, access to all the information and to the services of that machine is lost. Therefore, competent personnel are required to manage client/server architectures.

Peer-to-peer networking

Peer-to-peer networking is a low-cost way of providing some of the more popular benefits of client/server networking at a fraction of the cost of a full-blown NOS. Similarly, its major benefit is the sharing of resources such as printers, files, faxes, etc. The fundamental difference between client/server computing and peer-to-peer computing, however, is that with peer-to-peer networks, there is no central server (*see Figure 1.8*). The tasks normally performed by a server are shared between the client machines themselves. For example, a shared printer would be connected to a client machine rather than being connected to the server. Similarly, data to be shared would reside on a client machine rather than on the server. Often all that is needed to establish a peer-to-peer network is the network cabling itself and a version of an operating system that supports peer-to-peer networking (e.g. Windows 3.11, 95, 98, 2000, XP, Vista, etc.).

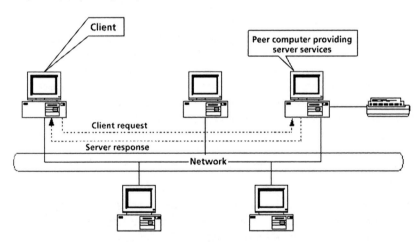

Figure 1.8: A typical peer-to-peer network

Peer-to-peer networks obtain their name from the fact that while each machine is being used by a user (a client), it may also be serving another computer (therefore acting as a server). Thus the conventional terms 'client' or 'server' are not applicable as the machines are a community of 'equals' (peers) in this network. As there is no requirement for an expensive server and the machines usually have the appropriate software installed, peer-to-peer networking is a low-cost solution for smaller businesses or isolated pockets in large organisations. As this type of networking is often found in small offices and homes, it is sometimes referred to as **Small Office Home Office (SOHO)** networking.

With peer-to-peer networking, it is the method of accessing resources that differs from client/server networking. In peer-to-peer networking, there's no server, and access to files, printers and other resources is provided by the peer machines.

Microsoft recommends a maximum of ten machines in a peer-to-peer network.

Whilst it is possible to have a peer-to-peer network of large servers (e.g. UNIX servers), this is not the generally-held definition of peer-to-peer networking and certainly not what is meant here. Peer-to-peer networking is really only suitable for small installations. Microsoft recommends a maximum of ten computers. If there are more computers than the recommended maximum, not only is it likely that throughput deteriorate, but also the general performance of the machines will suffer. It is not possible to give an exact figure because it depends upon how the computers are being used – if lots of disk sharing and file sharing happens, performance issues may arise with only four computers. Conversely, if there is little sharing of devices, both the network and the computers might operate satisfactorily with up to ten or more machines.

The vendors of peer-to-peer network operating systems have made their set-up very simple, thus avoiding the need for specialist network management skills. Overall, peer-to-peer networks are particularly useful to smaller organisations that wish to try out networking on a small scale or to larger organisations wishing to solve small problems. Usually there is little or no planning; such environments are usually fairly stable in terms of the user base; and peer-to-peer networks are only used for sharing a few resources. Examples would be a Managing Director and a Personal Assistant (PA) in a large organisation who link their machines to transfer data (files, letters, reports, etc.); small office computing (e.g. a small law firm or a small estate agent who require file and printer sharing) and more commonly sharing an Internet connection and printers in the home. Whilst encouraging the existence of isolated pockets in large organisations is not recommended, peer-to-peer networking can sometimes help provide limited connectivity as a stop-gap measure until the IT department is able to connect all the users. Small businesses, on the other hand, can use peer-to-peer networking whilst they expand and grow. The relatively low start-up costs, however, must be weighed against the possibilities for limited expansion, although investment in a company's peer-to-peer technology would not necessarily be lost when it reaches a sufficient size to expand into a full client/server situation.

Peer-to-peer networking has many advantages for the small organisation, but it also has its disadvantages. In a client/server network, the server is a powerful machine, reflecting the amount of work it does. If a peer-to-peer network is installed, the processing normally associated with a server has to be undertaken by the client machines themselves. This means that, as well as processing the task in hand, the machine must also undertake additional processing at someone else's request. Ultimately, this results in an overall degradation in the machine's performance.

Security is also an issue. Whilst peer-to-peer NOS manufacturers have made setting up these networks relatively easy, they have placed security in the hands of inexperienced users who might be unaware of the consequences of their actions. Therefore, there are often glaring security gaps in such installations.

The random distribution of resources can be a further problem with peer-to-peer networking. If the data is shared among many machines and one fails or cannot be started, it can be difficult to predict the consequences of such failure. For example, peer-to-peer networking often won't begin until a certain user has logged into his or her computer. Imagine a situation in a small business where someone powers off his or her PC on a Friday evening before going on holiday for two weeks. If that machine cannot be started without the password, no one in the organisation can access the data on it. If the data is payroll information, staff might not be paid until the user returns from holiday. For security reasons, however, the password should not be shared.

Summary

Both client/server networking and peer-to-peer networking have their advantages and disadvantages and careful consideration should be given to these when choosing the correct networking system for an organisation. It is always best to choose client/server architecture unless there are compelling reasons for choosing a peer-to-peer network. It is also important to note that both architectures need a network technology (cables, cards, etc.) to operate on (technologies are covered in *Chapter 5*).

Quick test

Briefly list the differences between client/server network and peer-to-peer network architectures.

Section 3: Network categories

Networks can be classified into five distinct types, although the boundaries between these types are somewhat blurred. This section reviews the different categories of network and identifies the key differences between them.

Introduction

Networks are often classified into five types depending upon the geographical area they cover and according to other distinguishing factors. It is necessary to understand the differences between them in terms of performance, geographic coverage, limitations of connection speed and degree of choice in the service provided, etc. The five common categories are:

- **Local Area Networks (LANs)**;
- **Metropolitan Area Networks (MANs)**;
- **Wide Area Networks (WANs)**;
- **Personal Area Networks (PANs)**;
- **Vehicular Area Networks (VANs)**.

Local Area Network (LAN)

LANs cover, with the exception of PANs, the smallest geographical area for networks. Despite this fact, they are the widely used, and LANs often have hundreds, if not thousands, of connections. LANs, as their name suggests, are intended to be local and small, although now this is not necessarily the case. When this type of network was first devised, a typical LAN would have been a classroom, an office or, at most, a small number of offices. Now LANs cover entire floors or even entire buildings, and with buildings such as universities, colleges and call centres, that can be a lot of connections!

LANs usually offer the highest speed of all network types as the media used in such networks are controlled by the organisations themselves and so, any constraints on the implementation of the technology are the responsibility of the organisations. For example, an organisation in the middle of the countryside is free to implement whatever media it desires for its LAN: it simply needs to buy the necessary equipment and install it. It could also have whatever speed LAN is supported by current technology. Should the organisation wish to connect to a telecommunications provider (e.g. BT), the speed of such a connection would have to be within the range offered by the provider, which, in some parts of the countryside, is likely to be limited.

Virtual Local Area Networks (VLANs)

Often, an organisation wishes to subdivide its LAN – for example, the accounts or personnel department may wish to keep its network secure whilst still being connected to the organisational LAN. This can be achieved using VLANs. VLAN technology is a by-product of switching technology (see Chapter 6), allowing a LAN to be subdivided into several virtual LANs. There is no difference in the physical structure of the LAN, but the switches deployed are configured to segregate traffic. Figure 1.9 shows a typical VLAN configuration. Here the network is divided into three separate VLANs. As with a normal LAN, the data passes through the organisation's backbone, but using this configuration, it is tagged, identifying the VLAN to which it belongs. Data is only distributed within the VLAN, which provides greater security.

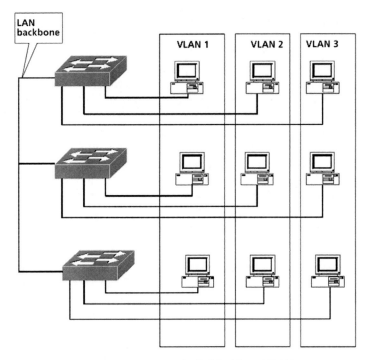

Figure 1.9: Network divided into VLANs

VLANs can be configured in one of three ways:

- Making the switch port a member of the VLAN. Thus any computer plugged into the port will become a member of that VLAN. This is known as a **port centric**.

- Via the **MAC address** (*see Chapter 3*). Each machine has a unique address (called the MAC address). This can be used to determine VLAN membership. Thus VLAN membership is determined by the computer's MAC address, irrespective of the port to which it is connected. This is more secure than port centric as a potential hacker would need to gain access to a computer that is a member of the VLAN. This type of configuration is known as **dynamic**.

- Based on the users login – **Identity Based Networking Services** (**IBNS**). Here an **Authentication, Authorisation and Accounting** (**AAA**) server is queried with the user's login details. For a successful query, the server then responds (to the switch) with the appropriate VLAN information. This is becoming increasingly common (*see Chapter 12*) especially with wireless networks (*see Chapter 9*).

TIPS & ADVICE

Not all switches support VLANs – they are typically only supported by high-end managed switches such as the Cisco 2960 series.

KEY CONCEPT

MANs occupy the area between LANs and WANs (*see below*). They can be contained within an organisation's site or they may be a regional resource. They generally operate on lines leased from a communications provider and hence operate at a lower speed than a LAN.

Metropolitan Area Networks (MANs)

Metropolitan Area Networks (**MANs**) are defined by **IEEE 802-2001**; they are larger than LANs, yet they are contained within a defined geographical area. A good example of a MAN is a university's campus network where several buildings are connected together across a city or town or where several universities or colleges are connected across a region. The media used in a MAN may be within the jurisdiction of the organisation itself or may belong to one or more telecomms providers (in which case the speed may be restricted). The overriding factor in determining which company provides the media, however, is cost. Although UK law currently allows for any organisation to lay its own cables, the cost of doing so safely and without risk to the public is high. The longer the cable run, the more expensive this becomes, and so it is often cheaper to contract with a telecomms provider who can provide the link at a lower cost.

MANs frequently don't belong to a single organisation but are a city or regional resource. An example of this is the **NORthern Metropolitan Area Network** (**NORman**), which is a network in the north east of England linking together the universities in the area and providing them with a very high-speed Internet connection. MANs usually run at a slower speed than LANs. However, they span a larger geographic area than LANs; usually use the services of a telecomms provider; and are usually managed and maintained jointly by both the organisation and the telecomms provider. Occasionally, they can be the sole responsibility of the organisation.

TIPS & ADVICE

One of the most common mistakes made by students is to forget that networks are measured in megabits per second (Mbps) and that data is measured in megabytes (MB). There are 8 bits in a byte and failure to work in bits rather than bytes puts your calculations out by a factor of 8. Thus 1 MB of data to be transferred is 8 Mb.

Wide Area Networks (WANs)

WANs cover a geographical area beyond that of a MAN – perhaps all an organisation's offices in a country or even beyond national boundaries (a good example would be a multinational organisation with offices in different countries). WANs are almost always dependent upon telecomms providers, as the length of the media runs are huge and prohibitively expensive.

As WANs are dependent upon telecomms providers, the speed of the link is likely to be limited compared with a MAN or a LAN and the costs significantly higher. In general, organisations lease a WAN connection from the telecoms provider for a fixed annual charge. This charge will vary depending upon factors such as the distance covered by the WAN link, the facilities at the telephone exchange etc. Normally there will also be an installation cost. This cost generally depends upon the distance from the end points of the link to the local telephone exchange and the facilities in that exchange. Due to these varying factors, a standard formula for pricing is not available and individual cases will require a quotation from the telecoms provider.

Until 1998, the fastest link available externally was only about 2 Mbps, and this speed (or slower) can still be encountered in many parts of the world where a WAN may have to make a link. Maintenance of the WAN is shared between the organisation and the telecomms provider. When selecting a WAN link, it is important to ensure that the provider will correct any faults in a timely manner – especially if the organisation is critically dependent upon the link.

TIPS & ADVICE

Just as a chain is only as strong as its weakest link, so the speed of a network is usually only as fast as its slowest link – thoroughly research the areas where you wish to deploy a WAN.

Personal Area Networks (PANs)

The PAN category started in approximately 2000. PANs are intended to link personal computing devices such as **Personal Digital Assistants (PDAs)**, mobile phones and laptops within a personal area – the absolute maximum is usually 10 metres, although 100 metres is now possible with some device classes. PANs are intended to remove the wires we all carry to link devices by utilising a wireless network. Each of the devices is fitted with a radio communications card (working in Ghz), which allows it to communicate with several other devices simultaneously. One of the better known PAN technologies is **Bluetooth**. Bluetooth is a consortium of manufacturers that developed a worldwide standard that allows connection of compliant devices. More information can be found at **www.bluetooth.com**.

Bluetooth has enjoyed a rapid take-up and is used in a wide range of devices, including mobile phones (handsets and headsets), digital video cameras and digital cameras as well as PDAs and laptops. Indeed, some car manufacturers have built in Bluetooth mobile phone connections. One of the likely limiting factors to Bluetooth is its speed. In 2009, Bluetooth operated at a maximum 3 Mbps.

In 2005, the **USB Alliance** (**www.usb.org**) launched a wireless USB standard 'for next generation consumer electronic devices'. Speeds quoted are 480 Mbps at 3 metres and 110 Mbps at 10 metres. Given the vastly superior speeds offered, the relatively low take-up is surprising.

Vehicular Area Networks (VANs)

The VAN category started in approximately 2004. VANs are usually wireless networks whose reach is bounded by the vehicle in which they are deployed. For example, in the UK, Virgin and GNER trains have wireless LANs that are available to train passengers throughout their journey.

As the travelling public demand Internet access, VANs are sure to become commonplace on aircraft as well as buses and other forms of public transport.

Technically, VANs are just wireless networks (*see Chapter 9*) that are available within a vehicle. The wireless access point is located somewhere within the vehicle maintaining the connection for those travelling inside the vehicle. The actual connection to the Internet is made separately from the vehicle using a variety of technologies.

Summary

The five types of networking are important as they represent the key attributes of that particular type of network. For example, if we are talking about a LAN, we would expect it to be under the control of the organisation, be of high speed and be limited to the size of the building. Knowing these types of network greatly assists the learning of computer networks.

Quick test

Briefly compare and contrast the five main categories of networking.

Section 4: Intranets/Internet/Extranets

Networks are also classified according to their connection to the 'general public'. Categorised as intranets, the Internet and extranets, this classification can be used to determine whether access to the network is from a closed group or from all groups.

Intranet

Intranets are networks that provide the facilities we have come to expect from the World Wide Web, such as web pages, file transfer, form filling, etc., but they only provide these to a closed group. Access is normally controlled by a password. For example, the XYZ Widget Company may have several sales executives who travel to meet with customers. To support these executives, the company wants them to have access to production schedules, customer information and costing details. If they had been based in the company offices, the network would provide them with this information. As the information will constantly change, it isn't feasible to continuously send them disks containing the information. The dilemma is that they need the facilities of the network but they need them outside the building. Using the Internet would solve the physical problem, but the data is confidential.

This is an ideal candidate for an intranet – the executives can go to the company's website and then select the private area (or a more secure method is to have a separate URL that isn't advertised). The executives are authenticated in some way and then allowed access to the sensitive data contained in the site.

The name 'intranet' is sometimes used to describe an 'internal' Internet, based upon files that are only open to users of the company's LAN. Although this is not exactly what is meant by the term intranet – which is providing web facilities to a closed group – it can be regarded as an intranet.

Most colleges and universities have intranets to support learning.

Typically, access to an intranet is based on either:

Authentication – user enters username and password. This means the user always has to login but can be used both on and off site/campus.

IP address – access is limited to a given range of IP addresses (perhaps those of a college or university). This means users don't have to login but access will only be on site/campus.

Virtual Private Networks (VPNs)

Whilst the facilities provided by intranets are extremely useful, there is a potential security risk in that the data can be 'eavesdropped' as it travels across the Internet. VPNs offer a solution to this potential problem by encrypting the data before it travels across the Internet. VPNs are set up by configuring the roaming machine as a VPN client, and a machine in the organisation as a VPN server (specialist hardware is available to act as a VPN server, but this task can also be undertaken by a Windows server operating system from Windows 2000 server onwards or a third party package).

Once configured, the roaming machine can contact the VPN server through the Internet in a conventional manner. Once connected, the VPN server and client go into a predetermined encryption mode and the data is sent between the two in an encrypted format. Once received by the VPN server, the data is decrypted and passed on to the organisational LAN (*see Figure 1.10*). At this point, the data from the roaming machine has an identity inside the organisation, giving it access to the organisational LAN.

When sent back to the roaming client, the data passes through the VPN server where it is encrypted before being passed on to the Internet. Upon receipt, the client decrypts the data for presentation to the user. This is a standard feature of Windows from 2000 onwards and can be found in Network Connections (*see Windows Help*), although a specialist hardware solution is more robust.

As organisations adopt cost-saving measures (particularly in the 2009 economic climate), VPNs offer the opportunity for substantial cost savings by replacing WAN connections with site-to-site VPNs across the Internet.

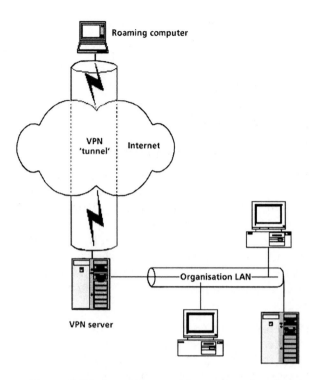

Figure 1.10: Roaming machine contacting the organisational LAN through a VPN

Internet

The word 'Internet' is an abbreviation of internetwork – literally meaning a 'network of interconnected networks' – a definition that can be applied to many networks that could be part of the Internet or independent of it. Thus the Internet we all know (i.e. carrying web traffic) is effectively a worldwide internetwork of networks.

An example of an internetwork is a college or university that has a large number of network connections. An internetwork can be compared to a road; the more users who use it, the more congested it becomes and the slower everything runs. To ease such problems, the number of machines connected to a network is restricted and divided up into several, smaller networks. To provide the same functionality, the networks have to be 'internetworked' together, thus forming an Internet. In a large college or university, this internetwork is likely to comprise many smaller networks and can itself be connected to the Internet.

The Internet itself, when conceived, was a network of networks. Designed by the **Advanced Research Projects Agency** (**ARPA**) of the US **Department of Defense** (**DoD**) in the 1960s, the Internet was developed to span military bases across the world and to connect their networks. It needed to be robust and to be able to operate in the event of a nuclear strike. It was later extended to those organisations that worked with the DoD – e.g. universities and suppliers. As the Internet became more widely known, more and more institutions wanted to be connected (especially academic institutions), so the number of connections on the Internet rose.

Until the early to mid-1990s, the Internet mainly carried text-based traffic (such as emails and files), although the standards for file transfer and remote login, etc. already existed. Any search was performed by a text-based utility called **gopher**. In the early 1990s, the **European Organization for Nuclear Research** (**CERN**) introduced a hypertext system allowing text to be linked over the Internet. By 1994, the **National Center for Supercomputer Applications** (**NCSA**) enhanced this with its **Mosaic browser**, providing a **graphical user interface** (**GUI**) hypertext-based system. As anyone who has created a web page will know, the majority of a basic web page is text. Text elements are enclosed in tags (e.g.), which are recognised by the browser and displayed in a particular way. This revolutionised the Internet and created the **World Wide Web** (**www**) that everyone wants to be a part of. However, it is the Internet that is the carrier of the web.

Extranets

Extranets are a popular discussion topic at the moment. An extranet essentially means extending access to an institution's network to its suppliers. Extranets are very popular because they can bring huge benefits. For example, a car manufacturer could extend access to its production network to its existing suppliers. By using this access, the suppliers could determine what cars were to be made that week and could ensure that they manufactured the correct components (e.g. seats) to go into the cars. Obviously, the seats would need to be the correct model and colour. In turn, by making their production schedule available to their own suppliers, the suppliers can ensure that the correct fabric is produced. In this example, none of the companies would need to hold as much stock of finished goods but they can still fulfil the orders. By not holding stock, they reduce storage and overall operating costs – hence the popularity of extranets.

Summary

This particular classification of networking relates to how the network connects to the outside world. As organisations strive to gain a competitive advantage, they often make use of these categories of networking. For example, by utilising extranets, organisations are generally able to reduce the amount of stock they hold and so save costs.

Quick test

Briefly compare and contrast the classifications of intranets, extranets and the Internet.

> **KEY CONCEPT**
>
> The Internet is a network of networks and is a publicly accessible information resource. An intranet is essentially an internet for use only within an organisation. An extranet is effectively an intranet that is typically shared among an organisation and its suppliers.

Section 5: Voice over IP

Organisations for a long time have had two distinct networks connecting their offices – one for data and one for voice (and possibly even one for video).

Obviously the cost of maintaining separate networks is expensive, and with the merging of telephone and data standards it has only been a matter of time before a solution became available.

Introduction

Voice over IP (VoIP) is a technology by which an organisation's data network can be used to carry voice traffic as well as data. There are numerous pieces of software available, such as Microsoft's Netmeeting, Skype, and Tesco Internet Phone, which allow you to chat over the Internet. One of the key differences between these types of software and true VoIP is quality.

VoIP is intended to replace the telephone service and therefore must be at least as high a quality in regard to key functions such as: reliability, ability to operate in the event of a power failure, switchboard functions, etc.

VoIP

VoIP requires special phones (*see Figure 1.11*), which are essentially computers with a built in Ethernet switch. When the receiver is lifted or a button is pressed, the phone communicates over the network with a server such as Cisco's CallManager. When a number is dialled, CallManager looks up the telephone number and finds the IP address of the dialled phone (*see Chapter 3*). It then passes this back to the dialling phone, which can then communicate directly over the network. VoIP is extremely sensitive to delays and the organisational network must be configured to prioritise VoIP traffic.

The data packets required to send VoIP are small, and can usually be easily accommodated by the existing network. VoIP allows organisations to make significant savings by only having a data link between buildings and as such is likely to pay for itself within less than three years. VoIP also has many other features:

- Extension mobility – you can 'login' to your phone. Using this method no matter where you login, that phone will have your extension number.

- Features – many IP phones are actually PCs and can be programmed using Java. Applications can be written for IP phones such as a register system in a school, further increasing the usefulness of the phone.

Figure 1.11: A Cisco 7970G VoIP phone

> ### TIPS & ADVICE
>
> VoIP is fundamentally different from Internet Telephony – VoIP has a guaranteed **Quality of Service (QoS)**, meaning that calls made with VoIP are normally slightly higher quality than those made with a conventional telephone.

- Wireless IP phones can move around access points providing coverage right across an organisation, rather than within reach of a traditional cordless phone's base station.

- Relatively easy to relocate a phone.

The major disadvantage is the initial cost – the phones themselves are many times more expensive than a conventional phone, and they require specialist Ethernet switches (*see Chapter 6*) that can provide **Power over Ethernet (PoE)** .

Section 6: Grid/Cluster computing

Some organisations, e.g. NASA, need vast amounts of compute power and traditionally achieved this through the use of supercomputers. These are very specialist computers costing many millions of pounds. They require specialist accommodation (air conditioning, etc.), and very specialist technical support, operators and development staff. In short, they cost an absolute fortune to own and run and are beyond the reach of most organisations and universities.

Many organisations would like such compute power but simply cannot afford it and so alternatives have been sought.

Introduction

PC compute power has increased dramatically since their inception, especially with the introduction of multi-core processors. The so-called 'high-end' PCs offer massive processing power to the organisation. By utilising the speed and capacity of today's networks, it is possible to connect together a number of such PCs to approximate the compute power of super computers. In general there are two terms given to such systems:

- **Cluster computing**; and

- **Grid computing**.

Both are essentially the same – it is simply the geographic distribution of the compute power which varies.

Cluster computing

Cluster computing refers to a collection of compute nodes (PCs) within one specific location (*see Figure 1.12*), for example, in a university, a research institute or an organisation. As the networks used in Cluster computing are the responsibility of the organisation, they are likely to be very high-speed networks – usually 1 Gbps minimum.

Typically, Cluster computing has three networks (usually each node will usually have three networking cards):

- **Data Network** – used for passing data.

- **Inter Process Communication (IPC)** Network – used for sending information between processes on different nodes.

- **Inter Process Management Interface (IPMI)** Network – used for node management.

Figure 1.12: The University of Sunderland Cluster computer

Grid computing

Grid computing derives its name from the electricity grid networks where many producers supply their electricity to the national grid. Consumers can then use (and pay for) that electricity. In a similar fashion, Grid computing is about sharing geographically separate compute power (usually clusters) over high-speed networks. For example, two universities could collaborate allowing the other institution to use its cluster computer when it was not using it. It is possible for many institutions to collaborate in such ways.

Grid computing is highly dependent upon the speed of the networks interconnecting the institutions. As these are likely to be **Wide Area Network (WAN)** links, speed is likely to be lower than Cluster Computing.

This is a rapidly growing area of computing and is sure to continue to grow as organisations demand more compute power.

Benefits

For those organisations that traditionally wanted such compute power, the benefits are that it will probably be available at a much lower cost. It can also be relatively easily assembled from 'off the shelf' components.

If more compute power is needed, then very often it is possible to simply add additional nodes to realise the required power.

For organisations that could traditionally not afford such compute power, then Grid computing makes this power available to them. It is likely that new types of applications will materialise to take advantage of such compute power. For example, consider an electricity company with traditional and renewable energy resources. If it were able to process weather forecasts and trends and simultaneously control its renewable energy sources concurrently and in real time, it could make much more efficient use of its resources.

Quick test

Define what is meant by the terms Grid and Cluster computing.

Section 7: Benefits of networking

We are now truly starting to appreciate the power of networking. There can be few people whose everyday lives have not been touched by networking. We use online shopping, online banking, emails, web access, instant messaging, etc. as part of our everyday lives and very often our livelihood may depend on it, without giving a second thought to the networks that make this possible.

Network centric world

Whether we like it or not, we are living in a world where we are becoming more and more reliant upon networking services – in a so-called network centric world. In this world, we can communicate effortlessly with colleagues, friends and family across the world and across time zones. Photographs can be taken with digital cameras and emailed or uploaded to websites virtually instantly. The same is true of digital video.

We can also talk to colleagues, friends and family cheaply (often for free) using instant messaging. We can connect our games consoles and play with other gamers across the world. We can watch TV via the Internet and even access programmes we may have missed. Many of us now simply turn to the world wide web for information using a variety of search engines such as Google.

We don't need to be static to connect to these services because wireless networks have made it possible to access services on the move. For example, we can have real time traffic information delivered direct to our car or perhaps our car-based satellite navigation system.

It is the power of the Internet carrying this traffic that makes all of this possible . . . . and yet we still haven't realised the full potential of the Internet!

Teleworker services

Technology is changing the way we work and has been doing so for some considerable period of time. The Internet is allowing organisations to make rapid advances in this area. The idea of the 'teleworker' is to enable someone to be able to work at home, or on the move, to carry out their job as though they were at their desk in the organisation's office.

Since **Integrated Services Digital Networks (ISDN)** came to the forefront in the early 1990s, teleworking has been a possibility, even though bandwidth was limited, costs were high and ISDN wasn't universally available.

With the wide availability of broadband services and high-speed wireless services, these three barriers have essentially been lifted. It is now entirely possible to work at home, or on the move, and have the same access to data at (relatively) the same speed as working in the office.

The technologies, which make this possible, are high-speed broadband and wireless connections. Although organisations were naturally concerned about security of the information in transit, VPNs have largely solved this problem and now it is possible to have a very secure high-speed connection between the home, a mobile location and the office. As VoIP is widely and rapidly adopted, then it will be entirely possible to use your office phone from home or on the move. Again, this can be sent across the VPN and so calls made in such a fashion will also be very secure.

Distributed call centres are now possible – where staff work from home and the organisation can make massive savings by not having large buildings to accommodate staff. Although this is probably some way off, there are already cases where organisations (such as breakdown services) have home based staff 'on-call' so that at times of peak demand they can easily increase their capacity by bringing these staff on stream.

There are also cases where staff simply can't afford to live near work – for example, Silicon Valley in the USA. There are a number of technology workers, who work for organisations based in Silicon Valley but who live all across the USA and, in some cases, across the world.

These massive changes in the way some people work is still set in the context of not having realised the full potential of the Internet.

Quick test

Define what is meant by the terms teleworker 'services' and 'network centric world'.

Section 8: End of chapter assessment

Questions

1. Outline the major developments that have led to today's networks.

2. Explain the differences and similarities between peer-to-peer networks and client server networks.

3. Explain what is meant by the terms LAN, MAN, WAN, PAN and VAN.

4. Explain what is meant by the terms intranet, extranet, the Internet and VPN.

5. Explain what is meant by the term VoIP.

6. Explain what is meant by the terms Grid computing and Cluster computing.

7. Explain the major benefits of networking and the terms 'Network Centric World' and 'Teleworking'.

Answers

1. To answer this question, you need to review the development of networks from the early days, when computers had no real networks up to the introduction of local area networks. In your answer, you should include local interactive terminals and remote access through both modem and leased lines. Remember that diagrams are important. If you can draw a diagram it makes your answer easier to mark (always a good ploy), and it shows the assessor you understand. The diagrams are relatively simple and drawing them serves as a prompt for you. At each stage, you should also discuss the reasons why networking developed and the benefits each particular phase gave to the users of the network. Ideally, you should also discuss any weaknesses of the stage and relate these to the next stage of development to enable your answer to flow smoothly.

2. As you progress through higher education the aim is to make you a reflective practitioner – someone who can review an idea or a concept critically. The earlier you learn this technique the better – it will allow you to pick up additional marks at Level 1 (HNC and Fd Level 1) and Level 2 (HND and Fd Level 2) because a critical review is not expected at these levels; instead, assessors expect descriptions or explanations – you can go one better! In answering this question, you need to provide the assessor with a discussion of both the client/server network architecture and of the peer-to-peer network architecture. If you begin with the discussion of client/server architecture, you can highlight its composition, the benefits it has brought to organisations and any limiting factors (the major one being cost). This will lead you smoothly into a discussion on peer-to-peer networks since these are meant to provide similar benefits to organisations, but at less cost.

   Again, diagrams may help illustrate your answer and will impress the assessor with your command of the subject. Diagrams allow assessors to see at a glance what the physical difference is between peer-to-peer and client/server networking. Extra marks will come from discussing limitations or problems with the architectures – for example, that Microsoft recommends no more than ten computers in a peer-to-peer network. Concluding the answer by discussing which network architecture is appropriate for an example organisation will demonstrate an understanding of the implementation of the subject and gain extra marks.

3. Again, an explanation and diagrams can help with the explanation. The assessor wants you to demonstrate that you

know and understand the five major categories of networking:

- LANs;
- MANs;
- WANs;
- PANs;
- VAN.

A successful answer would list the five categories and then discuss the properties of each of the categories – the geographic area they cover, speed, costs, who administers, any involvement from telecomms providers, etc. Typical applications and uses of the category will help demonstrate you have the ability to apply the knowledge. Don't be afraid to quote a university or college campus, classroom or national/multinational company in the categories, as these are perfect textbook examples.

You will also need to discuss what is meant by the term VPN and (ideally) show how it can be beneficial to a modern organisation.

4. To answer this question, you need to give a basic discussion of each of the categories of networking. For each, you should detail what it is, how it operates (e.g. IP address restricted or authenticated), the user group to whom it would normally be available and the advantages/disadvantages to various organisations.

5. To answer this question, you need to give a basic discussion of VoIP detailing, what it is, what equipment is needed and what the advantages/disadvantages of this technology are. VoIP is a benefit or a use of networking so you shouldn't be asked too technical a question on it – unless you are studying a VoIP course!

6. To answer this question, it is necessary to give a little background as to the need for such processing power. Next the assessor is looking for you to define what is meant by the terms Grid computing and Cluster computing. It is probably better to start with Cluster computing and discuss what a cluster is. It also a good idea to discuss the networking aspects. You can then go on to discuss a Grid computer – it is essentially a cluster of Cluster computers! Finally, for extra marks it is worth discussing new applications which may arise.

7. In this question the assessor is not really asking for technical information (although some content such as VoIP, VPNs etc. will be useful). This is more of a technology impact question. To answer it, you need to explain what is meant by the terms and discuss the impact that networking is having on our everyday lives. You should attempt a balance here – giving the negative as well as the positive impact.

Section 9: Further reading and research

Cisco Networking Academy Program (2004) CCNA 1 and 2 *Companion Guide* (3rd edn). Cisco Press. ISBN: 1-58713-50-1. Chapters 1 and 2. (Older but still useful).

Network Fundamentals, CCNA Exploration Labs and Study Guide (2008). Cisco Press. ISBN: 1-58713-203-6. Chapter 1.

Accessing the WAN, CCNA Exploration Labs and Study Guide (2008). Cisco Press. ISBN: 1-58713-205-2. Chapter 6.

Network Fundamentals, CCNA Exploration Labs and Study Guide (2008). Cisco Press. ISBN: 1-58713-203-6. Chapters 1 and 2.

www.bluetooth.com

www.usb.org

Chapter 2
The networked system

Chapter summary

Networked computer systems are part of almost every organisation in the western world, and not without good reason: networked computer systems allow organisations unparalleled access to their information, irrespective of geographic location. They make communicating between different machine types possible and, when coupled with the Internet, make e-commerce possible.

Organisations are constantly looking for ways in which they can save money or gain a competitive advantage – networks offer the promise of both.

Learning outcomes

After studying this chapter you should aim to test your achievement of the following outcomes. You should be able to:

Outcome 1: Networked resources

Understand the essential components of any networked system and be able to identify these components. Question 1 at the end of this chapter will test your ability to do this.

Outcome 2: Facilities of a networked operating system

Understand the facilities and benefits a networked operating system (NOS) can provide to an organisation. Question 2 at the end of this chapter will test your ability to do this.

Outcome 3: Capacity issues

Understand that a network has limited bandwidth (capacity) and that applications that run on the network need to be both suitable and within the capacity of the network. Question 3 at the end of this chapter will test your ability to do this.

Outcome 4: Security implications

Understand that connecting a computer to a network will greatly increase the security risks and be aware of such risks. Question 4 at the end of this chapter will test your ability to do this.

Outcome 5: Licensing issues

Understand the licensing issues associated with networked software and be able to provide advice. Question 5 at the end of this chapter will test your ability to do this.

How will you be assessed on this?

This chapter is very much an introduction to the topic – setting out the major components of networking and identifying the benefits and issues associated with their use. The ideal assessment in this case would be a case study of an organisation that wished to install a network. A case study would allow you to discuss all you have learnt from this chapter in a manner relevant to the organisation. It is therefore likely that such an assessment will be an assignment. The questions at the end of this chapter form such a case study.

Section 1: Networked resources

Computer networks are essential to most organisations and critical to a high number – that is to say, if the organisation was deprived of its network, it would no longer be able to carry out its mission. Such networks are considered 'mission critical'.

It might be thought that such mission critical networks would be restricted to large organisations, but this is not the case. A reasonably large taxi company, whose bookings are stored on a computer system and dispatched by that system, would consider its network as mission critical. If it was unable to access the server, it would be unable to dispatch the taxis; if it couldn't do that, it couldn't carry out its mission.

There are essential components to any networked system and this section explores these critical components.

Overview of network resources

From *Chapter 1* we know that a network provides a means by which two or more computers can communicate. It is desirable to have such communications as they allow the efficient sharing of files and printers and make possible such communications as the web and email. In short, they tie together data, communications, computing and file servers. They also provide a mechanism by which data can be transferred between differing machine types – for example, Apple Macs and PCs.

When considering resources, the best starting point is the computer itself: somehow the computer needs to be enabled to use the network. This is achieved by the installation of a Network Interface Card (or NIC). A NIC interfaces the computer's architecture with that of the network and facilitates connection between the two. Because of this, the NIC is said to be both network media dependent and computer hardware dependent. In short, the NIC you select needs to match both the internal architecture of the computer (e.g. PCI, ESIA, ISA) and the technology/media of the LAN (e.g. 100BaseT Ethernet). *Figure 2.1* shows a selection of NICs, whilst *Figure 2.2* shows the installation of a NIC. All computers that are to communicate over the network need to have NICs installed, although most modern PCs have Ethernet NICs already built onto the system board.

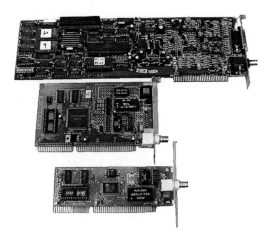

Figure 2.1: A selection of network interface cards (NICs)

Figure 2.2: The installation of a NIC

The computer is now electrically able to transfer data outside itself but doesn't have any form of connection with other computers and requires communications media. Most commonly, copper cables interconnect the machines. However, there is a variety of other media that are used in computer networking to carry the data – for example, fibre optic and infrared are used to carry light, and radio waves (wireless LANs, Bluetooth) are also used. To keep things simple, we will look at a common medium – copper. *Figure 2.3* shows **Unshielded Twisted Pair** (**UTP**) cabling, which is the most common form of connection today (terminating in an RJ-45 plug).

Figure 2.3: The correctly made-up end of UTP cabling

> **KEY CONCEPT**
>
> The NIC must match the computer architecture, LAN technology and media. For example, a 100BaseT PCI Ethernet card is meant for computers with a PCI slot and for Ethernet technology that runs over UTP cabling (*see Chapters 3 and 5*).

The media needs to be connected to the computers that are being networked, which may require the use of networking devices such as a hub or switch (see *Figure 2.4*) (for further information, *see Chapter 5*). Our computers are then able to communicate and are physically connected together. The final requirement is the software itself. On a Microsoft Windows platform, two pieces of software are necessary:

- driver software for the NIC;
- Windows itself.

KEY CONCEPT

Networking requires hardware, software and media. The hardware provides the electrical connection from the computer to the outside world, whilst the media connects the computers together. Networking 'kit' may be used to extend the media. The software uses this connection to carry bits of data. This data could be used to share or move anything that's digital.

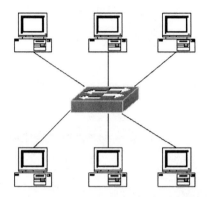

Figure 2.4: Computers networked using an Ethernet switch

As with most accessories purchased for a PC, NICs are shipped with a driver disk. The driver disk simply allows the computer to use (or 'drive') the hardware and needs to be installed before attempting to network the computer – otherwise the operating system won't be able to find the NIC. Since **Windows for Workgroups** was launched in the mid-1990s, the Windows operating system has had the ability to communicate through networks. The network settings can be found in the **Control Panel** (*see Figure 2.5*).

Figure 2.5: Control Panel settings; note the networking icon

Quick test

List the essential components of a networked operating system and briefly outline their purpose.

Section 2: Facilities of a networked operating system

Quite simply, networked operating systems (or NOSs) enable almost any make of computer to communicate with almost any other make of computer. Although this sounds relatively simple, it is not – and the power such simple communication provides to an organisation is tremendous. As the digital revolution continues more and more can transported by a computer network, for example, low cost telephone calls, video, music, etc.

Why are computer networks so popular?

Networking has, throughout its history, brought huge benefits to organisations. For example, the ability of early programmers to work online was immeasurable in terms of efficiency and effectiveness. Before the advent of PCs in the 1980s, computing was undertaken on either mini or mainframe computers. As these were hugely expensive, organisations with such machines needed to ensure maximum use was being made of them whilst the machines themselves were kept secure. The most effective way of achieving this was via remote access through the network. Thus, in local authorities and large companies throughout the world, the resources of the computer – processing power, disk storage, printing, etc. – were shared, providing maximum benefits for the cost.

In the early 1980s, IBM introduced the first PC, which was an instant success with organisations across the world. Processing power was brought to the desktop, as were files and printing devices. Having the files and printers local to a machine was, at first, a novelty – users were in charge of their own data, printing and processing power. Organisations very quickly realised that, although there were benefits to this approach, there were also drawbacks. Files, which needed to be shared, had to be swapped physically (sometimes referred to as **sneakernet** – a term which comes from walking around with a disk); expensive printing resources had to be duplicated; and the organisation's data was decentralised, difficult to locate, access and back-up. In the example of the booking office, taking bookings for a popular gig which we looked at briefly in *Chapter 1*, the seating area (file) needs to be shared amongst everyone taking the bookings, otherwise over- or under-booking may occur. This cannot be efficiently undertaken by sharing a floppy disk! As this example illustrates, the sharing of information in an organisation is critical. To most organisations, communication and the sharing of information are critical. A sales department may ask: 'Can production handle this extra order if we take it?' If production keep their data local, this will be a difficult question to answer and the order might be lost.

Soon PCs were added to the LAN providing a means whereby the users could have their processing power locally, but could share information and other resources such as expensive printers. The first LANs introduced to the PC environment were client/server LANs and, today, the majority still follow this pattern. However, such are the benefits provided by LANs that smaller organisations have introduced peer-to-peer LANs to emulate these similar benefits. As LANs have evolved, so have the benefits they provide. Early LANs provided facilities for file and printer sharing. Today, LANs provide many more benefits to the organisation, for example:

- distributed processing (where the server can process, for example, a database query before returning the results to the client);
- email facilities and file transfer;
- remote backup;
- video conferencing;
- fax;
- shared applications, such as accounting and payroll systems (subject to licence terms);
- shared data;
- telephony services;
- instant messaging;
- wireless access.

To emphasize the importance of these benefits, most people would argue that email has revolutionised communication. For example, in 2002, a fire at a chemical plant sent a toxic cloud over the north east. The university, in which I work, had one call from the police advising everyone to stay inside. Relaying this life-threatening information to 1500 employees and thousands of students was achieved in seconds using email.

KEY CONCEPT

Networking has brought many benefits to organisations, allowing them to realise huge savings. Such a positive cost-benefit has fuelled the development of networks. Organisations can almost always benefit from enhancing their networks.

Sharing information (such as working documents) with colleagues is difficult and time-consuming without email (the file would have to be copied to one disk per colleague and put in the internal post). It is much more efficient to use email and simply attach the file. The network, therefore, also has to provide the translation between different machine types. Thus a Mac computer can send and receive emails to and from a PC, which is easier than sharing floppy disks (due to the different formats between MACs and PCs). The phrase 'information is power' is certainly true – the organisation that can share and access the information the quickest is likely to be the one that progresses the fastest. In every sense, networks provide an organisation with many ways of communicating more effectively. The fact that the cost of providing these facilities is relatively low means that the networks are providing low-cost/high-benefit solutions to an organisation – hence their popularity and continued growth.

Quick test

Identify the benefits networks bring to an organisation and, hence, why they are so popular.

Section 3: Capacity and performance issues

Computer networks bring enormous benefits to an organisation and, therefore, organisations often become critically dependent upon their networks. Unfortunately, computer networks do not have unlimited capacity, and it is important to realise that this can often be a limiting factor. This is particularly so when connecting externally, either via a WAN or the Internet. (*Chapter 7* covers capacity in more detail.)

Capacity limitations

Perhaps the single most limiting factor of a computer network is its capacity to carry data. Unfortunately, networks lag behind computer architectures in terms of the amount of information they can pass from point to point although they are quickly reaching an acceptable level. This is due, in part, to networks providing serial as opposed to parallel transmission. It is also due to the fact that the network is shared amongst many computers, where the faster internal architecture of a computer is reserved for its own use.

It is often helpful to think of a computer network in terms of plumbing. No one would dream of supplying the water needs to a twenty-storey hotel from a garden hose! There obviously isn't enough capacity in a garden hose – it isn't big enough to let the required amount of water through and neither is the tap. If such a water supply was used, the water would slow to a trickle for each user, and the problem would become more acute during peak times – early morning and when many people wanted a bath (high-volume users) or a shower. In fact, if the water was fed from the bottom of the building it is likely that, during peak times, only the bottom floor would have a supply. This is because there is insufficient capacity. We can substitute the hotel for a computer LAN (say, 30 stations) and the garden hose for the LAN technology. If we have 10Base2 (*a type of Ethernet cabling which is explored in more detail in Chapter 5*), we have a maximum of 7 Mbps (technically 10Base2 has a theoretical maximum of 10 Mbps but in practice it's nearer 7 Mbps) shared amongst every user of the LAN. Thus in every second we can transfer a maximum of 7 Mbps for all computers. To take an example, poor-quality video is approximately 10 MB per minute: 10 MB x 8 = 80 Mbits. 80 Mb/60 secs tells us that each machine requires 1.34 Mbits per second (Mbps) capacity to show the video over a LAN. If we have 30 machines, there is no way the LAN can cope.

When considering placing an application on the LAN, the effects of doing so must be taken into account. If the LAN in our example was mission critical, by adding the video we would slow the information on the LAN to a trickle – which would mean the organisation would be unable to carry out its mission. This could seriously damage the

TIPS & ADVICE

It is important to remember that data is measured in megabytes (MB) and networks work in megabits (Mb). To convert you need to multiply MB by 8.

KEY CONCEPT

Networks don't have unlimited capacity. When introducing applications or data to the LAN or making changes, we must ensure that the LAN can cope with the new load (*see Chapter 7*).

---

organisation. For a store at Christmas, if an employee chose to watch a video over the LAN, slowing it to a trickle, it might well take 30 minutes to serve each customer! The one thing that is certain about bandwidth is that we can never have enough. An organisation's requirements will constantly grow, just as LAN capacity will grow.

Quick test

Describe briefly what is meant by the term 'bandwidth'. Discuss why it is important to assess bandwidth and its impact when considering installing a networked application.

Section 4: Security implications

Whilst computer networks undoubtedly provide unparalleled access to information, they can also allow it to be seen by prying eyes. As soon as information is networked, it is shared with people we want to share it with and those we don't want to share it with. Hence the need for security measures. (Security is given fuller treatment in *Chapter 12*.)

Security implications

Information security is often as paramount for commercial organisations as it is for military organisations. Companies have commercially-sensitive information as well as obligations under such legislation as the Data Protection Act 1984 to keep it secure. Before the widespread use of computers, information security was provided by robust filing cabinets, perhaps a security guard and, usually, a personnel-screening system. The aim was simple – to limit access to sensitive information. Unauthorised access to such information could be damaging to the company. Consider a car dealership – access to customer lists would be very helpful to other dealers.

Before the widespread use of computers, it was relatively easy to spot someone stealing information – long periods spent at the photocopier and carrying large boxes of paper out of the building. The widespread use of computers makes it much easier to steal information. By using a memory stick, it is possible to steal up to 64 GB of data on a device small enough to fit into a shirt pocket (to put 64 GB in context – the entire *Encyclopaedia Britannica* is around 1 GB!). Essentially, anyone connected to the corporate network has access to the information held on its computers and the information travelling across the network. Organisations need to take steps to protect the contents of their servers and other computers. Access to servers should be via authentication only (e.g. biometric or passwords), and users should be given the minimum access rights necessary for them to carry out their work. Computers (including PCs) that are connected to a corporate network should be reviewed to ensure that only the files and directories that need to be shared are shared and that all others are protected. Again, access to shared drives should be via authentication only.

Quick test
Briefly discuss why security is a vitally important issue with reference to information held on a network.

Section 5: Licensing issues

Breaking licence agreements is a civil offence, as is a breach of copyright or copying software. Software piracy is a serious issue and is reported to be costing the software industry billions of dollars each year. In 1984, the British Computer Society's Copyright Committee established the Federation Against Software Theft (or FAST). The aim of FAST is to safeguard software and, contrary to popular belief, the organisation represents both users and software producers. FAST can assist in identifying and prosecuting organisations or individuals who copy or use copied software or who breach licence agreements. Unauthorised copying of software and breaches of a software licence are serious crimes and there can be severe penalties for those caught. The network manager is often the one who is nominated to oversee an organisation's licence agreements, and must understand licensing issues fully.

KEY CONCEPT

Security should be paramount. To ignore security is to risk the organisation's entire existence – it cannot be treated in a piecemeal fashion. All organisations must take a professional approach to computer security.

Licensing issues

Discussion of software licensing has necessarily been limited here. Network managers must ensure they understand their position fully and the wider issues involved. Before computer networks, licensing issues were relatively simple – a licence was bought for every machine the software was to be installed upon. If an organisation had 25 machines but only ten were in use at any one time, it still needed 25 copies of the software or one per **Central Processing Unit (CPU)**. With the advent of computer networks, software could be held centrally and downloaded to a machine when required. Software manufacturers realised this and released appropriately designed networked versions of their software. Central to these licences is the issue of concurrency. Thus, a ten-user licence of networked software usually means a maximum of ten machines can be using that software at one time. When an eleventh user downloads and runs the software, this is a breach of the licence agreement. Some manufacturers include the word 'normally' in the licence agreement: 'the number of users of the software will normally not exceed x'. The intention here is that, in exceptional circumstances, they would not be averse to more users than the licence permits, although there will be restrictions. An example of this could be the student records system. Normally it may only have eight users but, during times of enrolment, extra staff may be needed to cope. The term 'normally', however, does not apply to all software and its meaning should be checked with the manufacturers.

Some argue that a user logging into a network and starting a piece of networked software may be unaware that the maximum number of licences have been used and that it is the software itself that should enforce the licence agreement. The argument about the user logging in is, however, valid – an organisation should know how many people

KEY CONCEPT

An organisation must ensure it has sufficient software licences for the software in use. In the case of operating systems this will usually mean one licence per computer (as all computers need an operating system). Other software may be available in a networked version. An organisation should also ensure that the maximum number of concurrent users allowed under the licence agreements is never exceeded. Exceeding the licence agreement may result in prosecution, and the authorities often take a serious view of such cases.

Software licences and agreements do change over time, so remember to keep abreast.

are likely to be using a piece of software at one time. For example, if a university has three classes of 25 students using Microsoft Office, it should know it needs 75 licences. Some software does, on the other hand, enforce the licensing agreement through a licence meter. This works by the software either refusing to start if the maximum number of licences has been reached or – more ruthlessly – logging out the user who has been connected for the longest period of time. Whilst the use of a meter sounds good, in practice it can be problematic. If a machine crashes whilst using the software, it may not release the licence and, when restarted, may consume another licence. Eventually, this could lead to the situation where all the licences have been consumed through faults and so no one can use the software. This would obviously lead to frustration and to increased technical support costs.

Quick test

Briefly discuss the main issues concerning software licensing.

Section 6: End of chapter assessment

Questions

1. You have been approached by a local charity that wishes to network their office. It has limited funds and has asked you to identify the minimum resources it would need to network its office. It currently runs donated copies of Windows 98.

2. The charity is aiming to help the unemployed over-fifties to get to grips with computing in the hope they can find employment. Typically, it intends to train ten students at a time in the use of word processors. The charity also has a small administration team of three. Two of the team typically use Microsoft Word and Microsoft Access on a daily basis, handling confidential files on the charity's students and producing references for employment. A further administrator uses Microsoft Excel. The functions provided by this team can be considered mission critical. As the charity does not have sufficient printing resources, it would like the administration team to be connected to the network. Outline the benefits a network would offer the charity.

3. The founder of the charity has recently acquired a high quality 1.5 GB AVI video which, over a period of 15 minutes, introduces the trainees to the benefits of word processing and many of the techniques they need. She feels that the class can use the video throughout the lesson rather than having formal instruction. As the charity will be networked, she feels that delivery of the video over the network will be ideal and has sought your advice.

4. The charity has also asked your advice on the security implications of connecting the administrative staff to the teaching network.

5. The charity has a ten-user licence for Microsoft Word, which is

currently used by two administrators. It wishes to use the same licence for the classes it intends to teach and has asked for your advice on the licensing issues of such a move.

Answers

The questions above are all interrelated and are based upon a small case study. This is deliberate as it is likely that assessment of such topics will be in this form. Thus the answers below are likely to form subsections of your overall answer. In practice, the case study would go into far greater detail and would be tied in with capacity planning covered in *Chapter 7*.

1. To answer this question, you need to pick up on the key facts – the organisation is a charity and has limited funds. It is seeking your advice on the minimum resources it needs to get its network operational. Obviously there are two sides to this question, as it is meant to test your academic knowledge – the assessor is not just looking for a shopping list, but for a list of items the charity requires together with an **explanation** of why it needs them and some form of explanation of what the items actually do/a justification of why they are needed. Don't forget: for a network to be successful, you need both hardware and software – the software they have, albeit outdated, would appear to support their requirements.

2. This question is asking you to outline the benefits a computer network would bring to the charity. Although this is a case study, there is considerable scope in the benefits it can provide. Again, don't forget that the assessor isn't simply looking for a list of benefits: he or she is looking to see that you understand the benefits (shown through discussion) and that the benefits you propose are realistic and achievable within the charity's limited budget.

3. This question is about managing the expectations of the end-user. Networks are useful and do provide enormous benefits, but they have limited bandwidth. In this example, the founder of the charity has great expectations of the network, which it won't be able to deliver within her limited budget (assuming the charity will install a 10 or 100 Mbps Ethernet network – *see Chapter 5*). You need to discuss the fact that networks have limited bandwidth and advise her on what is and is not realistic.

4. Although this question seems to be simple, the answer is more complex and, as usual in such an assessment, some of the clues are hidden elsewhere. If you review the earlier questions, you will see what information is actually being held and processed on the computers connected to the network. You need to outline to the charity the security implications of its intentions. Again, a list isn't required – the assessor is looking for evidence of thought and wants to see discussion of the issues as well as guidance for the charity.

5.   The answer to this question centres on software licensing issues. To answer it you need to provide a general discussion of the software licensing issues and relate this to the case of the charity. It has a networked ten-user licence for Microsoft Word, but it is likely that, at peak times, it will exceed this licence. You need to inform the charity of the implications of this.

Section 7: Further reading and research

Cisco Networking Academy Program (CNAP) Network Fundamentals CCNA Exploration Companion guide. Cisco Press. ISBN: 1-58713-208-7. Chapters 1 and 2.

Cisco Networking Academy Program (2004) *CCNA 1 and 2 Companion Guide* (2nd edn). Cisco Press. ISBN: 1-58713-150-1. Chapters 1 and 2. (Older, but still useful).

Cisco Networking Academy Program (2003) *CCNA 3 and 4 Companion Guide* (2nd edn). Cisco Press. ISBN: 1-58713-113-7. Chapter 18. (Older, but still useful).

Chapter 3

Fundamentals of networks

Chapter summary

Networks operate by taking binary data from a computer and encoding it onto transmission media which forms a circuit. These signals either occupy the entire frequency range or only part of it. As the signal traverses the media, it can suffer from interference. 'Networkers' need to be aware of such issues and how to address them. This chapter presents these issues with minimal technicality.

Networks also have a shape which is dependent upon their type and need to use **addressing** to correctly send the data from the sending machine to the recipient. Design of IP addressing is now becoming a critical issue as more organisations want to divide their network into subnetworks.

Saving the use of real (Public) IP addresses is also becoming a priority for network designers. This is achieved through the use of **Network Address Translation (NAT)** and **Port Address Translation (PAT)**.

Finally, the **IP version 4 (IPv4)** address space is depleted and its replacement **IP version 6 (IPv6)** is complex, but it is necessary to have a basic understanding of this later version for today's larger networks.

Learning outcomes

After studying this chapter you should aim to test your achievement of the following outcomes. You should be able to:

Outcome 1: Network basics

Understand the basics of computer networking and be familiar with some of the terms. Question 1 at the end of this chapter will test your ability to do this.

Outcome 2: Network topologies

Describe the common network topologies and be able to identify each one. Question 2 at the end of this chapter will test your ability to do this.

Outcome 3: Network addressing

Understand the basics of network addressing and be able to discuss the addressing formats. Question 3 at the end of this chapter will test your ability to do this.

Outcome 4: Classless Subnetworking and Variable Length Subnet Masking (VLSM)

Understand the process of dividing a network address through subnetworking and VLSM. Question 4 at the end of this chapter will test your ability to do this.

Outcome 5: Network Address Translation (NAT)/Port Address Translation (PAT)

Understand how the number of Public IP addresses in use can be limited through the use of NAT and PAT. Question 5 at the end of this chapter will test your understanding of this.

Outcome 6: IP version 6 (IPv6)

Understand the limitations of IPv4 and a limited introduction to IPv6. Question 6 at the end of this chapter will test your understanding of this.

How will you be assessed on this?

The topics covered in this chapter form the fundamental principles of networking – how data is encoded; the different topologies; logical/physical addressing mechanisms; IPv4/v6 addressing and NAT/PAT. The most popular form of assessment for such topics is by examination or time-constrained test (TCT). The questions at the end of this chapter provide you with sample questions that may well be asked in such assessments.

Subnetting is usually assessed through a design exercise – perhaps as part of an assignment.

Section 1: Understanding network basics

Computer networking is subject to the laws of physics, and therefore a basic understanding of the physics of networking will aid understanding. The laws of physics also govern the speed and development of networking. This section introduces some of the basic physics that impact on networking. It is assumed that you have a basic understanding of binary – that binary is the basis of all data held and transmitted by a computer. If this is not the case, it is recommended that you consult a book on computer architectures to understand these basics before proceeding.

TIPS & ADVICE

Although it might seem odd, difficult concepts can be visualised from comparing networking to plumbing. Here, how a wire carries data (represented by a voltage) is compared to a pipe carrying water.

Encoding

Computer networking is about moving data (in the form of bits) along some sort of transmission media (most commonly a piece of wire). For transmission, the data needs to be encoded into an electrical voltage that can then be carried by the wire.

Figure 3.1 shows data encoding using +12 v to represent a 0 and -12 v to represent a 1. It is common usage to employ two voltages to differentiate a no signal state from a signal state. Thus, if the sender is at the right and the receiver at the left, the data 0101010 is being transmitted.

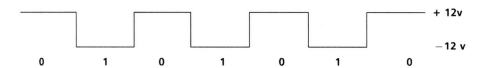

**Figure 3.1: Data encoding
(diagram courtesy of Professor Peter Hodson,
University of Glamorgan)**

Any good computer architecture book will detail how alphanumeric characters are encoded using an encoding mechanism such as the **American Standard Code for Information Interchange (ASCII)**.

Circuits

To carry data, a circuit is required. In most cases a circuit comprises two wires. Consider *Figure 3.2*, which is a simple torch circuit. Here, when the switch is closed, the electrons move, providing electricity to the bulb, which lights up. Opening the switch stops the flow of electrons and the light goes out. This circuit could be used to represent basic binary digits (either 1 (on) or 0 (off)).

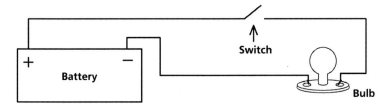

Figure 3.2: Simple torch circuit

Networking also needs complete circuits – we call the cables the 'signal' and the 'signal ground'. As can be seen from *Figure 3.1*, determining the height of the signal (the voltage) accurately is of crucial importance. The signal wire carries the signal, whilst the signal ground completes the circuit and allows the height of the signal to be determined. In practice, networks often use multiple voltage levels to represent many bit patterns. For example, by using four voltages we can encode two bits to each voltage, which allows transmission of twice as much data by each voltage level:

Voltage 1   00

Voltage 2   01

Voltage 3   10

Voltage 4   11

Three types of circuits are commonly used in networking:

- **simplex** – can carry signals in one direction only (e.g. a one-way street or a public address system);

- **half duplex** – can carry signals in both directions, but only one direction at a time (e.g. a walkie talkie or a narrow bridge where traffic from only one direction can cross at a time – under traffic light control);

- **full duplex** – carries signals in both directions simultaneously (e.g. a telephone or a dual carriage way).

Signal problems

Electrical signals are susceptible to a wide range of interference. For example, as the signal travels along the wire it loses some of its strength and arrives at the destination weaker (at a lower voltage), which makes it more difficult to determine how it was originally encoded – hence the big difference in the voltage levels used to represent a 0 and a 1. This loss of strength is known as **attenuation** and limits the distance a signal can travel without being amplified or regenerated. Attenuation can be addressed in analogue networks by amplifying the signal, or in digital networks, by repeating or regenerating the signal. Repeating is preferable as the signal generated by repeating is a perfect signal like the original, whereas amplifying also amplifies noise – similar to the quality difference between a DVD (digital) and a video (analogue).

TIPS & ADVICE

You must understand these three types of circuits, as they are often referred to in a range of networking situations.

TIPS & ADVICE

Assessors quite like the topic of sources of error as an examination question.

The following is a summary of the common sources of error:

- **Attenuation** – As the signal travels along the cable it becomes weaker. On long-distance runs, unless it is aided, the signal received can be too weak to use.

  On 100BaseT Ethernet, it is recommended that the cable lengths be no more than 100 m.

- **Impulse noise** – Sometimes known as **electromagnetic interference** (**EMI**), electrical signals given off by some electrical devices (e.g. fluorescent lights and electrical motors) can cause severe degradation to the signal or even destroy it. Lightning is also a cause of impulse noise. Care should be taken when routing the network cable to avoid close contact with such devices.

- **Thermal noise** – Thermal noise is the interference that comes from the cable itself – the distortion caused by moving the electrons. Very little can be done to address this.

- **Crosstalk** – Crosstalk is when two or more pairs of cables lying near each other interfere with the signals on the other cable. This used to be common on older telephone networks where you could hear someone else's conversation if you were quiet. Crosstalk can be largely eliminated by twisting the two wires in the circuit together (hence twisted pair cabling).

- **Intermodulation noise** – Similar to crosstalk except that the signals which interfere are being transmitted on the same cable (*see Broadband/baseband below*). A good example of this in the UK is Channel 5 TV, which is transmitted on a frequency used by most video recorders – if the video recorder and Channel 5 are switched on together they often interfere with each other. This problem can be addressed by altering the frequencies used for transmission.

- **Radiation** – Just as atmospheric conditions interfere with TV signals, they can also interfere with computer networks and telephone networks. Thankfully, such interference is rare and can be addressed by using shielded cabling.

- **Radio frequency interference** (**RFI**) – RFI is interference caused by devices emitting radio signals in the proximity of the network cable. Again, electric motors and fluorescent lights can be a source of this interference. Other sources include mobile phones and other devices that transmit radio signals. Reduction of such interference is identical the methods used to reduce to impulse noise.

- **Signal reflection** – If a network cable is not terminated correctly, the transmitted signal is reflected back from the open end of the cable and interferes with the remainder of the signal and others that follow. This was a particular problem with 10Base2 and 10Base5 networks. Network cable testers (**Time Domain Reflectors** (**TDRs**)) use this principle to determine cable length and broken circuits.

Electrostatic discharge (ESD)

Often referred to simply as **static** or **static electricity**, ESD is caused by the electrons becoming loosened and staying in one place, where they look for an opportunity to 'jump' to a conductor. ESD is the shock we feel when we have built up a charge from, for example, dragging our feet on a nylon carpet and then touching something – perhaps a metal stair banister. Other than a shock, it is usually harmless to human beings, but to sensitive electronic components, such as those found inside a computer or networking devices, it can be fatal. ESD can be as high as 40,000 volts, which can wreak havoc on a 5-volt computer circuit.

Broadband/baseband

A TV aerial cable carries many channels (e.g. BBC1 and ITV1). Although there is only one piece of cable, the TV stations are able to transmit using discrete frequencies – a different frequency for each channel. Technically, this is known as **broadband signalling**.

Computer networks can operate in a similar fashion – the available frequency range of the cable can be divided up and used to transmit different signals. Broadband services from telecommunications companies use this concept (e.g. **Asymmetric Digital Subscriber Line (ADSL)** – two channels for Internet access and another, separate channel for telephone. Thus a device (a microfilter) needs to be employed at the socket to divide the signals.

Alternatively, a signal can occupy the entire frequency range, which is known as **baseband signalling**. This allows the signal to use all the frequency range available on the cable and, hence, it has a higher throughput (more bandwidth). Ethernet uses this principle.

Packets

Data to be transmitted across the network is broken down into chunks known as **packets**. There are two main reasons for breaking the data down into chunks. To:

- reduce the amount of data lost to noise; and
- ensure fair access to the medium.

Let's imagine we need to transmit 2 MB of data – 2 x 8 gives us 16 Mb. Let's assume that, on average, the network can transmit only 2 Mb before an error occurs. Thus we could never transmit the data as a 16 Mb entity successfully – each transmission will be corrupted by an error and require retransmission. If we break the data into packets of, say, 0.5 Mb each, on average we will successfully transmit three packets before an error occurs, requiring only 0.5 Mb to be retransmitted. By reducing the size of the packet further, we can prevent even more data loss. However, as each packet needs to contain the sender and receiver addresses and some mechanism for detecting errors, if we reduce the packet size too much, these overheads will also reduce performance. Consequently and due to other reasons, packet size is fixed by network technology designers and cannot usually be altered by the user.

> **TIPS & ADVICE**
>
> Remember, data is measured in megabytes (MB) and data on a network is measured in megabits (Mb).

Breaking data into packets also provides a fairer way of sharing the medium – users each send a packet at a time rather than 'hogging' the medium until their transmission is over.

Error detection/correction

We cannot prevent errors from occurring in data transmission and it is imperative we detect all errors, since data with an error must not be used – consider a spreadsheet with financial information – if an error has occurred we don't know that the amounts are correct and so it is unsafe to use the data. You will most likely have studied parity as an error detection method in the past. Parity is one method of error detection but it is not accurate enough for today's networks because it does not detect all errors. Instead, we use **Cyclic Redundancy Checks (CRCs)** based on **32 bit polynomials** to detect errors. All that needs to be known is that they detect 99.997% of all errors and that correction requires the data to be retransmitted.

Quick test

1. Briefly describe how data can be sent over a computer network. Your answer should include encoding.

2. Describe the differences between full duplex, half duplex and simplex circuits.

3. Briefly describe the kinds of interference that can occur in computer networks and how these can be addressed.

Section 2: Network topologies

The words 'technology' and 'topology' are often used when discussing networks, and it is important to clarify these terms. Technologies are the hardware devices and their operation, whereas topology is the physical shape of the network. Different technologies require different topologies. In this section, the differing topologies available for computer networks are discussed, and the differences between logical and physical topology are distinguished.

Early star networks

In *Chapter 1*, we discussed the ways that local interactive terminals were connected to the mainframe computer – each had its own cable running back to the central computer forming a star pattern (the early star network – *see Figure 3.3*).

TIPS & ADVICE

Naming and drawing diagrams of various networking topologies is a popular type of examination question. Examiners may also ask you to discuss which topologies support a networking technology (*see Chapter 5*).

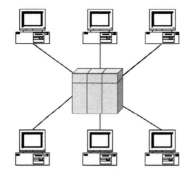

Figure 3.3: An early star network

Such cabling resulted in hundreds of cables descending upon the main computer and was costly in terms of cable and labour. Organisations often encountered problems in handling the sheer volume of cables, and relocating the central computer was a major issue.

The advantages of this type of topology, on the other hand, are:

- **robustness** – a cable break will only affect one machine;

- **performance** – each terminal has a dedicated cable.

RS232-C connectors (*see Figure 3.4*) are the standard connectors used here (known as D.25). The cable used was a variety of twisted pair (*which is illustrated in Figure 3.19 later in the chapter*).

Figure 3.4: D.25 serial connector

Point-to-point network

The point-to-point network is the simplest of all topologies. In the point-to-point topology (*see Figure 3.5*), two computers are connected together via a physical wire. It is a network because it has networking hardware and software to facilitate the exchange of information. The costs can be less than £20 at early 2009 prices (when implementation is based on Ethernet technology using a low cost switch and 100BaseT) and assuming that the computers are fitted with 100BaseT NICs. This is explored in more detail in *Chapter 5*. If a cross over cable (which can be used to connect two computers directly without the need for a switch) is used to create the network, then the costs can be as low as the price of a cable (less than £5 at early 2009 prices). This topology is useful in small organisations or the home where two computers may share costly resources, such as a colour laser printer, or to facilitate file transfer.

Figure 3.5: Point-to-point network

Bus network

The bus network (*see Figure 3.6*) used to be very common and was used by a number of technologies – most notably, Ethernet. In this topology, a central 'backbone' cable spans the area and computers 'tap' into this backbone for their connection. In a bus network, the communications medium is shared between the computers attached to it. The standard connector used in this type of network was the **British Naval Connector** (**BNC**) (*see Figure 3.8*). The cable used was coaxial cable (similar to that used by TV aerials and cable TV) (*see Figure 3.9*).

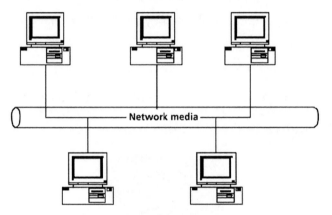

Figure 3.6: Bus network

The advantages of a bus network include the following:

- it was easy and inexpensive to install;
- it was easy to add further devices by tapping into the wire (avoiding the costs of expensive recabling);
- bandwidth was higher than in early star networks;
- facilitates communication with the interconnected device without going through the central computer.

The disadvantages include the following:

- the media was shared – therefore there was contention for access that required an algorithm to ensure fairness;
- data was sent in a broadcast fashion, meaning that all computers could 'see' the information – a security weakness;
- a cable break on the main bus cable took down the entire network;
- although the cable had higher capacity, it was shared among

many more users. As network traffic increased, capacity became an issue.

This kind of topology was popular (along with ring and tree networks, which are discussed in the next sections) from the mid-1980s until around 1992, when the volume of network traffic started to increase dramatically and consequently performance became an issue.

Tree network

It is possible to connect bus networks together to form a network that has branches with other bus networks. Such a topology is known as a **tree network** (*see Figure 3.7*). As it is essentially a bus network, a tree network has the same advantages and disadvantages as a standard bus network. The devices used at the joints are known as **hubs** and are a specialist piece of hardware. The standard connector used in this type of network was the **British Naval Connector** (**BNC**) (*see Figure 3.8*). The cable used was coaxial cable (similar to that used by TV aerials and cable TV) (*see Figure 3.9*).

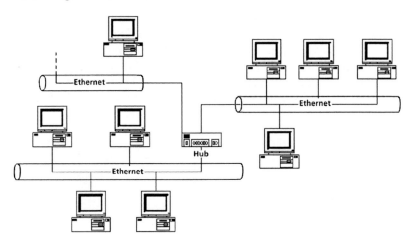

Figure 3.7: Tree network

Figure 3.8: British naval connector (BNC)

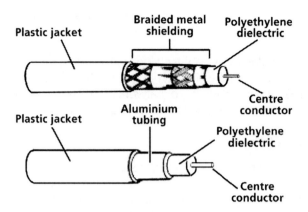

**Figure 3.9: Coaxial cable
(diagram courtesy of Professor Peter Hodson,
University of Glamorgan)**

Ring network

In the ring topology (*see Figure 3.10*), computers are connected to one another in a circular fashion and therefore form a ring. Although several companies and several implementations were involved, the two most notable were the Cambridge Ring (developed in Cambridge University and used extensively by Acorn in the BBC microcomputer series) and the Token Ring (developed and used extensively by IBM). The dominant network in this topology was IBM's Token Ring network.

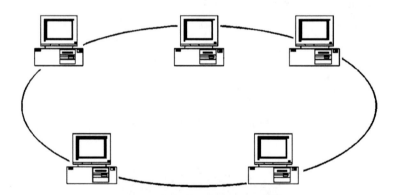

Figure 3.10: Ring network

The advantages of the ring topology are as follows:

- robustness – there are two links to each PC;

- in the case of Token Ring, higher capacity than 10Base2, 10Base5 (usually bus or tree networks) or 10BaseT Ethernet (modern star);

- a fairer method of access than standard Ethernet (*see Chapter 5*).

The major disadvantage was cost. As the equipment used in the Token Ring topology was IBM proprietary technology (which had a royalty fee attached to it), it was substantially more expensive than bus networks. Eventually, Ethernet gained the lion's share of the market (due to costs) and later versions of Ethernet outstripped the Token Ring's capacity.

Star with logical ring

Occasionally, ring networks (especially IBM's Token Ring) appear to be a star network (*see Figure 3.11*) as they run to a piece of hardware called a **Multistation Access Unit** (**MAU**). This essentially connects all the computers together and gives the network a star appearance. However, the network is very much a ring and operates as such.

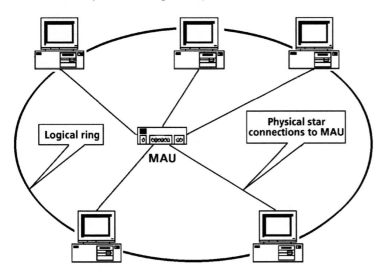

Figure 3.11: Logical ring

Connectors used in the IBM Token Ring are a proprietary technology (*see Figure 3.12*), although most are now RJ-45. The cable used was shielded twisted pair (*see Figure 3.13*). Shielded RJ-45 connectors are also commonly used with this technology (*see Figure 3.14*) – note the metal sides (where grounding provides shielding) to the RJ-45.

Figure 3.12: Typical Token Ring connectors

**Figure 3.13: STP cabling
(diagram courtesy of Professor Peter Hodson,
University of Glamorgan)**

Figure 3.14: STP RJ-45 connector (note the metal grounding)

Mesh network

With a **mesh network** (*see Figure 3.15*), a number of connections exist between machines so a route must be established in order to get from one machine to another. Mesh networks are complex and are designed to provide resilience in the event of a cable break. A mesh network can be either full or partial. In the case of a full mesh network, every node is directly connected to every other node – there is more than one route to every node in the mesh (*Figure 3.15* shows a full mesh network). As its name suggests, a partial mesh network is not complete. The Internet itself is a mesh network, as part of its original design specification was resilience. The major advantage of mesh networks is resilience, and the major disadvantages are cost and complexity. Mesh networks are almost always used for WAN links and, therefore, the cabling is provided by the service provider. A typical connector (V.35) is shown in *Figure 3.16*.

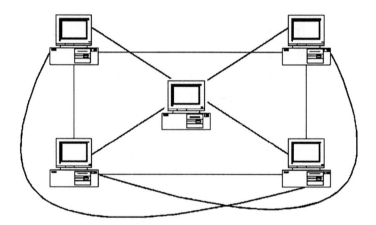

Figure 3.15: Full mesh network

Figure 3.16: Typical WAN serial connector (V.35)

Structured cabling solutions/modern star

Modern organisations experience a great deal of change during their lifetimes and have high demands for networks in terms of capacity and reliability. The original star network offered capacity that was dedicated to a terminal and that was extremely robust. Due to these advantages, the star network has been developed further and is the preferred solution for modern cabling. A modern star network (see *Figure 3.17*) has, at its centre, a wiring closet to which all communications points (telephone sockets, computer sockets, etc.) on that floor are connected. Inside the wiring closet, each connection terminates in a patch panel which can then be connected to a service using a patch lead. Services would typically include different computer networks, telephone services and perhaps ISDN lines.

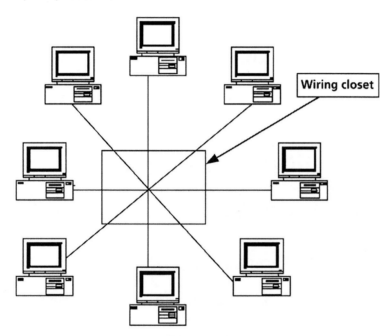

Figure 3.17: Modern star network

Known as a structured cabling solution, this is the recommended wiring structure for new installations, each installation requiring one wiring closet per 1000 m² floor space, interconnected by cable (usually fibre) known as **backbone** or **vertical cabling**. Structured cabling specifications require a minimum of two connection points to be installed per user and provide a very flexible communications solution. *Figure 3.18* shows a typical structured cabling solution. The PC is connected through an interface card (*see Chapter 5*) via a **drop cable** to the floor socket. This is connected directly to the patch panel in the wiring closet, this cabling is known as **horizontal cabling**. A patch lead then 'patches' the required service from the service point to the patch panel. In this case, the service is an Ethernet network. The standards for structured cabling recommend that **Category 5e**, or higher, **unshielded twisted pair** (**UTP**) cabling (*see Figure 3.19*) is used throughout the installation, terminated by RJ-45 plugs (*see Figure 3.20*) and sockets.

TIPS & ADVICE

Structured cabling is the standard in all new installations.

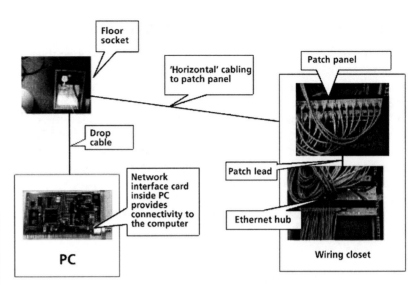

Figure 3.18: Typical structured cabling

KEY CONCEPT

It is important to be able to remember the various topologies and to be able to draw these topologies.

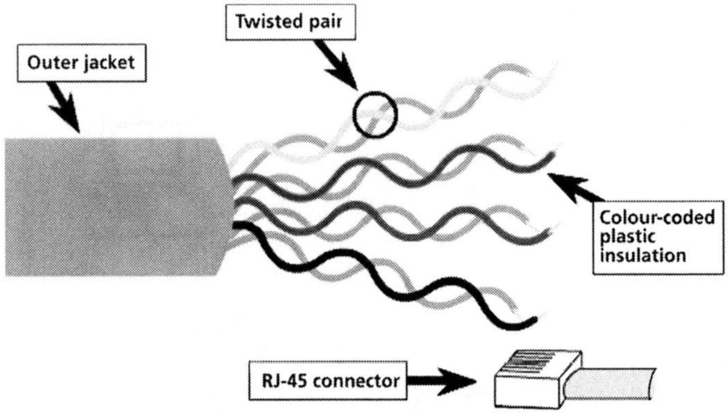

Figure 3.19: UTP cabling (diagram courtesy of Cisco Systems Inc.)

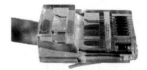

Figure 3.20: RJ-45 connector

Technologies

As well as having a physical shape, networks also need equipment in order for them to operate – for example, a **network interface card** (**NIC**), switch, etc. The equipment to support a network is known collectively as the technology (examples being Ethernet and Token Ring). The most popular technologies are discussed in detail in Chapter 5.

Quick test

1. Name the most common network topologies and discuss the differences between them.

2. For each of the topologies given, list any advantages/disadvantages.

Section 3: Network addressing and protocols

Computer networking is a complex business and requires rules to govern the communication. Such rules are known as protocols and are critical to computer networking. Most crucial of all is the **Open Systems Interconnection (OSI) seven-layer model** for computer communication (sometimes known as the **International Standards Organisation (ISO) seven-layer model**), which defines standards and protocols that are used extensively in the networking industry today.

Protocols

Computer communications are extremely complex, and there are many parameters that must be agreed before communication can take place. What was needed, therefore, where standards (or protocols) for communication between computers. In other areas, this problem has been resolved by breaking down one large, complex problem into several smaller ones – for instance, with personal CD players the jack for headphones is a standard 3.5 mm, which means that any headphones can be used; it can play any audio-compatible CD; a standard battery compartment means any make of batteries can be used; and, if the player has a mains adaptor, it can be plugged into any mains outlet that fits the adapter. This is because tight standards have been set that govern the production of all the pieces of equipment.

The same is true with networking: standards for networks were established and a model devised. This model, known as the **Open Systems Interconnection (OSI) seven-layer model**, was devised by members of the **International Standards Organisation (ISO)**. The layers of the OSI seven-layer model are shown in *Figure 3.21*, and the model is discussed in detail in *Chapter 4*. Prior to the model (which was devised in the early 1980s), vendors tended to produce proprietary network solutions, which reduced the end-user's choice and limited the connectivity of the machine.

| Application |
| Presentation |
| Session |
| Transport |
| Network |
| Datalink |
| Physical |

Figure 3.21: The OSI seven-layer model

The benefits the layered model brings are as follows:

- it breaks network communication down into smaller simpler parts that are easier to develop;

- it facilitates the standardisation of network components to allow multi-vendor development and support;

- it allows different types of hardware and software to communicate with each other;

- it prevents changes in one layer from affecting the other layers so that layer technologies can be developed more quickly;

- it makes networks easier to learn.

Whilst the seven-layer model brings many benefits, it has several disadvantages:

- redundant functions and facilities are retained;

- simple communication is made over complicated because of structure overheads;

- the structure overheads reduce the overall performance.

Logical and physical addressing

Devices on a network must be able to communicate directly with one another and must be uniquely identified. Communication can then take place in a similar way to the postal system: the sender addresses an envelope or package to a recipient (including a return address). The postal system examines the recipient's address and forwards the package as appropriate. This may involve the package being forwarded to another postal network or sorting office before being delivered to the recipient.

Computer networks operate on an almost identical principle. Each machine on the network has an address to which data can be forwarded. In order to reach its recipient, the package may have to cross multiple networks before it is delivered. On a computer, there are two possible addressing mechanisms:

- physical; and

- logical.

Physical addressing (also known as layer two addressing as it occurs in layer two of the OSI model) mechanisms are used internally within an organisation. They use an address that is hardcoded on to the **Media Access Control unit (MAC)** – usually part of the networking card (i.e. the NIC). With Ethernet networks, this is usually a 48 bit field that is unique across the world. Burnt into ROM (on the NIC) and unable to be changed, the first half of the address identifies the manufacturer; the second half is the unique serial number within the manufacturer's ID. Thus replacing a card will change the MAC address. Whilst this is acceptable for local area networks where the address is circulated as the machine interacts, it would clearly be impossible to know the physical address of every machine in the world (and to keep that list up to date!). Thus another mechanism for addressing machines globally is needed – the logical addressing mechanism.

Logical addressing is used for three main reasons. To:

- overcome the problem of a card change;
- allow the demarcation of networks;
- provide a structure to the addressing scheme.

The best analogy that can be drawn to logical addressing is the telephone network. If you purchased a phone and the serial number of that phone was your phone number, each time you changed the phone you would need to notify all your friends of your new number – something that is clearly undesirable. Also, as phones could be located anywhere in the world, when friends call you , the telephone network would have to try every phone in the world to find out if it was yours – a huge waste of resources. Instead, the telephone network is structured. For example, if you were to ring the University of Sunderland helpline from outside the UK, you would dial the following number:

00 44 191 5153000

The 00 routes the call from the local telephone exchange to an international one; the 44 routes the call to the UK; the 191 to the north east of England; the 515 to the University of Sunderland; and the 3000 is the number of the student helpline. This structure allows the telephone network to make much better use of its resources, and it allows demarcation of telephone networks – once the call has left one country/ service provider, it becomes the responsibility of another. Also, you can change your phone at will without having to notify your friends because your telephone number remains the same.

Logical addressing for networks is very similar. The most popular logical addressing mechanism is that used on the Internet – **Internet Protocol (IP)** addressing. With IP addressing, an organisation is issued with a block of IP addresses from its **Internet Service Provider (ISP)**, who is issued these by the **Network Information Center (InterNIC)** in the USA, or their **Regional Internet Registries (RIRs)** – (these organisations are examined in more detail later in the book). In the early stages of Internet development, the Network Information Center would issue blocks of numbers, known as licences, directly to large organisations – *see below*). There are two possibilities **IP version 4 (IPv4)** and **IP version 6 (IPv6)** we will examine IPv4 as it is easier to understand. IPv4 is a 4 byte dotted decimal. For example:

157.228.102.1

Computers are thus grouped under the organisation's or ISP's network address, which are issued in licenses. Although these numbers are dotted decimal, they are actually a decimal representation of 4 x eight bit binary digits (a byte). The largest number that can be represented by a byte is 255 (all 0s are reserved for the network address and all 1s are reserved for the broadcast address; therefore the maximum available is 254). There are three possible types of licence:

KEY CONCEPT

We need to use logical addressing to provide a means by which we can structure traffic on the Internet and maintain independence from the MAC address.

The Network portion of an IP address refers to the part of the IP address which identifies the network. The broadcast address is a special address (usually all binary 1s) within the network portion which is used to contact all devices on a network.

- **Class A licences** These were intended for very large organisations and were mainly issued to universities in the USA. In a class A licence, the first byte is fixed but the organisation is free to allocate addresses in the other bytes, giving it a maximum of 254 x 254 x 254=16.3 million possible addresses on its network. Class A licences are no longer issued. In a class A licence, the leftmost bit (the **Most Significant Bit (MSB)**) is always zero. The largest number that can be represented is therefore 127 and thus the range is: 1 –126. *X. X. X* (127 is reserved for the loopback address – a means of testing the network hardware and software on a computer). Thus, there are 126 class A licences each with 16.3 million addresses.

- **Class B licences** These were also issued to large organisations – many universities in the UK hold a class B licence. With a class B licence, the first two bytes are fixed, giving the organisation a maximum of 254 x 254 = 64,516 possible addresses on its network. Thus 157.228 uniquely identifies the University of Sunderland; the remaining parts of the address identify specific networks and machines within the University of Sunderland. Class B licences are very rarely issued now. The first two bits (the **Most Significant Bits (MSBs)**) of a class B licence are always 10. Therefore the effective range is 128 –191. *X. X. X.*

- **Class C licences** These are the most common and are still issued. In a class C licence, the first three bytes are fixed, giving the organisation 254 possible addresses on its network. The first three bits (the **Most Significant Bit (MSB)**) of a class C licence are always 110 therefore the effective range is 192 –223. *X. X. X.*

Internet service providers (ISPs) either allocate IP addresses statically – that is to say, a machine always has the same IP address (a necessity for a web server), or dynamically – leased for a period (usually 24 hours), after which it needs to be reviewed. Logical addressing is also known as layer-three addressing because it occurs at layer-three of the OSI seven-layer model.

Clearly, few organisations will ever have 16.3 million computers (which is the capacity of a class A licence) and few organisations holding a class B licence will ever have 64,516 computers – such allocation of IP addresses has meant huge wastage.

Classful Subnetworks (subnets)

As can be seen from the above explanation, with class A and B licences there would be a huge number of hosts on a network. If we take class A as an example, it is possible there could be 16.3 million computers on a single network. This is akin to having all the cars in the country on one road at the same time – there would be too much traffic and everything would grind to a halt. But just as the road network comprises many roads, the computer network can also be divided into smaller networks or subnetworks (often referred to as subnets). In a similar way to road networks, such a division reduces the load in each subnetwork enabling traffic to flow more freely. The key to good network design is traffic management (*see Chapter 7*).

The network is therefore divided using a subnetwork (or subnet) mask. As its name suggests, this is a mask (in the form of 4 bytes dotted decimal) that is applied to the IP number to determine the correct network for the traffic. The subnet mask is local to the network (i.e. it is not transmitted outside the network) and is found in a computer's settings. In Windows this can be found in the Network Connections box or by running **ipconfig** in a DOS command box (Windows XP, Vista and 2000) or **winipcfg** (in Windows 98) (*see Figure 3.22*).

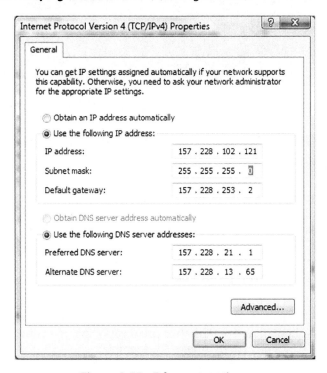

Figure 3.22: Ethernet settings

In this example, we can see that the IP address is class B (157 is in the class B range). Where there is a value other than zero in the subnet mask, the corresponding part of the IP address is treated as part of that network. Each part of the IP address is a byte (with a maximum value of 255) – in the *Figure 3.22* the subnet mask identifies that all the first, second and third bytes of the IP address relate to the network. Thus, host 121 is to be found on subnetwork 102 of major network 157.228 (*see Chapter 11* for an example).

Figure 3.23 shows how the **ipconfig** command displays similar information (note that this is for a different computer than the one shown in *Figure 3.22*).

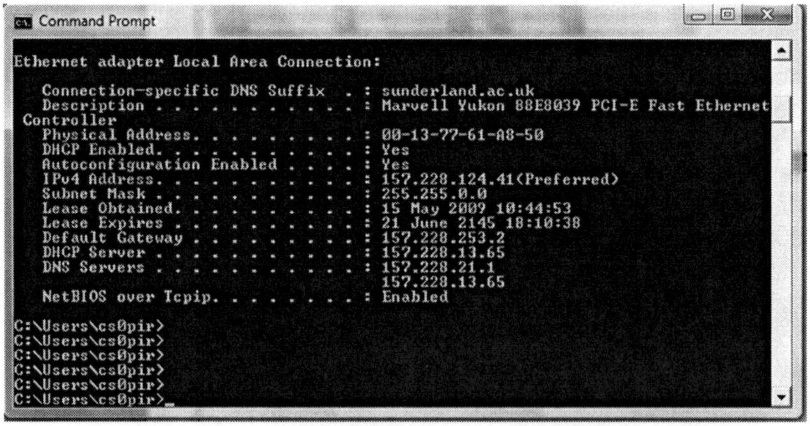

Figure 3.23: Ethernet settings (ipconfig in Windows Vista)

Section 4: Classless subnetworking and VLSM

The sub networking (subnetting) in the previous section is known as classful subnetting or classful addressing because the network address is broken into subnets at the dot (.). Thus 157.228.102.121 with a subnet mask of 255.255.255.0 means that the first 3 octets (157.228.102) define the network address and the 121 is the host address. However, there is also classless addressing.

Let us consider an example. Irving's Manufacturing has 5 departments (Sales, HR, Finance, Directorate and Production). If they had a class B licence (say beginning 157.228) they could easily split the network into 5 subnets – 1 for each department. For example:

157.228.1.X for Sales

157.228.2.X for HR

157.228.3.X for Finance

157.228.4.X for Directorate

157.228.5.X for Production

Thus the first 3 bytes (or octets) form the network portion of the address and the last octet the host portion.

The subnet mask would indicate that all bits in the 1st, 2nd and 3rd bytes are used to identify the network portion (255.255.255.0).

This would allow them to keep the traffic from each department separate, which would enhance network performance and tighten security. However the address space for Class A and B licences has been depleted to an extent that in 1994 there was an IP address ing crisis where the world effectively ran out of IP addresses.

In the IP address ing crisis of 1994 there were two main issues:

1. IPv4 address space largely depleted – only class C licences available;

TIPS & ADVICE

Because of the way IP addresses are distributed, approximately 75% of all IPv4 addresses are wasted. Consider a Class A licence, the first octet is fixed meaning the organisation can have 254 networks of 254 networks of 254 hosts – over 16.3 million addresses tied to one organisation. How many organisations have 16.3 million hosts?

Also, the special address 127.0.0.1 is reserved as the loopback address – 16.3 million IP addresses wasted here!

2. Class C licences cannot be subnetted in the traditional classful method.

Two solutions were found to the problem:

1. **Network Address Translation (NAT)** and later **Port Address Translation (PAT)** - *see later* and;

2. **Classless Inter Domain Routing (CIDR)**.

Thus if Irving's Manufacturing were instead allocated a class C licence – say 193.63.148.X then they could have up to 254 hosts but no subnets or any of the benefits that they bring. The solution to this lack of subnets was CIDR.

Classless Inter Domain Routing (CIDR)

CIDR essentially ignores the dots (.) in the dotted decimal notation and allows bits to be borrowed from the host portion of the IP address to represent networks. Thus if Irving's Manufacturing were allocated the above class C licence (193.63.148.X), some bits from the host portion of the address (the last octet in a class C licence) could be borrowed so they could be used to represent 5 subnets. Irving's Manufacturing wants subnets for:

- Sales

- Production

- Finance

- HR

- Directorate

How many bits do we borrow? Well, how many bits do we need to represent decimal 5? 5 in binary is 101, so we need 3 bits. With 3 bits we can have the following networks:

001

010

011

100

101

110

> **KEY CONCEPT**
>
> You must 'borrow' at least 2 bits and leave at least 2 bits. You can't use all 1s or all 0s.

We can't use 000 (as it is the network address) nor can we use 111 as this is the broadcast address. Thus by borrowing the first 3 bits from the last octet we can achieve the number of networks we desire.

We do, however, need a mechanism to tell the device that we are treating the first 3 bits of the last octet as belonging to the network portion. We do this by setting the 3 corresponding bits in the subnet mask to 1. Thus the last octet of the subnet mask becomes 11100000.

Let's take the first network (001) as an example. 001 is the network address, the first host on that network will be 00001 which makes the last octet look like this: 00100001. The **logical AND operator** is then used to calculate the network portion of the address, thus:

00100001 (address)

11100000 (subnet mask)

00100000 (The 'ANDing' result provides the network portion of the address)

Identifying that this address is for the first host on subnet 001 (decimal 32). If we convert the last octet to decimal we get 33 and the subnet mask to decimal gives 224. So what we actually enter into the device is:

IP Address: 193.63.148.33

Subnet mask: 255.255.255.224

Completing the example:

Dept	Binary	Decimal	IP addresses	Net Address	Broadcast
Sales	001	.32	.33-.62	.32	.63
Prod	010	.64	.65-.94	.64	.95
Fin	011	.96	.97-.126	.96	.127
HR	100	.128	.129-.158	.128	.159
Direct	101	.160	.161-.190	.160	.191
Spare	110	.192	.193-.222	.192	.223

Although CIDR seems to be the answer, it is not without its problems:

- IP addresses are wasted – in the above example, without CIDR Irving's Manufacturing would have had 254 usable IP addresses. As they have deployed CIDR they now have six networks of a maximum 30 hosts – 180 usable IP addresses;
- Not all devices (mainly legacy devices) are CIDR compatible;
- Not all routing protocols (for example RIP and IGRP – *see Chapter 6*) support CIDR.

Let's discuss another example. Irving College of Technology (ICoT) has been allocated a class C licence of 193.63.148.0 and wants to divide this into 8 networks:

- ICT
- Design
- Admin
- Product Design
- Faculty
- Finance
- HR
- Directorate

We need 8 networks, converting 8 to binary gives us 1000. Thus we need to borrow 4 bits from the host portion of the address to represent networks. The subnet mask needs to have the first 4 bits in the last octet set to one to identify that it is now part of the network portion of the address: 255.255.255.240

Addresses for the networks always begin 193.63.148 and we need to increment the 4 binary digits of the last octet to give the network address:

Binary	Decimal	IP addresses	Net Address	Broadcast
0001	.16	.17-.30	.16	.31
0010	.32	.33-.46	.32	.47
0011	.48	.49-.62	.48	.63
0100	.64	.65-.78	.64	.79
0101	.80	.81-.94	.80	.95
0110	.96	.97-.110	.96	.111
0111	.112	.113-.126	.112	.127
1000	.128	.129-.142	.128	.143

Thus our networks are:

Dept	Decimal	IP addresses	Net Address	Broadcast
ICT	.16	.17-.30	.16	.31
Design	.32	.33-.46	.32	.47
Admin	.48	.49-.62	.48	.63
Product Dsn	.64	.65-.78	.64	.79
Faculty	.80	.81-.94	.80	.95
Finance	.96	.97-.110	.96	.111
HR	.112	.113-.126	.112	.127
Directorate	.128	.129-.142	.128	.143

Variable Length Subnet Masking (VLSM)

The key difference between CIDR and VLSM is that with CIDR all subnets created need to have the same number of bits allocated to each subnet – they are of a fixed length. VLSM is an advancement which makes the number of bits allocated to each subnet variable. Let's look at Irving's Manufacturing again. From the CIDR example, we know that they have 6 usable subnets of 30 hosts. What happens if they have more than 30 hosts in one network but fewer in the other networks? Well, with CIDR they are stuck – they could use their spare network, but the hosts would still be on a separate network. The answer lies with Variable Length

Subnet Masking (VLSM). Let's have a look at the actual number of hosts per network in Irving's Manufacturing:

Dept	No. of hosts
Sales	9
Prod	33
Fin	4
HR	2
Direct	3

In total they have 51 hosts across 6 networks, however, because of the number of bits borrowed for CIDR to gain 6 subnets, they only have a maximum of 30 hosts per network. They are therefore in a position of having sufficient IP addresses (they have 6 x 30 = 180), but not enough per subnet. VLSM may help to solve the problem. In VLSM we calculate the number of bits we need to leave for hosts in each of the subnetworks:

Dept	No. of hosts	Binary	Bits needed for host portion of address
Sales	9	1001	4
Prod	33	100001	6
Fin	4	100	3
HR	2	10	2
Direct	3	11	3 (11 is a broadcast address so leave an extra bit)

To simplify this procedure, we then rank this from most required to least:

Dept	No. of hosts	Binary	Bits needed for hosts	Left for net
Prod	33	100001	6	2
Sales	9	1001	4	4
Fin	4	100	3	5
Direct	3	11	3	5
HR	2	10	2	6

We now calculate the subnet mask per required subnet:

Dept	Binary Net Address	Binary Host addresses	Subnet Mask
Prod	01	000001 – 111110	11000000
Sales	1000	0001-1110	11110000
Fin	10010	001-110	11111000
Direct	10011	001-110	11111000
HR	101000	01-10	11111100

We can now turn this into decimal:

Dept	Decimal Net Address	Decimal Host addresses*	Dec. S/Net Mask
Prod	.64	.65-.126	.192
Sales	.128	.129-142	.240
Fin	.144	.145-.150	.248
Direct	.152	.153-.158	.248
HR	.160	.161-.162	.252

* This includes the base network address, thus 65 is 01000001.

KEY CONCEPT

A very common mistake is not ensuring the next network starts above the current network. For example Production starts binary 01, therefore the next network above must start binary 10 – the network binary 0100 is inside of the network binary 01, whereas binary 1000 is in the next network.

Irving's Manufacturing class C licence is:

193.63.148

Thus the first valid IP address for the production network is: 193.63.148.65 with a subnet mask of 255.255.255.192.

Let's discuss another smaller example. Irving's Primary school wants three networks – we'll use the same class C IP address 193.63.148:

Name	Hosts
Children	62
Staff	9
Admin	4

Dept	No. hosts	Binary	Bits needed for host portion of address
Children	62	111110	6
Staff	9	1001	4
Admin	4	100	3

They are already ranked, so we can now calculate the subnet mask per required subnet:

Dept	Binary Net Address	Binary Host addresses	Subnet Mask
Children	01	000001 – 111110	11000000
Staff	1000	0001 – 1110	11110000
Admin	10010	001 – 110	11111000

We can now turn this into decimal:

Dept	Decimal Net Address	Decimal Host addresses*	Dec. S/Net Mask
Children	.64	.65-.126	.192
Staff	.128	.129-.142	.240
Admin	.144	.145-.150	.248

TIPS & ADVICE

This section has shown the easier way to determine addresses based on CIDR and VLSM – no account has been taken of route aggregation (or supernetting) as it is beyond the scope of this book.

Thus the first usable IP address for Children is 193.63.148.65 with a subnet mask of 255.255.255.192; for Staff it will be 193.63.148.129 with a subnet mask of 255.255.255.240; and for Admin it will be: 193.63.148.145 with a subnet mask of 255.255.255.248.

Quick test

Unfortunately with CIDR and VLSM, there are no quick tests – you need to be able to do it. Normally you won't be given this as part of an exam or time-constrained test but probably as part of an assignment.

Irving's Stores have a class C licence (193.63.148) and require four networks. Using CIDR, determine an addressing scheme.

Supposing Irving's stores required the following hosts per subnet:

Handheld devices	42 hosts
Checkouts	17 hosts
Admin	9 hosts
Directorate	4 hosts

Prove that CIDR won't allow this flexibility and so, using VLSM, determine an addressing scheme.

Section 5: Network Address Translation (NAT) and Port Address Translation (PAT)

Another response to the IP addressing crisis was to limit the number of real or Public IP addresses which needed to be assigned. For example, if an organisation wanted to use an IP addressing scheme internally, but never wanted to connect to the Internet, they wouldn't need IP addresses which can be routed across the Internet (Public IP addresses). Instead they can use any IP addressing scheme they wish – as long as they don't connect to the Internet. In 1994 not all organisations wanted to connect to the Internet and so this was still a possibility,However, the **Internet Engineering Task Force (IETF)** wanted to ensure that should such organisations decide to connect to the Internet in the future that these internally allocated IP addresses wouldn't cause disruption to the Internet. The IETF made a recommendation (called a **Request For Comments (RFC)** which created **Private IP addresses**.

Private IP addresses are a widely-known range of IP addresses which are not routable across the Internet. This means that the routing devices in the Internet are configured to drop any packets using these well-known addressing schemes. An organisation, which wanted an addressing scheme internally but which didn't want to connect to the Internet, was (and still is) advised to use Private IP addresses.

Private IP addresses

RFC 1918 defined three private address ranges:

Class A	10.0.0.0	with a 8 bit prefix (the 1st octet is fixed)
Class B	172.16.0.0	with a 12 bit prefix – 1st octet and first 4 bits of the 2nd octet are fixed
Class C	192.168.0.0	with a 16 bit prefix – 1st two octets are fixed

It is strongly recommended that anyone wishing to use an IP address range for internal purposes only uses one of the above ranges. In the event they connect to the Internet, these address ranges aren't routable and therefore won't corrupt the routing of information on the Internet.

There is also a range of Private IP addresses for IPv6 (*see later*).

This preserved the pool of legitimate or Public IP addresses which are needed by organisations if they are to connect to the Internet.

Network Address Translation (NAT)

As discussed above, an organisation only needs a **Public IP address** if it is connecting to the Internet and only when it is connected to the Internet. In other words, it would be possible for an organisation to use Private IP addressing for internal communication and to use a Public IP address only when it wants to connect to the Internet. **Network Address Translation (NAT)** makes this possible by allowing devices

> **KEY CONCEPT**
>
> **Public IP address allocation is controlled by the Network Information Center in the USA (InterNIC) through its five Regional Internet Registries (RIRs):**
>
> **RIPE for Europe**
>
> **AFRINIC for Africa**
>
> **LACNIC for Latin America**
>
> **APNIC for Asia Pacific Region**
>
> **ARIN for North America and Canada**

on a network with Private IP addressing to share one or more Public IP addresses.

Figure 3.24 shows a typical deployment of NAT. The router (carrying out NAT) sits between the organisation's internal network and the ISP. Computers on the inside of the network are using a Private IP address range (as defined by RFC 1918). When a computer on the inside network wishes to communicate over the Internet, the router translates the internal private network IP address (192.168.1.1) to the external IP network address (157.228.1.1) – hence the term 'network address translation'. The packet originating from 192.168.1.1 cannot be routed over the Internet (as it is a Private IP address) and has its source address replaced by that of the router before being placed on the Internet. The router keeps a table of internal and external mappings to use when a reply is received (*see Figure 3.25*).

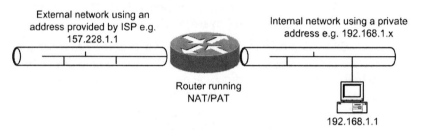

External network using an address provided by ISP e.g. 157.228.1.1

Internal network using a private address e.g. 192.168.1.x

Router running NAT/PAT

192.168.1.1

Figure 3.24: A router (see chapter 6) using NAT/PAT connecting an internal and external network

Inside IP address	Outside IP address
192.168.1.1	157.228.1.1

Figure 3.25: Sample IP address mapping

When the reply is received, the router looks up the destination IP address in the map and translates it to the internal IP address before placing the packet on the internal network where it will be received by the machine that sent it. The translation can then be deleted from the map.

In this simple example, only one IP address is used for translation. This gives the restriction that only one internal computer can use the Internet at any one point in time – requests will be queued. In reality this solution wouldn't work and so a pool of external IP addresses can be defined that will allow a number of computers to access the Internet up to the maximum number of addresses in the pool.

Most household routers (DSL or cable) use NAT or PAT.

Port Address Translation (PAT)

In the case of smaller organisations or even in the home, only one IP address may be allocated preventing multiple computers from accessing the Internet at the same time. Another technique – **Port Address Translation (PAT)** – is used to overcome this issue. PAT works in an identical fashion to NAT except that in addition to the IP address a port address is appended to the IP address. Wherever possible, PAT attempts to preserve the original source port number. However, if this is not possible then PAT assigns the first available port number from the beginning of the port groups (0-511, 512-1023 or 1024-65535). Port addresses are a normal part of an IP address , for example when we make a web request the port number 80 is automatically appended to the destination IP address . With PAT we are using unused source port numbers and appending them to the outside source IP address . The router then maps the IP address and the port numbers; and by using different port numbers for the different computers, it is able to allow multiple computers to share one IP address . *Figure 3.26* shows an example of this.

Inside IP address	Outside IP address
192.168.1.1	157.228.1.1:1024
192.168.1.2	157.228.1.1:1025

Figure 3.26: An example of PAT. Note two PCs now using the single IP address

The examples in *Figure 3.26* show NAT being used dynamically for outbound traffic only. However, there are instances where we want NAT to be applied to inbound traffic. *Figure 3.27* shows a typical organisation with a web server. The web server needs to be accessible via a real IP address. In this case, one of the two IP addresses provided by the ISP is statically mapped using static NAT to the address of the web server (e.g. 157.228.1.2), the remaining address being used for dynamic NAT. Thus, 157.228.1.2 is statically mapped to 192.168.2.1. Any inbound packets to 157.228.1.2 will be translated to 192.168.2.1. 157.228.1.1 will be used for dynamic NAT outbound.

Key Concept

The PAT example (left) is simplified to aid understanding. In reality, the inside IP address will also use a port number as part of its source address. The usual cause for this is that a PC may have many Internet enabled applications in progress at once – perhaps several web browser windows, MSN, etc. The PC uses port numbers on the source IP address to keep track of which application the returning packets should be sent to.

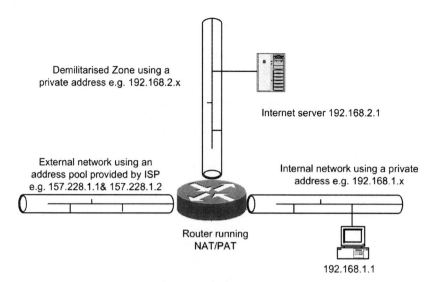

Figure 3.27: Typical deployment using static and dynamic NAT

Static NAT provides a means by which the web server can be accessed from a real IP address whilst the internal LAN is still protected. Notice that the Internet server is on a less secure network than the internal network – the so called **DeMilitarised Zone** (**DMZ**).

Quick test

Briefly describe what is meant by the terms NAT and PAT and give an example of how they are used (ideally use diagrams to illustrate your answer).

Section 6: IPv4 and IPv6

One of the key factors causing the IP addressing crisis of 1994 was that the address space of IP version 4 (IPv4) was depleted, and that IP version 6 (IPv6) with its extended IP address ranges was not yet ready.

Throughout this book IPv4 is used for examples as it is by far the most common IP addressing scheme (and easier to understand). However, it is important that you know about IPv6 and the differences between them.

Although creating expanded addressing capabilities was the primary motivation for IPv6, the IETF also took the time to consider other issues, the result being that IPv6 is not merely a new layer 3 protocol – it is a new protocol suite. As NAT, PAT, CIDR and VLSM have been so successful, IPv6 will rarely be seen in an organisation, however, it is now deployed in the Internet itself . You may notice that Windows Vista also has the option for setting an IPv6 address (*see Figure 3.28*).

TIPS & ADVICE

Wondering what happened to IPv5?

IPv5 did exist for research purposes but was never publicly released.

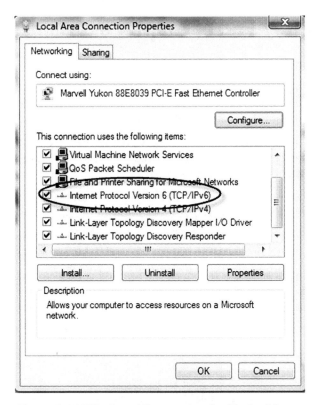

Figure 3.28 Windows Vista option for IPv6 address.

An IPv4 address is 32 bits in length – four octets of dotted decimal. For example, 157.228.102.121. IPv6 extends this addressing space by increasing this to 128 bits which is in hexadecimal (base 16) format. For example, a valid IPv6 address is: 2031:0000:130F:0000:0000:09C0:876A:130B. The subnet mask is now replaced with a subnet prefix length.

There are rules about shortening IPv6, but these are beyond the scope of this book. It is suffice to say that IPv6 offers:

- improved packet handling and security;
- larger addressing space; and
- **Quality of Service** (**QoS**) mechanisms.

Key Concept

IPv 6 dramatically extends the addressing space of the Internet and will be used for years to come in a world where we have more and more connected devices.

Section 7: End of chapter assessment

Questions

1. Discuss how data is encoded on to a transmission medium and why a packet structure is used. You should use any necessary diagrams to illustrate your answer.

2. For each popular networking topology, draw a diagram illustrating the topology and highlight any advantages/ disadvantages of the topology.

3. Discuss the terms 'logical' and 'physical' addressing. Highlight any differences and give an example of the use of each.

4. You may be asked to design an addressing scheme for a fictional organisation using, CIDR and VLSM techniques.

5. Describe what is meant by the terms NAT and PAT. Using diagrams to illustrate your answer, show how NAT and PAT can be deployed in a network to preserve Public IP addresses.

6. Outline the key differences between IPv4 and IPv6.

Answers

1. This question tests your knowledge of network basics. The assessor is trying to find out if you understand the fundamentals of computer communications – that we need to encode data as a voltage for transmission, that we use at least two voltages (and why), and that a packet structure is necessary. To answer it, you need to discuss how data is encoded on to the medium and why a packet structure is used. Wherever possible, you should illustrate your answer with diagrams.

2. Topologies are a common question and come in a variety of guises. Once you have learnt the topologies, tackling such a question is fairly easy – all you need to do is to draw a diagram of each of the topologies and to list their advantages and disadvantages. Drawing the diagrams is an essential part of the answer.

3. This particular question is trying to establish whether you know about the addressing mechanisms used in computer networking. The ideal answer to this question would discuss both terms separately, highlight any differences between them and discuss why these differences are necessary. You should illustrate your answer with examples of both addressing mechanisms and, for extra marks, highlight why the Internet could not run with physical addressing mechanisms. Comparing addressing schemes to either the postal service or the telephone network will impress the assessor and will earn you extra marks.

4. Subnetting, CIDR and VLSM are almost always used in a design scenario (usually as part of an assignment). You will usually be

given a fictitious organisation and asked to use CIDR and/or VLSM techniques to design their network addressing scheme. You should practice with the examples given in *Section 4* until you feel confident. Most of the questions you face should be at this level and you should answer as per the examples in section 4

5.   This question is trying to establish what you know about NAT and PAT. The ideal answer would start with NAT, outline what the term means and why it was used. It would then give an example diagram (similar to the one in section 5) and discuss how NAT works showing the Private and Public IP addresses. Ideally it would conclude the NAT section by highlighting the benefits of NAT and the limitations. The answer would then give PAT similar treatment and show how PAT addresses the limitations of NAT.

6.   IPv6 is a very complex protocol. It is unlikely you will be given a question on it as it is beyond the scope of this level. What is important is that you understand it is available and that it extends the addressing space and that there are other enhancements.

Section 8: Further reading and research

Cisco Networking Academy Program (2004) CCNA 1 and 2 *Companion Guide* (3rd edn) Cisco Press. ISBN: 1-5871315-0-1 . Chapters 1, 7 and 8.

Network Fundamentals, CCNA Exploration Labs and Study Guide (2008). Cisco Press. 1-58713-203-6. Chapter 6.

Accessing the WAN, CCNA Exploration Labs and Study Guide (2008). Cisco Press. 1-58713-205-2. Chapter 7.

Computer Systems Architecture (2002) R. M. Newman, E. Gaura and D. Hibbs Lexden Publishing. ISBN 978-1-904995-09-8.

'A Brief History of the Internet,' www.isoc.org/internet/history/brief.shtml

'Internet Protocol v4 Address Space,' **www.iana.org/assignments/ipv4-address-space**

'Classless Inter-Domain Routing (CIDR): an Address Assignment and Aggregation Strategy,' www.ietf.org/rfc/rfc1519.txt

Chapter 4

Standards

Chapter summary

One of the most important things to understand when studying networking is the standards that have been established in this area. The main set of standards that has helped networks evolve so quickly is the **Open Systems Integration (OSI)** seven-layer model. This provides a model for the development of computer communication and is fundamental to the study of networking. Other models exist, however, the most important being the transmission control protocol/Internet protocol model. TCP/IP is of great importance as the Internet is built around this model. This chapter concentrates on the OSI and TCP/IP models. (The benefits of the seven-layer model were discussed in *Chapter 3*.)

Learning outcomes

After studying this chapter you should aim to test your achievement of the following outcomes. You should be able to:

Outcome 1: OSI seven-layer model

Understand the concept of, and each layer of, the OSI seven-layer model. Question 1 at the end of this chapter will test your ability to do this.

Outcome 2: TCP/IP model

Understand the TCP/IP model and each of its layers. Question 2 at the end of this chapter will test your ability to do this.

Outcome 3: Comparison of the models

Understand the differences and similarities between the OSI seven-layer model and the TCP/IP model. Question 3 at the end of this chapter will test your ability to do this.

How will you be assessed on this?

Of all the topics in networking, assessors feel obliged to assess your knowledge of this subject – the study of these models is like the study of the human body to medicine! Assessment usually takes place in an exam or TCT – the subject lends itself well to this. In my experience of writing exam papers in the last 14 years, each paper has had at least one question on these models.

TIPS & ADVICE

This chapter is probably the most important in this book, and understanding the concepts explained in this chapter is key to the study of networking. *You should study this chapter repeatedly until you understand it.* This study shouldn't be in vain – you are almost guaranteed to be assessed on it. This is even more true of MCSE or CCNA professional qualifications.

Section 1: The OSI seven-layer model

Early computer networking evolved slowly and in a proprietary fashion until those bodies involved in networking came together under the umbrella of the **International Standards Organisation (ISO)** and developed the **Open Systems Interconnection (OSI)** model. This model has been critical to the rapid development of computer networking and will continue to influence the future development of networking. Understanding the seven-layer model is an absolute necessity for the continued study of networking and for most professional qualifications.

The OSI seven-layer model

The OSI seven-layer model (sometimes referred to as the ISO seven-layer model) basically divides the complex process of computer communication into smaller, tightly defined parts that aid understanding and network development (the benefits of a layered approach are discussed in *Chapter 3*). Breaking the process into smaller parts, has meant that opportunities have been provided for vendors to specialise in particular areas of networking rather than offering a complete service. This is common practice in other industries (for example, as we saw in *Chapter 3*, with portable CD players). The layers of the OSI seven-layer model were given in *Figure 3.21* in the last chapter but are shown here again for convenience in *Figure 4.1*.

Application
Presentation
Session
Transport
Network
Data link
Physical

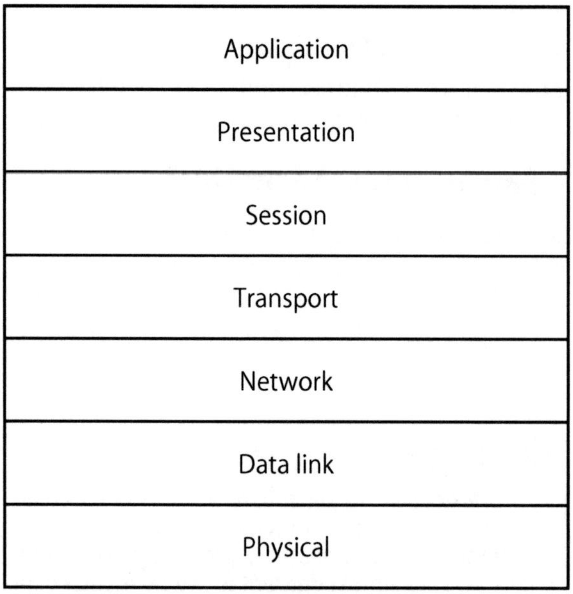

Figure 4.1: The OSI seven-layer model

The seven-layer model facilitates communication between any two computer systems that support the model, even though their underlying architecture, encoding mechanisms (e.g. ASCII, **Extended Binary Coded Decimal Interchange Code (EBCDIC)**) and method of storage may be totally incompatible. The model therefore allows totally incompatible machines (such as Apple Macs and PCs) to share data, to send email and to browse the web. The model achieves this by converting the data into an abstract data type that can be understood by both machine types and through handling all aspects of communication between the machines.

To understand the process of conversion, it might be helpful to consider an abstract example. A French businessman wishes to speak to a Greek businesswoman over the phone. Neither can speak the language of the other and so they decide to use interpreters. Unfortunately, they cannot find a French-to-Greek interpreter in either country but can find a French-to-English in France and a Greek-to-English in Greece. By using the common language of English, they have found a basis for communication, albeit one step removed. They also need to set up the call (through the company telephone operator), to have mechanisms in place to redial should the connection be broken, to establish mutual standards of speaking courteously, etc. They may also need to handle delays in the telephone network. *Figure 4.2* shows how such a communication structure might look.

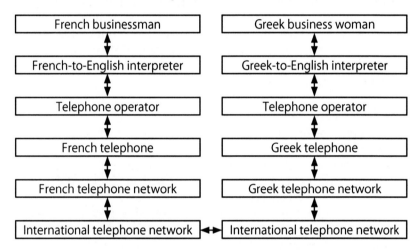

Figure 4.2: Communicating using telephones

As can be appreciated, this process is quite complex: the business people don't need to know how the telephone networks operate or how the telephone operates, the language of the other person or even the number to dial. They simply rely on services provided by the others, but the services must meet standards. The seven-layer model uses the same concept for computer communication, although the functions of each layer are clearly different.

The upper layers

The top three layers of the model are application orientated – that is, they are machine and operating-system specific, converting the data received from the network into a usable form and vice versa.

Layer 7: the application layer

The application layer is the network layer that is closest to the user. It differs from the other layers in that it doesn't provide services to any other OSI layer. It provides the user's application (e.g. browsers, telnet, word processors, spreadsheets) with network services, such as file access, Internet access and shared printing. One of the best ways of remembering the application layer and its function is to think of it as the interface for browsers.

Layer 6: the presentation layer

The presentation layer is responsible for converting between data formats – putting the data to be sent into an abstract form and converting data received into a format suitable for the machine. The presentation layer is also responsible for data compression and is associated with such formats as JPEG, GIF and applications such as Quicktime. The easiest way to remember it is to think of it as the French-to-English translator.

Layer 5: the session layer

The session layer is responsible for establishing, managing and terminating sessions between two communicating hosts. It also provides for the synchronisation of dialogue between the hosts, for session regulation, for efficient data transfer, for class of service and for exception reporting. Effectively, the session layer controls the dial-up box that springs up when we attempt to use the Internet without having a connection. It also controls dialogues and conversations. Think of the session layer as springing up the dial-up box.

The lower layers

So far we have been discussing information to be sent as data. As discussed in *Chapter 3*, the data, however, must be broken down into packets to be transmitted effectively across the network. It is in the lower layers that the data enters the process of being broken down. Hence, the lower layers of the model are concerned with data transport, whereas the upper three layers are concerned with application issues. This boundary can be thought of as that between application protocols and data-flow protocols.

Layer 4: the transport layer

The transport layer breaks the data from the sending host down into units called **segments** and reassembles the segments received into data. This layer also provides the session layer with a transport service and shields it from details such as reliability and flow control. In order to provide a reliable service, transport error detection, error recovery and information flow control are used (think of flow control and reliability for ease of memory). **Transmission Control Protocol (TCP)** and **User Datagram Protocol (UDP)** are used extensively in the transport layer.

Layer 3: the network layer

The network layer is a complex layer where logical addressing resides. It is the layer that provides connectivity and path selection between the host systems. The Internet operates at this layer. The devices in it (often represented by the 'cloud' in diagrams) switch the data packets to the appropriate path using the logical address (this is known as routing and is examined in detail in *Chapters 6* and *11*). The hosts can be on geographically separate networks.

In this layer the data continues to be broken up as the segments are broken into packets suitable for transmission across the Internet. Headers and footers are added to the packets to make them suitable for transmission. The most important elements in the header are the destination address (the network address of the destination machine) and the source address (the network address of the sending machine). Nowadays these addresses are almost always IP addresses – and we can think of them as such (*see Chapter 3* for more information on IP addresses). The most important element in the footer is the **Cyclic Redundancy Checks** (**CRC**) – *see Chapter 3*). Note that the size of the data is increasing as we add the headers and footers. (To remember this layer, think of path selection, routing and logical addressing.)

Layer 2: the data link layer

The data link layer provides for the transit of data across a physical link, and as such, it uses physical addresses. These addresses are particular to the networking technology in use – i.e. a situation of network dependency. Whilst the technology itself embraces this layer, it also covers access to the communications medium (*see Chapter 5*).

The data continues to be broken up. The packets are taken from the network layer and are broken into frames suitable for transmission over the implemented network technology. Different network technologies – for example, Ethernet and Token Ring (*see Chapter 5*) – have different frame sizes and composition – just as the envelopes used for letters differ in size between the USA and the UK. Again, headers and footers are added to the data. The headers contain the physical addresses of the source and destination machines, and the footer contains another CRC for the frame. (To remember this layer, think of frames and access control.)

Layer 1: the physical layer

The physical layer is the very bottom of the model and is concerned with the electrical, mechanical, procedural and functional specifications for activating, maintaining and deactivating the physical link between end systems. The data is sent from this layer one bit at a time, perhaps as voltages on a wire. Thus the data needs to be broken up into further bits at this layer of the model. The properties that allow the data to be sent and received accurately (such as voltage levels, timing of voltage changes, physical data rates, etc.) need to be defined in this layer. Maximum transmission distances, physical connectors and other similar attributes are defined in this layer's specification. (The best way to remember this layer is to think of physical properties and bits.)

Quick test

List the seven layers of the OSI seven-layer model and briefly describe each. Now amend your answer to show how the data is encapsulated at each layer.

TIPS & ADVICE

In this discussion of the seven-layer model we have looked at five distinct formats in which the data is converted or encapsulated. From the smallest units upwards these are:

- bits;
- frames;
- packets;
- segments;
- datastream.

Again, a phrase might help you to remember this. My favourite is:

British

Forces

Postal

Service

The data simply comes at the end!

TIPS & ADVICE

The seven-layer model will almost certainly crop up as an examination question at some point. The model is so fundamental to networking that an examiner is almost duty-bound to ask it! You may as well, therefore, make life simple and learn it thoroughly now.

Section 2: The TCP/IP model

Although the OSI model is recognised and used universally, the open standard for the Internet is **Transmission Control Protocol/Internet Protocol (TCP/IP)**. TCP/IP makes data communication possible between two computers (running appropriate software) anywhere in the world at almost the speed of electricity (consider emails). The US Department of Defense (DoD) design specification for the Internet was for a computer network that allowed military bases to communicate across the world and which was also capable of surviving a war (including a nuclear war). Thus the Internet is a mesh network (*see Chapter 3*) with multiple paths to each location to allow the data packets to get through every time under any conditions. This presented challenges for the designers (remember the Internet was developed in the late 1960s) who went on to develop a four-layer model (*see Figure 4.3*). It is important to bear the original intention of the Internet in mind as we examine this model.

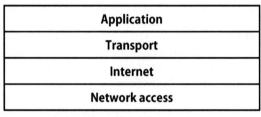

Figure 4.3: The TCP/IP model

Application layer

The designers of the Internet chose to create a layer that could handle all the higher or application-orientated protocols. Thus the application layer (sometimes referred to as the process layer) handles high-level data protocols, issues of representation, encoding and dialogue control. Just like the seven-layer model, this layer ensures the data is properly packaged for the next layer.

Transport layer

Also known as the host-to-host layer, the transport layer is in the same place in this model as it is in the seven-layer model. As with the seven-layer model, data is segmented within this layer ready for the next layer. The transport layer provides some of the protocols that are used to send data across the Internet. Specifically, it provides the **Transmission Control Protocol (TCP)**, which supports connection-orientated services such as **File Transfer Protocol (FTP)**, **Hypertext Transfer Protocol (HTTP)**, **Simple Mail Transfer Protocol (SMTP)** and **Domain Name Services (DNS)** (for domain name look-ups). It also provides a connectionless service known as **User Datagram Protocol (UDP)**, which provides a faster but unreliable service. Generally, UDP is used for **trivial FTP (TFTP)**, **Voice over IP (VoIP)** and sometimes DNS.

Internet layer

This is best thought of as the postal service that delivers the letters (or, in this case, packets) you send. Segments are accepted from the transport layer and converted into packets. It allows these packets to be transmitted from any network on the Internet so they arrive at their destination independent of the path and networks it took to get there. The best route must be selected at this layer (e.g. it mustn't select a link that is down), which is known as **path determination**. The placing of the data on to the link is known as **switching**. **Routers** (*see Chapter 6*) handle these tasks. The Internet layer is roughly equivalent to the network layer of the seven-layer model.

Network access layer

This layer is essentially a combination of the seven-layer model's physical and data link layers. As such, it is concerned with all the issues an IP packet requires to cross a physical link from one device to another directly-connected device. This is sometimes called the host-to-network layer. Data encapsulation into frames and bits is also handled by this layer.

Quick test

List the four layers of the TCP/IP model and briefly describe each one.

Section 3: Comparison of the models

The OSI seven-layer model and the TCP/IP model perform a similar function in that they allow any connected computers to communicate. *Figure 4.4* compares the seven-layer model and the TCP/IP model.

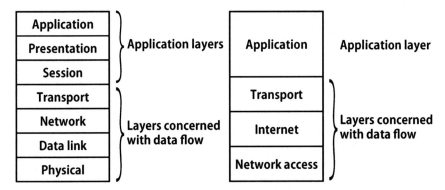

Figure 4.4: Comparison of the OSI seven-layer model and the TCP/IP model

The similarities between the two models can be summarised as follows:

- both are layered models and, as such, have the benefits of layering (*see Chapter 3*);

- both have application layers, although the TCP/IP application layer incorporates the session and presentation layers;

- the transport layer is comparable in each;

- the Internet layer (TCP/IP) and the network layer (OSI) are comparable;

- both have packet switched technology.

- networking professionals need to understand both models.

The differences can be summarised as follows:

- TCP/IP appears simpler because it has fewer layers;

- TCP/IP combines the presentation and session layers into the application layer;

- TCP/IP combines the OSI data link and physical layers into one layer, known as the network access layer;

- The OSI seven-layer model is used as a guide around which networks are built.

TCP/IP protocols are the standards around which the Internet was developed. These protocols are in use across the entire Internet, which gives the model great credibility.

Quick test

Draw a diagram that compares the OSI seven-layer model with the TCP/IP model. Briefly identify the similarities and differences between the two models.

Section 4: End of chapter assessment

Questions

1.   Identify the layers of the OSI seven-layer model and briefly describe each one.

2.   Identify the layers of the TCP/IP model and briefly describe the function of each one.

3.   Compare and contrast the OSI seven-layer model and the TCP/IP model.

Answers

1.   In this kind of question the examiner is looking for two things:

- your knowledge of the layers;

- your understanding of what each layer does.

Using a phrase (perhaps 'please do not throw sausage pizza away'), you can construct a diagram showing the OSI seven-layer model. For that 'finishing touch', you can show you understand which are application-related layers and which are networking related. You can also impress by stating that the seven-layer model is used as a guide around which networks are built. Next you need to discuss each layer in turn, highlighting the services and functions in each layer. If you can remember some of the standards (e.g. JPEG, GIF, RTF, etc., in the presentation layer), mention them. Remember each layer (apart from application) provides a service to the layer above and utilises the services of the layer below (apart from the physical layer). For really high marks, you could also discuss data encapsulation at layers 1–4 and the fact that it is a data stream at layer 5 (remember 'British Forces Postal Service').

2. Again, the examiner is looking for two things:

    • your knowledge of the layers;

    • your understanding of the functions of the layers.

    Again, use a phrase ('A TIN') to help you remember the layers and their sequence. Draw a diagram and, to impress, show the difference between the application-orientated layers and the network-orientated ones. You may further impress by stating that the TCP/IP model, unlike the OSI seven-layer model, is actually implemented – it is the one around which the Internet is built. Next, a discussion of each layer and its functions is required. Remember to include that each layer provides services to the layer above. High marks will be assured by discussing data encapsulation in the model (using the same mnemonic 'British Forces Postal Service').

3. This time the examiner is looking for the differences between the two models. The starting point is to construct a diagram similar to *Figure 4.4*, which compares the two models. It is worth spending some time getting this diagram correct as it will almost completely answer this question! By using the word 'compare', the examiner is asking for the similarities and, by 'contrast', the differences. *Section 3* provides a summarised list of the similarities and differences. Your answer should include these, but in a more discursive way. However, make sure you make them easy to find and mark! Don't forget the major difference is that the OSI model is just that – a model – whereas the Internet is built around the TCP/IP model.

Section 5: Further reading and research

Most comprehensive texts on networking will provide you with further reading on this topic.

Cisco Networking Academy Program (CNAP) Network Fundamentals CCNA Exploration Companion guide. Cisco Press. ISBN: 1-58713-208-7. Chapters 2, 3,4 5, 7, and 8.

Chapter 5
Popular technologies

Chapter summary

A network has a physical shape (a topology – *see Chapter 3*) and an implementation, a set of protocols and hardware (technology). Over the years many technologies have been established but, like most industries, the market has largely settled on a small number. This chapter doesn't seek to cover all the technologies but only those most widely-used:

- **Ethernet** – without doubt the most popular LAN technology in the world. Hugely dominant and likely to stay that way.

- **Token Ring** – once a worthy alternative to early Ethernet, which is now hardly used.

- **FDDI** – up until early 2004, FDDI was the standard for backbone/vertical cabling (between wiring closets). Since 2004, Gigabit Ethernet has become more prominent.

- **ATM** – this is important as it harmonises the telephone network with computer networking, providing the highest speed transfer of external data to the organisation. It has also been implemented inside organisations as a LAN backbone before gigabit Ethernet.

Learning outcomes

After studying this chapter you should aim to test your achievement of the following outcomes. You should be able to:

Outcome 1: Ethernet networks

Understand the development, variants, method of access, typical uses and hardware components of Ethernet networks. Question 1 at the end of this chapter will test your ability to do this.

Outcome 2: Token Ring networks

Understand the development, variants, method of access, typical uses and hardware components of Token Ring networks. Question 2 at the end of this chapter will test your ability to do this.

Outcome 3: FDDI networks

Understand the operation, typical uses and hardware components of Fibre Distributed Data Interface (FDDI) networks. Question 3 at the end of this chapter will test your ability to do this.

Outcome 4: ATM Networks

Understand the operation, typical uses and hardware components of Asynchronous Transmission Mode (ATM) networks. Question 4 at the end of this chapter will test your ability to do this.

How will you be assessed on this?

The technologies covered in this chapter represent the range of technologies in use today. The assessment of your studies is almost guaranteed to include them. Commonly, assessments are in the form of a design (in an assignment) and, as part of a TCT, questions regarding their particular features. You are often asked to describe the method of access of either Ethernet or Token Ring, or to discuss Ethernet and its variants.

Section 1: Ethernet networks (IEEE 802.3)

Ethernet (IEEE 802.3) networks are the most popular networks in the world, and the technology is continuing to develop. It is widely implemented and has dominated the market for a considerable time and this position is likely to continue. As such, it is the network that is given the greatest treatment in this chapter.

Method of access

Initially Ethernet was a bus network (*see Chapter 3*), and its method of access is known as **Carrier Sense Multiple Access with Collision Detection (CSMA/CD)**. The assembled data is broadcast (like a TV programme but occupying the whole frequency) over the media. The steps involved in a transmission can be summarised as follows:

- listen to network.;
- if it is clear, begin transmission of the frame;
- continue to listen to the network;
- if a collision is heard (two frames colliding with one another), send out a jamming signal;
- if the jamming signal is heard, stop transmitting and wait for a random time period before retrying.

Figure 5.1 shows two Ethernet stations (A and C) that wish to transmit at the same time. Both are listening to the network: there is no transmission and so both begin to transmit. The frames eventually collide and both are lost, requiring retransmission. The time taken from transmission to collision to the end of the random time period is, therefore, wasted time.

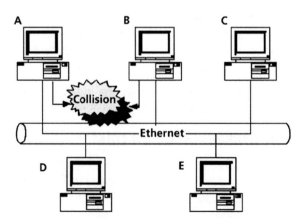

Figure 5.1: An Ethernet collision

The problem with traditional Ethernet (10Base2 and 10Base5) is that, the more frames that are transmitted, the higher is the probability of a collision. The greater the number of collisions, the more frames that require retransmission. Whilst all this is happening, very little data is getting through, and the users experience severe delays. This tends to happen when the data presented to the network exceeds 7 Mbps. Traditional Ethernet is therefore useful in situations of moderate load and particularly useful for traffic loads which transmit in short bursts.

KEY CONCEPT

It is very important to understand the way the medium is shared, as this is absolutely fundamental when moving on to discuss other networks and other variants of Ethernet. An easy way to remember this is to draw an analogy. Suppose that an army commander needs to get a message through enemy territory during a battle. He writes a note and gives this to the first dispatcher. Both listen and, if all is calm, the dispatcher goes out. Once he's gone the commander listens again. If a shot is heard, the commander knows the message didn't get through and so sends out another dispatcher. The more intense the battle, the more chance there is of a 'collision'. The more collisions, the longer it takes to get the message through.

Ethernet frame formats

Whatever variant of Ethernet is implemented, the same frame format is used. As discussed in Chapter 3, data needs to be broken into packets to be sent across the network. Packets are the units used by the Internet protocol (IP) structure (*see Chapters 3 and 11*). A particular technology uses a specific frame type. Ethernet frame type is shown in *Figure 5.2*. Being a CSMA/CD method of access, Ethernet requires a minimum frame size in order that errors can be detected properly. If the data to be sent makes the frame smaller than this minimum size, it needs to be 'padded out' (frame contents are discussed in more detail in *Chapter 3*).

8	6	6	2	0–1500	(46–0)	4
Preamble	Destination address	Source address	Length	Data	Padding	CRC

Figure 5.2: Ethernet frame structure

Ethernet variants

Ethernet is constantly being developed. Early Ethernet utilised a bus or tree topology, whereas later versions use a star topology. A naming convention (shown in *Figure 5.3*) has been adopted for Ethernet.

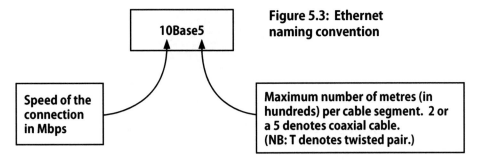

Figure 5.3: Ethernet naming convention

10Base5

Speed of the connection in Mbps

Maximum number of metres (in hundreds) per cable segment. 2 or a 5 denotes coaxial cable. (NB: T denotes twisted pair.)

The continual development of Ethernet has meant that it exists in many forms. *Table 5.1* summarises the variants.

Name	Cable type	Max. dist. /segment (m)	Max. speed (Mbps)	Topology	Max. nodes per segment	Max. segments per LAN
10Base5	10 mm coaxial	500	10	bus/tree	100	5
10Base2	5 mm coaxial	185	10	bus/tree	30	5
10BaseT	twisted pair	100	10	star	2	n/a
100BaseT	twisted pair	100	100	star	2	n/a
1000BaseT (gigabit Ethernet)	twisted pair	100	1000	star	2	n/a
10GE	fibre	up to 40 km on single mode fibre	10,000	star	2	n/a

Table 5.1: Ethernet variants

10Base5

This was the original Ethernet development. It is easily distinguished by the thick 10 mm coaxial cable on which it is based, and it operates on the bus/tree topology. 10Base5 was initially the standard Ethernet because of the great coverage length achieved for each segment of this cable. But it came to be used as the backbone connecting LANs formed with 10Base2 cabling as cabling 10Base5 was difficult because of the thickness and rigidity of the cable used. Attaching a computer to this cable required the use of a specialist device, called a **tap** (*see Figure 5.4*), whilst *Figure 5.5* shows how a tap is installed. Other than this, only one networking card per computer (with either in-built transceivers or external transceivers) and terminators were required. But 10Base5 was expensive because of the costs associated with the cables and taps. However, current prices are not available as this variant of Ethernet is no longer used.

Figure 5.4: Combined 10Base5 Ethernet tap and transceiver (courtesy of Blackbox Networks)

- The advantage of 10Base5 was the long length of cable run, which allowed the network to be extended to cover large buildings.

- The disadvantages were the difficulties in laying the cable (due to its rigidity) and the costs of the cable, taps and transceivers.

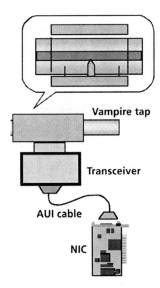

Figure 5.5: Installation of a tap
(courtesy of Surasak Sanguanpong, Kasetsart University, Thailand)

10Base2

This was a very popular variant of Ethernet; mainly due to its very low installation and hardware costs (hence it was also known as 'Cheapernet'). 10Base2 is based on 5 mm coaxial cable (very similar to TV aerial cable) and, in the main, **British naval connectors (BNCs)** (*see Figure 5.6*). Its price made it popular for use in classrooms and for small networking applications (e.g. lawyers' offices, estate agents, small companies and in the home). Adding machines to the network was also easy – all that was required was to disconnect the cable at the required point (when the network wasn't in use) and to connect the new computer. Providing certain standards were observed, the computer would operate. All that was needed to construct a two-station 10Base2 network were two 10Base2 Ethernet cards (NICs) (approximately £10 at the end-of-life price in early 2003), a piece of cable (around £5 at the end-of-life price in 2003) and two terminating resistors (50p at end-of-life-price in 2003) (*Figure 5.6* also shows these components). By 2005, UTP Ethernet had taken over and 10Base2 products became extremely difficult to locate.

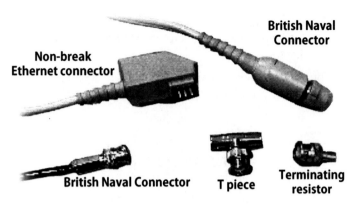

Figure 5.6: Typical 10Base5 connectors

The typical advantages of 10Base2 were:

- its low cost;
- ease of setup;
- the minimum kit requirements;
- the single cabling, which minimises disruption to the installation.

The typical disadvantages were:

- its poor performance for busy networks (e.g. college multimedia lab);
- cable breaks affect all computers (although connectors were later invented to minimise this – *see Figure 5.6*).

> **KEY CONCEPT**
>
> 10Base2 and 10Base5 are both based on differing versions of coaxial cable and represent the 'older' variant of Ethernet. Most new installations use twisted pair cabling, as detailed below.

10BaseT

Whilst 10Base2 probably ensured the success of Ethernet as a technology, compared to its competitors, it still suffered from cable break problems. Also, in the mid-1990s when many organisations were looking to structure their communications and cabling, Token Ring (its main competitor) was perceived to be better suited, 10BaseT Ethernet was developed in response.

10BaseT Ethernet is based upon a star technology with a device called a **hub** (*see Figure 5.7*) at the centre. 10BaseT uses RJ-45 connectors and twisted pair cabling (*see Figure 5.8*). This makes the system resilient to cable breaks and also makes it suitable for structured cabling. Thus the management and maintenance of the cabling have been made easier than in the past. The method of access is, however, no different. Inside the hub, all the ports are connected together just as in a bus topology and so collisions occur and capacity is lost. The network therefore still works as in the same way a bus topology.

Figure 5.7: 10BaseT hub

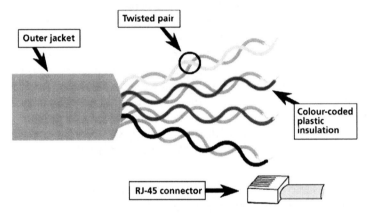

**Figure 5.8: Twisted pair cabling and an RJ-45 connector
(courtesy of Cisco Systems Inc.)**

10BaseT was popular for large organisations such as universities, colleges, large companies, call centres, etc. It rapidly took over from 10Base2 and as such is being utilised in most organisations as well as in the home. Structured cabling is recommended by **Electronic Industries Alliance (EIA)** and **Telecommunications Industry Association (TIA)** for all new installations; most new installations from the late 1990s have used this form of cabling.

Advantages of 10BaseT are:

- structured cabling;
- resilience to cable breaks;
- low cost of components;
- company reorganisation is easier to accommodate.

Disadvantages are:

- capacity is still lost to collisions;
- installation costs are high compared to 10Base2 (which requires more cable runs);

- hub represents a single point of failure (as with all star based technologies).

10BaseT has been replaced as a technology by 100BaseT as the price of 100BaseT equipment having fallen so much as to be comparable to 10BaseT.

At end-of-life, cabling, hubs and network cards for 10BaseT were priced at less than £10 for a NIC, a hub less than £20, 100 metre drum of cable £25 and the connectors about £0.05 each. The cabling and the connectors also being suitable for 100BaseT. Thus a two-station network could be set up for less than £40 with a hub and less than £20 with a crossover cable (a cable allowing two computers to be directly connected).

100BaseT

100BaseT was a major breakthrough in Ethernet technology. Whilst still a star-based topology and using the same connectors and cabling as 10BaseT, the hub used in 10BaseT was replaced with a 100BaseT switch. Through the use of the switch, the ports are no longer connected together internally but, instead, the connections between the ports are 'switched' together as and when necessary for data transfer (*see Figure 5.9*). This means collisions are virtually eliminated as only two devices are switched together at any one time. This allows for a far greater throughput to be realised. A full duplex switch will allow the connected NICs to realise 100 Mbps of data transfer, inbound and outbound simultaneously.

The switches also allow simultaneous 100 Mbps transfers between many pairs of ports, thus increasing substantially the throughput of the network and firmly establishing Ethernet as the network of choice for most organisations. Although 100BaseT still uses the CSMA/CD method of access, collisions are virtually eliminated because of switching. Furthermore, 100BaseT is available in full duplex, which uses two pairs of twisted pair – one for transmitting and one for receiving. This gives 100 Mbps data transmission and simultaneous 100 Mbps data receive.

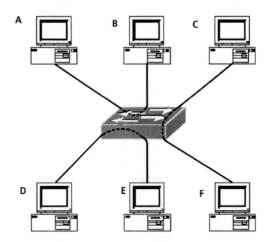

Figure 5.9: Switched ports

The costs of 100BaseT were initially high but, as with most computer products, their acceptance by the market has caused prices to tumble. Very basic switches can be bought from as little as £12 (at 2009 prices) and cards from as little as £8.50 (at 2009 prices) making 100BaseT the entry level network technology. Indeed most computers come with an inbuilt Ethernet NIC. These prices make it possible to build a two-station network for around £29 including a switch and NICs, or about £19 using crossover cable (i.e. just buying the NICs).

The major advantages of switch-based 100BaseT are:

- the virtual elimination of collisions;
- the high-speed data throughput;
- it is the quickest desktop networking solution;
- its costs are now very low, making it the obvious choice.

The main disadvantage of 100BaseT is the switch, which represents a single point of failure (as with all star-based technologies).

> **KEY CONCEPT**
>
> In 2009, 100BaseT was still the EIA/TIA's recommended desktop networking standard.

100BaseFx

In 1995, a version of 100Base Ethernet was devised for backbone applications that ran over fibre. It never really caught on as FDDI was also 100 Mbps, and faster technologies such as ATM took over. 100BaseFx is still available and seems to have found a niche market as a conversion technology to overcome noise problems. For example, if network cabling has to pass through a particularly noisy area such as a motor room, then a signal on a copper wire can be destroyed. By sending the signal as light on a fibre, it makes the data immune to noise. It is not a particularly common variant of Ethernet.

1000BaseT (or Gigabit Ethernet)

Following the successful development of 100BaseT (a process which took only 18 months), the Ethernet Alliance rushed to develop the next generation. Unfortunately, this took a lot longer than 18 months, but Gigabit Ethernet was finally launched at the end of the 1990s. Using the existing cabling (category 5) and the same frame format, Gigabit Ethernet is an easy upgrade path for 100BaseT users. Gigabit Ethernet can now be found on servers and in the networking infrastructure that provides connections between switches. It can even be found on more expensive PCs.

In 2003, a NIC cost £105, but the price of Gigabit Ethernet dropped from 2004 onwards. In 2009, a more advanced NIC cost just £12 with a basic switch costing £29. Like 100BaseT, Gigabit Ethernet provides both full and half-duplex operation, offering the possibility of simultaneous 1000 Mbps receipt and transmission. The majority of users do not need 1000 Mbps to the desktop and so for the foreseeable future, 1000BaseT will probably remain as a network infrastructure connection. .

> **KEY CONCEPT**
>
> In 2009 Gigabit Ethernet was the recommended backbone technology by EIA/TIA.

The major advantage of 1000BaseT is its very fast connection speeds. However, the major disadvantage remains the switch, which represents a single point of failure (as with all star-based technologies).

10 Gigabit Ethernet

Almost immediately following the completion of Gigabit Ethernet, 10 Gigabit Ethernet was proposed in February 2000 with Cisco Systems Inc. co-founding the 10 Gigabit Ethernet alliance. The **10 Gigabit Ethernet** (**10GE**) standard was formally ratified by the IEEE in March 2002 under IEEE 802.3ae, whilst the first 10 Gigabit networking products became available in March 2005.

There are essentially two types of 10GE:

- copper; and
- fibre.

There are two copper based 10GE standards – **10GBase-CX4** and **10GBASE-T**. 10GBase-CX4 requires special connectors and cabling and has a maximum working distance of 15 m , whilst 10GBASE-T uses **Shielded Twisted Pair** (**STP**) or **Unshielded Twisted Pair** (**UTP**) cabling with a maximum of 100 m cable length. Both of these Ethernet versions are designed to work primarily for data centres to attach servers to network uplinks, providing a high speed throughput for server traffic.

The fibre version of 10GE is designed to operate as uplinks between wiring closets aiming to support Gigabit Ethernet to the desktop. Fibre-based 10GE is capable of a transmission distance of 40 km over single mode fibre, making it suitable as a MAN and possibly a WAN technology as well as a LAN.

In 2009, 10GE was expensive, a 10GE fibre switch cost approximately £20,000. 10GE is deployed in large organisations that require high bandwidth backbones for capacity, backup/disaster recovery (*see Chapter 10*) or high availability such as server farms environments.

Wireless LAN (WLAN)

WLANs are an alternative to conventional wired networks. In 2001 many products were developed so that in 2002 they were first used in organisations (in particular, hotels and airports). Since 2002, the deployment of wireless LANs has been phenomenal and they are now commonplace just about everywhere – in the office, coffee shops, fast food chains, the home, railway stations, and even in the trains themselves.

WLANs offer a very flexible alternative to current wired networks by utilising radio waves as the medium of transmission rather than copper or fibre cabling (*see Figure 5.10*). WLANs operate in much the same way as conventional Ethernet – on a **Carrier Sense Multiple Access** but with **Collision Avoidance** (**CSMA/CA**) basis. However, they still provide less bandwidth than conventional wired systems.

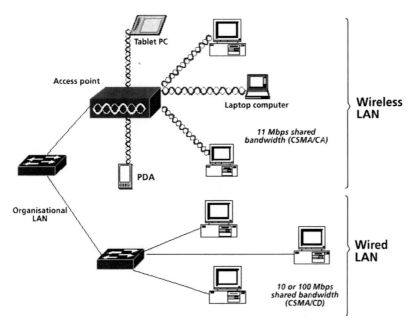

Figure 5.10: Typical WLAN implementation

Wireless LANS are discussed in more detail in *Chapter 9*.

Quick test

Briefly list the main variants of Ethernet, together with their advantages and disadvantages.

Section 2: Token Ring (IEEE 802.5)

Token Ring was developed by IBM and accepted by the International Standards Organisation and the IEEE. It was a popular alternative to Ethernet, particularly with companies who needed a guaranteed response time from their network. Unfortunately, Token Ring never became as cheap as Ethernet and, so, never became as popular. At one point, Token Ring was far faster than Ethernet with its 16 Mbps version (compared with Ethernet's 10 Mbps). Token Ring's method of access is also much fairer, which means it is able to use the whole bandwidth.

Token Ring has been included in this chapter to show there are alternatives to Ethernet, but it is regarded as an end-of-life technology. You may well come across Token Ring in your employment.

Method of access and operation

As Token Ring is based upon a ring technology (*see Figure 5.11*), the best place to start to describe it is with its method of access. A data frame (called the 'free token') circulates continually, passing through each machine on the network. When a machine (e.g. A) wishes to transmit data, it waits for the free token to pass through its interface. When the free token passes its interface, it sets the free token bit to indicate that this frame is now busy. It then inserts its data (including the source and destination address) into the frame. This data frame then circulates around the network until it reaches the destination machine (e.g. C). The destination machine copies the data and sets flags (in the frame) to say that the address was recognised and the data copied. The frame continues to circulate until it reaches the sender. When the sender receives the frame, it checks to see if the address has been recognised and if the data has been copied. If not, the frame continues to circulate. If the flags were set, the sender removes the data and resets the token to indicate that the frame is free once again.

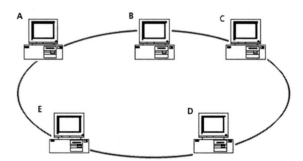

Figure 5.11: Token Ring

However, there are possible problems with this system. For example, what happens if the destination machine either doesn't exist (or goes down), or the sender goes down before the frame is cleared? In the former case, the data packet would circulate several times, but eventually, the sender would give up after several attempts and remove the frame. The latter case is more serious – Token Ring protocols require the sender to remove the data from the frame. If the sender goes down, the data will not be removed and the frame would circulate endlessly. There would be no free token and no other machine could access the network. To solve this problem, the monitor station was introduced. The monitor station, as its name suggests, monitors the frames sent round the network. When the network starts up, all the machines make a bid to be the monitor station, and protocols determine which machine will be the monitor station whilst the rest go on standby.

As a frame passes through the monitor station, the station sets the monitor bit in the frame to 1. Should the monitor station detect a frame with its monitor bit already set to 1, it knows the frame has traversed the entire ring once and therefore now seems to be circulating endlessly. The monitor station can then take action to clean up the network by replacing the frame with a free token frame. Using the same example as above with machines A and C, let us assume that machine B is the monitor station. Machine A transmits the data packet to machine C. The frame passes through machine B (the monitor station), which sets the monitor bit. The frame passes through machine C which copies the data. Machine C then sets the address recognised bit and the data copied bit. The frame then passes through machines D and E. Let's assume the sender (machine A) has suffered a failure and has gone down. The switching technology in Token Ring means machine A will be bypassed and so the frame passes to machine B. At this point, the frame is circulating endlessly and so no one else can transmit. The monitor station (machine B) notices that the monitor bit is already set, indicating it has seen the frame before. The monitor station generates a new free token and places it on to the network (in place of the data packet). As a further precaution, the machines 'on standby' to become monitor stations periodically inquire whether they can become the monitor station. Thus, if the monitor station should go down, the network will be able to continue.

> **TIPS & ADVICE**
>
> An analogy to help you remember Token Ring operation is a relay race – you can't run without the baton (the free token) and you must pass it on when you have run round the track once. The baton gives you access to the track (the media).

Token Ring hardware

Although a ring, Token Ring operates as a star format and has, at its centre, a Multistation Access Unit or MAU (*see Figure 5.12*). The MAU simply connects the stations together in a ring but, in the event of a cable being broken or a machine going down, the MAU can bypass the port. Every machine on the network needs a Token Ring networking card. The cable used for a Token Ring is, typically, shielded twisted pair (STP) (*see Chapter 3*).

**Figure 5.12: Token Ring MAU
(courtesy of Blackbox Networks)**

Token Ring frame structure

Token Ring has two frame formats – a free token frame and a data frame. *Figure 5.13* shows the free token and *Figure 5.14* the data frame.

Start delimeter (1 byte)	Access control (1 byte)	End delimeter (1 byte)

Figure 5.13: Structure of Token Ring free token

Start delimeter (1 byte)	Access control (1 byte)	Destination address (2–6 bytes)	Source address (2–6 bytes)	Length (2 bytes)	Date (no minimum size)	CRC (4 bytes)	End delimeter	Status flags (address recognised, frame copied, etc.) (1 byte)

Figure 5.14: Structure of Token Ring data frame

Unlike Ethernet, there is no minimum data size for a Token Ring frame. The monitor bits etc., are found in the access control part of the frame (*see Figure 5.15*). The operation of Token Ring lies in the detail behind this part. A free token is set to 0 bits but, when claimed, it is set to 1 bit. Similarly, the monitor bit has a value of 1 when set. As *Figure 5.15* suggests, Token Ring allows for priorities to be set. When it is waiting to transmit, if a station receives a busy token, it can place its assigned priority number into the reservation field. When the machine currently holding the free token releases it, the reservation field is moved to the priority field. Thus only the bidder (or one with higher priority) is able to claim this 'priority token'. This allows for the support of stations with priority traffic (e.g. real-time data for robot control or applications with synchronous data flows of (low-rate) video).

Access Control			
Priority bits (3)	Token bit (1)	Monitor bit (1)	Reservation bits (3)

Figure 5.15: Structure of the access control part of the data frame

Advantages/disadvantages of Token Ring

Token Ring has the following advantages:

- it is a much fairer method of access;
- bandwidth is not lost to collisions;
- performance is more predictable (adding an extra machine will slow the network down proportionately);
- speed (compared with standard 10Base5 and 10Base2 Ethernet);
- signal quality is greater as each machine regenerates the signal. Token Ring networks, therefore, can span a greater distance;
- it is able to prioritise data flows.

Its disadvantages are as follows:

- costs are much higher than Ethernet;
- Speed is not as great as 100BaseT.

Quick test

Briefly describe the mode of operation of a Token Ring network.

Section 3: Fibre-Distributed Data Interface (FDDI)

FDDI is also an end-of-life technology, but has been included as you may meet such legacy systems. In 2003, it was still the recommended network backbone – it has been replaced by Gigabit Ethernet.

Method of access and operation

FDDI operates in a similar manner to Token Ring and it is also based on a ring topology. It uses fibre optic cabling (*see Figure 5.16*) and offers speeds of up to 100 Mbps in private networks. Its dual concentric rings also provide greater resilience to cable breaks (if one cable is cut or breaks, the data can use the other cable). One of the rings operates in a clockwise fashion and the other anti-clockwise to ensure all nodes are in reach. FDDI uses the same method of operation and access to the media as Token Ring networks and it uses similar flags for recognised address and data copied. FDDI was used in backbone cabling and to link together networking devices, such as switches (*see Chapter 6*), as shown in *Figure 5.17*.

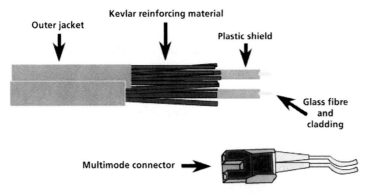

**Figure 5.16: Fibre optic cabling
(courtesy of Cisco Systems Inc.)**

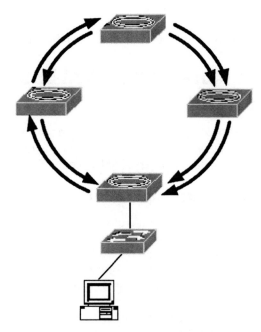

Figure 5.17: A typical FDDI deployment

Advantages/disadvantages of FDDI

The major advantages of FDDI are as follows:

- its speed as compared with such technologies as conventional Ethernet and Token Ring (FDDI was available when 10Base2 was the standard for LAN cabling);

- its robustness;

- the distance it can cover – fibre optic can carry data further than copper without the need for signal regeneration (2 km between nodes);

- its resistance to interference (fibre optic is virtually immune to interference from outside sources – *see Chapter 3*);

- its suitability for interconnecting buildings. (Copper can be dangerous as it could be struck by lightning and conduct the current.)

The major disadvantages of FDDI are as follows:

- its speed when compared to Gigabit Ethernet;

- it is not in harmony with the telephone network and therefore slower over public networks.

Quick test

Briefly describe an FDDI network and its uses.

Section 4: Asynchronous Transmission Method (ATM)

Introduction

The telecommunications standards up until the late 1990s were primarily designed to carry voice. This was a time when computers were less powerful and slower than today. The design criteria for these networks specified reliability rather than speed and, hence, the criteria included error-checking facilities. The computing world is now very different, and indeed in 1998, the quantity of data sent over the BT network overtook the quantity of voice transmission. ATM was devised as part of a review of telecommunications. ATM operates in harmony with the telecommunications network and provides organisations with a high-speed link to the outside world. As it is half as fast again as FDDI, it was also used as a backbone inside organisations.

ATM

ATM was a breakthrough in communications technology. When used as a network backbone, ATM provides 155 Mbps transfer speed – higher than any available before. However, that was only the beginning. ATM was originally developed for public broadband networks but became the technology of choice for private networks and LANs. ATM is a packet-switching multiplexing transmission technique that makes use of fixed-length packets (called **cells**). Based around switches (called **cellplexes**), like FDDI, the cellplexes identify the cells' destinations and then forward them. This means that ATM responds reasonably well to demands but, and more importantly, it can handle any type of content – cells could also be data, video, audio or speech. Just as network interface cards are a standard part of the ISO seven-layer model, ATM is standard in the digital telecommunications protocol. Because of this, it is able to work internally and externally at 155 Mbps. This speed was a major breakthrough: the best external data rate available in the UK jumped from 2 Mbps to 155 Mbps with the introduction of ATM. *Figure 5.18* shows a typical ATM implementation. Many high-end server manufacturers (e.g. Sun Microsystems) manufactured servers with in-built ATM support.

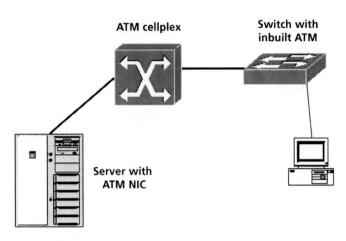

Figure 5.18: A typical ATM configuration

Advantages/disadvantages of ATM

ATM has the following advantages:

- it is harmonised with the telephone network, providing 155 Mbps connection external to the organisation;

- it has a higher speed than FDDI.

The disadvantages of ATM include the following:

- costs (compared with the gigabit Ethernet);

- speed (compared with the gigabit Ethernet).

Quick test

Briefly describe an ATM network and outline why it is so revolutionary.

Section 5: End of chapter assessment

Questions

1. Discuss the mode of access of Ethernet technology, and outline the major developments of this technology.

2. Discuss the way Token Ring operates. Highlight its advantages and disadvantages compared to conventional (10Base2 and 10Base5) Ethernet.

3. Discuss FDDI technology, highlighting its mode of operation and typical uses.

4. Discuss ATM technology, explaining why ATM is so revolutionary.

Answers

1. This question in one form or another is very popular in assessments and exams. Such is the importance of the technology that the examiner is almost obliged to test you on

it! What the examiner is essentially looking for is that you:

- understand the method of accessing the media (CSMA/CD);

- understand that it is unfair and can result in a large amount of wasted bandwidth;

- can sensibly discuss its shortcomings.

  Once you have demonstrated this you should aim to discuss each variant within the technology. For each you should discuss:

- its topology and typical configuration;

- the speeds attainable;

- the distances covered and typical costs;

- typical connectors and wiring;

- typical applications;

- advantages and disadvantages.

You should then summarise your answer, drawing conclusions relevant to the question.

2. To answer this question, you need to highlight the way in which Token Ring technology operates and draw out the fact that it is a much fairer method of access than CSMA/CD. You should outline the typical structure of Token Ring, its topology and typical applications. It is important that you highlight that the expected delay for Token Ring is proportional to the number of stations connected. You should next compare and contrast Token Ring with Ethernet and highlight the relevant advantages and disadvantages of each. In doing this you will need to discuss each one with respect to the various stages of Ethernet development.

3. To answer this question you will need to highlight the mode of operation of Token Ring networks and the fact that FDDI is very similar. You should outline the topology and typical cabling solutions of the network and ideally show these diagrammatically. You should also outline the speeds attainable by FDDI and its typical applications. It is worth pointing out that fibre covers a longer distance than copper and is less susceptible to noise and errors than copper. Also highlight the fact that FDDI was the EIA/TIA recommended backbone for many years.

4. To answer this question, you will need to discuss ATM technology. In particular, the assessor is looking for your ability to discuss what is so radical about this technology and the major breakthrough it represents. Demonstrate your knowledge by describing it as an internationally agreed

standard in harmony with the telephone network. You should also mention that it was used by organisations for a number of years as a backbone as it was faster than FDDI technology. However, you should note that take-up lessened as Gigabit technology appeared on the horizon. You must make sure you mention that ATM is in harmony with the telecommunications network and that it can be provide high-speed links externally to the organisation.

Section 6: Further reading and research

Cisco Networking Academy Program (2004) *CCNC 1 and 2 Companion Guide* (3rd edn). Cisco Press. ISBN: 1-58713-150-1. Chapter 6. (Older but still useful.)

Cisco Networking Academy Program (CNAP) Network Fundamentals CCNA Exploration Companion guide. Cisco Press. ISBN: 1-58713-208-7. Chapter 9.

www.bt.com (you can find the prices for external lines from here – e.g. ATM).

Chapter 6
Popular networking devices and Routed/Routing Protocols

Chapter summary

The purpose of a network is to interconnect computers to facilitate the transfer of data. To achieve this, a number of networking devices are available. The principal ones are:

- NICs;
- modem;
- repeater;
- hub;
- bridge;
- switch;
- router;
- Router Switch Module (RSM)/Multi-Layer Protocol Switch (MLS);
- gateway;
- Wireless Access Point;
- Wireless Router.

Routers also need to exchange routing information as well as data. Routed and routing protocols are also briefly discussed in this chapter.

Learning outcomes

After studying this chapter you should aim to test your achievement of the following outcomes. You should be able to:

Outcome 1: Interconnection provided by a Network Interface Card (NIC)

Understand what a NIC is and its essential role in networking.

Outcome 2: Collision and broadcast domains

Understand what is meant by the terms collision and broadcast domain and understand which devices provide containment.

Outcome 3: Interconnection based on a repeater

Understand the function, interconnections and typical uses of a repeater.

Outcome 4: Interconnection based on a hub

Understand the function, interconnections and typical uses of a hub.

Outcome 5: Interconnection based on a bridge

Understand the function, interconnections and typical uses of a bridge.

Outcome 6: Interconnection based on a switch

Understand the function, interconnections and typical uses of a switch.

Outcome 7: Interconnection based on a Multistation Access Unit (MAU)

Understand the function, interconnections and typical uses of a MAU.

Outcome 8: Interconnection based on a router

Understand the function, interconnections and typical uses of a router.

Outcome 9: Interconnection based upon RSM/MLS

Understand the function, interconnection and typical uses of a RSM/MLS.

Outcome 10: Interconnection based around a gateway

Understand the need for a gateway and its role in internetworking.

Outcome 11: Interconnection based upon Wireless Access Points and Wireless Routers

Understand the function, interconnection and typical uses of Wireless Access Points and Wireless Routers.

Outcome 12: Routed and routing protocols

Understand and be able to discuss what are meant by the terms routed and routing protocols.

How will you be assessed on this?

Understanding the function of networking devices is usually assessed in one of two ways: either directly in an examination or TCT question, or indirectly through a design-type assignment. A typical TCT/Exam question is given at the end of this chapter.

Section 1: Interconnection provided by a Network Interface Card (NIC)

Introduction

NICs are a crucial part of networking, allowing the computer to be connected to the network.

A NIC is a printed circuit board that goes inside a host computer (known as a **host**) to provide it with LAN connectivity. NICs fit into a PC's expansion slot (*Figure 6.1* shows three NICs, the oldest being from the 1980s and the smallest from 1998). NICs are also known as **network adaptors**. They are manufactured to operate with a particular networking technology and particular variants of that technology. For example, a 10Base2 networking card is usually different from a 10BaseT networking card because of the difference in the cabling type.

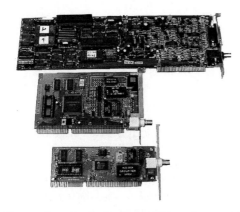

Figure 6.1: Typical network interface cards

In laptop computers, NICs are usually PCMCIA devices. Such is the popularity of Ethernet that most computers (including laptops) come with Ethernet NICs built in.

The NIC's function is to connect the host to the network media, and it is the basic hardware component of network communications. The NIC translates the parallel signals produced by the computer into serial signals suitable for transmission across the network. The binary 1s or 0s are usually turned into electrical pulses or, sometimes, into light or radio waves suitable for transmission over the medium. To make this transmission, the NIC needs a transceiver unit. Most NICs for Ethernet (except 10Base5) also have this in built.

NICs are layer two devices in the OSI seven-layer model as they work on frames and have media access control capabilities – including (in the case of Ethernet) an address that is unique in the world. This address is a 48-bit number (usually expressed in hexadecimal). The first 24 bits are a vendor ID and the second 24 a vendor-assigned unique serial number within that ID (*see Chapter 3*).

It is important to consider the computer's architecture when selecting an NIC, for two reasons. First, the NIC must match the host computer's architecture (e.g. an ISA will not connect to a PCI-only architecture). Secondly, and less importantly – except for high-end networks, the architecture should be capable of supporting the NIC's speed requirements (e.g. a 100BaseT ISA network card could never achieve more than 8 Mbps as that is the speed limit of the ISA architecture). Other important factors to consider when selecting a NIC are:

- the operating system (are the NIC drivers supported?);
- the media type (UTP, coaxial);
- the network architecture;
- the data transfer speed.

Quick test

Briefly outline the function of an NIC and the factors that should influence which one is chosen.

Section 2: Collision and broadcast domains

Introduction

There are two major considerations when discussing networking kit based upon Ethernet technology. As was discussed in *Chapter 5*, Ethernet method of access (CSMA/CD) causes collisions, which can be a major problem as these waste bandwidth and can cause delays. There is also the possibility of broadcasting a transmission to all the stations on the network. It is essential you appreciate these considerations before looking at networking hardware in more detail.

Broadcast domain

As noted above, it is often necessary to send a message to every machine on a network. System administrators often need to alert all users about a problem, an impending shutdown, etc. Indeed, broadcasts are a normal part of Ethernet operation. To obtain a **MAC address** of a destination computer, the sender will broadcast asking for the machine with a given IP address to respond with its MAC address (this is known as **Address Resolution Protocol** (**ARP**)). To broadcast, the broadcast address (all the 1s in Ethernet) is placed into the destination address field of the frame. Every machine on the network will then receive this frame. If a great many machines send out broadcasts at once, this places an unnecessarily heavy load on the LAN. Ideally, the number of machines that receive this broadcast should be limited or they should be grouped together in some way. Such groupings are termed **broadcast domains**. A networking device is available to contain such broadcasts – the router (*see Section 8*).

Collision domain

As we saw in *Chapter 5*, Ethernet relies on collision detection to operate and, the busier the network, the more collisions. The more collisions, the more capacity is wasted. Thus it is necessary to control the number of collisions to make better use of the available capacity. Given that stations have unrestricted access when transmitting on Ethernet, the only way to control collisions is to limit the number of stations on a network without reducing connectivity. The solution to this problem is to divide the network up by establishing collision domains that will contain the collisions. Again, networking devices are available that contain collisions – bridges (*Section 5*), switches (*Section 6*) and routers (*Section 8*).

The terms 'broadcast' and 'collision domains' will become clearer as we explore each piece of hardware in turn.

Quick test

Briefly discuss what is meant by the terms 'broadcast domain' and 'collision domain'.

Section 3: Interconnection based on a repeater

Introduction

Repeaters were an essential part of early Ethernet technology as they provided a means by which the length of a cable run could be extended. They are still sometimes used today for the same reason. As was seen in *Chapter 5*, there are limits to the length of cabling used on Ethernet. These restrictions can often pose problems but repeaters can help to overcome them. There are three types of repeaters – coaxial repeaters, UTP repeaters and repeaters that convert between UTP and coaxial cable.

As an Ethernet signal nears the end of its cable run or gets close to the maximum number of nodes per segment the technology can handle, it becomes weaker – timing signals move out and the signal can become distorted. A repeater restores the signal to its original state and passes it on. To do this, the repeater must regenerate rather than amplify the signal (amplification would amplify the distortion and wouldn't address the timing issues). Thus a signal is received on one port of the repeater, is regenerated and then re-timed before being transmitted to the other ports. Repeaters are bi-directional devices that regenerate at the bit level and as such, they are layer one networking devices. As they need to listen to a bit before regenerating it, they introduce a delay into the network of at least 1 bit. Repeaters have no effect on collision or broadcast domains.

TIPS & ADVICE
Imagine there was only one road to serve an entire country. Every car journey made involved using that road. Also imagine there were few regulations governing access to that road – a quick look and on you go! Obviously, there would be a great number of accidents (collisions). One solution would be to provide local roads for local traffic, thus reducing the number of collisions on that main road. Hence, collision domains would have been created to prevent unnecessary traffic from entering the main road. Junctions would join the roads providing access but resulting in fewer collisions.

Coaxial repeaters

As their name suggests, coaxial repeaters are used in 10Base2 and 10Base5 networks but there are strict limits to their use. For example, in a 10Base2 network, all that is allowed between the sender and the receiver are:

- a maximum of five segments (of which two must be free from nodes);
- a maximum of four repeaters;
- a maximum of three active segments;
- two transit segments (free of nodes).

(Alternatively, it is possible to have two active segments and three transit segments.)

In 10Base2, segment ends when 30 nodes or 185 m are reached. At that point the signal is too weak to continue and needs to be repeated. *Figure 6.2* shows a typical 10Base2 layout using a repeater. *Figure 6.3* shows the limit between a sender and a receiver in a 10Base2 network – five segments (two empty) and four repeaters. This rule obviously limits the extent to which the network might grow but can be overcome by good design. By using a segment(s) as a backbone and by using multi-port repeaters, it is possible to design a network with more segments which still conforms to the 5-4-3-2 rule. In *Figure 6.4* there are numerous segments but, between the nodes there are never more than five. For example, between points A and B there are only three segments (including segments A and B).

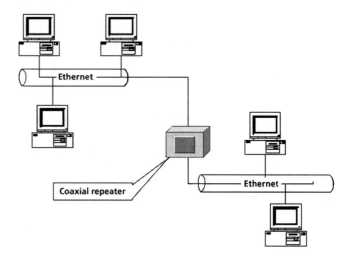

Figure 6.2: Two Ethernet segments connected by repeaters

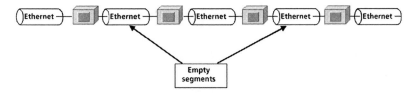

Figure 6.3: A typical 10Base2 network using repeaters

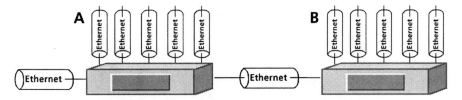

Figure 6.4: A well designed 10Base2 network with many segments which still conforms to the 5-4-3-2 rule

UTP repeaters

UTP has even more restrictions than coaxial cabling:

- it can only have two nodes per segment;
- a segment can only be 100 m long.

These restrictions are a result of the 1XBaseT Ethernet being a star topology and because interconnection is carried out in the hub or switch. However, there are occasions when a machine might need to be placed more than 100 m away. On such occasions, a repeater can be used to extend the distance (to a maximum of 100 m either side of the repeater). *Figure 6.5* shows a typical repeater implementation.

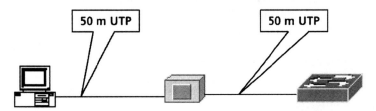

Figure 6.5: A typical UTP network with a repeater

TIPS & ADVICE

Conversions cannot be made between Token Ring and Ethernet using such devices. Token Ring has a completely different frame structure and method of accessing the network. However, Token Ring cards function as repeaters in a Token Ring network regenerating the signal, so repeaters aren't necessary.

Coaxial-to-UTP converting repeater

As was seen in *Chapter 5*, all Ethernet variants have the same frame format. Occasionally, however, there might be a need to connect machines (or even small LANs) that use coaxial cable to a network based on UTP and, rarely, vice versa. To achieve this, a coaxial-to-UTP repeater is used, as shown in *Figure 6.6*. Coaxial-to-UTP repeaters function in exactly the same way as other types of repeater. Their physical limitations depend on the media to which they are attached. As most installations now use UTP, these devices have become less common.

Figure 6.6: Coaxial-to-UTP repeater

Quick test

Briefly discuss the role of a repeater in a network.

Section 4: Interconnection based on a hub

Introduction

Hubs are part of Ethernet technology where they connect devices together. Basically, there are two types of hubs: those used to connect coaxial cables; and those that connect to UTP cabling. Although the media differ, essentially the hubs perform the same function. Hubs are layer-one devices of the OSI seven-layer model. They have little or no intelligence (as standard) and, basically they simply pass the data out across a number of ports. Hubs have no effect on collision or broadcast domains. UTP were the more commonly used hubs.

Coaxial hubs

Coaxial hubs have become almost redundant. They were used to connect multiple bus networks together to form a tree network (*see Chapter 3*). Technically, these hubs were multi-port repeaters. They took a coaxial cable and split it into many branches to form a tree network (with the original as the root) (*see Figure 6.7*). As with a standard repeater, the signal out of each port was regenerated.

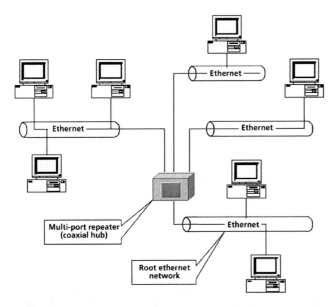

Figure 6.7: Ethernet network with a multi-port repeater

UTP hubs

These were by far the most common type of hub, forming the centre of a 10BaseT star network (*see Chapter 3*). The hub transformed the star topology into a logical bus network (*see Figure 6.8*). Whilst this type of Ethernet network was a star topology, because it is 10BaseT, it operated as a logical bus network. Thus when one machine sends data to another machine, the data is received on a port of the hub and transmitted on all ports of the hub rather than just the port that the receiver is connected to. For this reason, UTP hubs are sometimes called multi-port repeaters. As a signal is received, hubs regenerate and re-time the signal before sending it out on all the other ports. This is known as **concentration** and, rarely, hubs are referred to as **concentrators**. Such regeneration and re-timing are carried out at the bit level, which means that hubs operate at level one of the OSI seven-layer model.

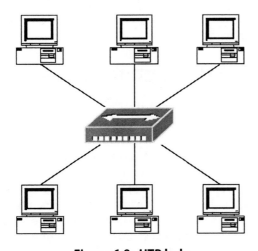

Figure 6.8: UTP hub

Essentially a hub:

- is used as a network concentration point;
- regenerates and re-times signals;
- cannot filter network traffic;
- cannot determine the best path for data;
- propagates signals across the network.

Hubs are most commonly used in 10BaseT networks, but most organisations now use switches at the centre of the star giving 100BaseT networks (*see Section 6* of this chapter).

Figure 6.9 shows the typical installation of a 24-port 10BaseT hub. In large installations such as this, the hubs are themselves connected together.

Figure 6.9: 10BaseT hub

Quick test

Briefly discuss the role of a hub in networking. Your answer should cover 10BaseT in particular.

Section 5: Interconnection based on a bridge

Introduction

Bridges were an essential piece of networking hardware but are less commonly used now. They enable traffic control; they also allow standards conversion and provide the essential connectivity. As was seen in *Chapter 5*, network technologies are often incompatible, but bridges provide the means by which they can be joined. As noted earlier, the maximum number of segments in Ethernet technology is five. Bridges, however, provide the means of extending such networks, and also provide collision containment (discussed earlier in this chapter). Bridges operate in layer two of the OSI seven-layer model. Being layer-two devices, they work at the data-frame level and are able to understand and forward frames. Bridges can be divided into two categories – those that perform technology conversions and those that work within a specific technology.

Technology conversion bridges

Often, data on a network needs to be available to machines that use different technologies. For example, a production department might use Token Ring technology but the sales department uses Ethernet. Emails and data, however, must be available to the whole company, irrespective of the technology. As bridges are intelligent devices and can see a frame in its entirety, they are able to extract the data from one frame and place it in another. In the above example, the bridge would take an Ethernet frame (from the sales department); extract the data and place it into a Token Ring frame before forwarding it on to the production department (see Figure 6.10).

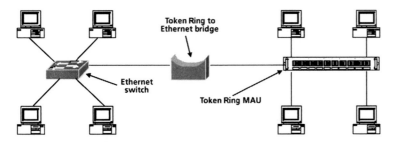

Figure 6.10: Bridging between Ethernet and Token Ring

Single technology bridges

Single technology bridges are the most common. They are used for one of two purposes:

- to extend a technology (e.g. 10Base2) when its maximum length or number of nodes have been reached;
- to perform traffic management by containing collisions and by preventing unnecessary traffic from crossing to the other side of the bridge.

10Base2 was useful in the early days of LANs when, for example, colleges and universities, had one LAN per classroom. When such organisations wanted to join their networks together, the limitations of 10Base2 became a problem (see Chapter 5). To extend their networks, a single technology bridge was used that divided the connected networks into distinct LANs.

The most common use of bridges was for collision containment and traffic management. As bridges are intelligent devices, they can prevent frames passing through unless they are bound for a computer on the other side of the bridge. In Figure 6.11, a bridge has been installed in the middle of a busy network. The network designer has made sure the servers and the machines they serve are on the same side of the bridge. This means the bridge will quickly learn the MAC addresses of the connected machines and also which side they are on. Once it learns the addresses, it will prevent frames from passing through the bridge unless they are bound for a machine on the other side. All things being equal, the effect will be to split the load on the network evenly – if the load was 6 Mbps before the bridge, it will be 3 Mbps (per segment) after installation of the bridge. The bridge will also reduce the number of collisions, thus breaking the network into two collision domains. Bridges have no affect on broadcasts.

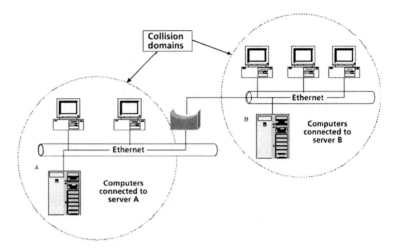

Figure 6.11: Bridged 10Base2

Quick test

Identify the two types of bridge and discuss briefly the situations in which they would be used.

Section 6: Interconnection based on a switch

Introduction

Switches are used at the centre of 100BaseT networks (as hubs were used at the centre of 10BaseT networks) and less commonly as the centre of 1000BaseT networks. As 100BaseT networks are currently the recommended standard for new desktop points, their importance cannot be emphasised enough.

Switches/switching

Switches can best be thought of as a combination of a bridge and a hub. As a layer-two device, a switch can read Ethernet frames and can make forwarding decisions according to the MAC address (unlike a hub, which makes no decisions at all). *Figure 6.12* shows the implementation of a switch. If machine A wished to transmit to machine D, in a hub environment the frame would be broadcast out of each port and would be heard by all the machines. The switch, just like a bridge, would know the MAC address of machine D and would know the port it was connected to. The switch would then send the frame out of that port only.

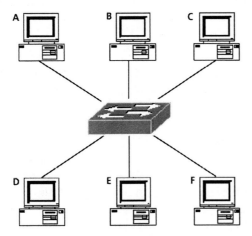

Figure 6.12: Implementation of a switch in a network

The effect of deploying a switch is to make the network more efficient and to increase throughput. As the data is sent out of the switch on one port only (with the exception of a broadcast), the number of collisions is dramatically reduced, thereby increasing available bandwidth. It is also possible for many groups of machines to communicate through the switch simultaneously at the network's full transmission speed. Thus, it would be possible for machines (A and D), (B and E) and (C and F) to communicate simultaneously, and each group to operate at the full bandwidth (*see Figure 6.13*). As the switch only switches the communicating ports together, it is only possible for a collision to occur within a group (in this case pairs) of machines, which greatly reduces the chances of a collision occurring. The switch thus creates multiple collision domains and this function is sometimes referred to as **micro-segmentation**.

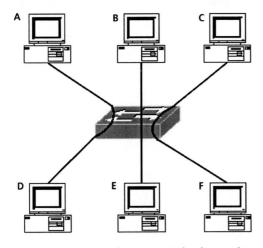

Figure 6.13: Ports being switched together

More expensive switches operate in full duplex mode (*see Chapter 3*), which means they provide each host simultaneously with 100 Mbps transmission and 100 Mbps receive. To use this facility, the NIC must also be full duplex. Most switches are able to accommodate 10BaseT networking cards by switching to a lower speed (known as **asymmetric** switches). Those that are 100BaseT only are known as **symmetric** switches.

Switches are a critical part of today's modern networks forming the main part of the Access layer (*see Chapter 7*). This is where the majority of devices connect into the network (commonly called the network edge), and so there needs to be many connection points. Consider the example of a school which has 300 PCs and 30 printers. It will require at least 330 edge connection ports.

Switches typically come in 12, 24, 48 and 96 port varieties. As such it is usually necessary to connect several switches together to achieve the required number of ports (port density). Switches often come with higher speed uplink ports. For example, the Cisco 2960 switch shown in *Figure 6.14* has 24 100 Mbps ports and 2 Gigabit Ethernet ports. Normal practice is to connect these Gigabit Ethernet ports to other similar switches to give a higher speed uplink.

Achieving high speed connection between switches is a hot topic and manufacturers basically have three solutions (*see Figure 6.15*):

- high speed uplink ports on fixed configuration switches;
- 'stackable' switches; and
- modular configuration switches.

Figure 6.14: Cisco 2960 Switch

SWITCH FORM FACTORS

Fixed configuration switches

Features and options are limited to those that originally come with the switch

Modular configuration switches

The chassis accepts line cards that contain the ports.

Stackable configuration switches

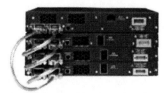

Stackable switches, connected by a special cable operate as one large switch.

Figure 6.15: Typical switch solutions (image Courtesy of Cisco Systems Inc – Network Academy Programme, Exploration Semester 3)

Fixed configuration switches, as their name suggests, are devices which have a fixed configuration. They may have high speed uplink ports to facilitate high speed connection to other switches and are more suited to the lower end of the market e.g. small businesses.

Stackable switches are connected by special backplane cables which provide high bandwidth connection between switches. These switches have a higher interconnection speed (typically 1 – 10 Gbps) than the uplink ports on fixed configuration switches and are more suited to medium-sized organisations.

Finally the **modular configuration switches** support very high port density (perhaps up to 1000 ports) on a single device. A special backplane supports very high speed communication between the modules in the device (typically around 720 Gbps full duplex).

Managed/unmanaged switches

There are basically two categories of switches available on the market.

Unmanaged switches are cheap devices suitable for the home or small office. Costing approximately £16 (in 2009) these provide the ability to interconnect a number of devices. Such switches do not have the management software necessary for connection onto an organisational LAN.

Managed switches tend to be a lot more expensive, costing around £300 (in 2009). These switches do have management software and are suitable for deployment in an organisational LAN.

One of the key differences between the two devices is the issue of redundancy. Consider *Figure 6.16* where there is a two switch network connecting many PCs. The switches are connected together using a crossover cable (link 1); at this point, either managed or unmanaged switches can be deployed. Supposing we wanted to put another link (link 2) between the two switches in case the first link failed. If we had a managed switch, a protocol called **Spanning Tree** would be running and it would detect the duplicate link and switch it into standby. With an unmanaged switch, no such protocol is running and the network would be brought down via a broadcast storm.

Consider machine A broadcasting an ARP request (sending a frame to all machines) looking for the MAC address of machine C. The frame will pass into switch A, the rule of switching is 'flood out of all ports except the receiving port', switch A applies the rule and forwards out of both link 1 and link 2. Switch B receives the frame (first on link 1) and immediately floods out of all ports including link 2; it then receives the frame on link 2 and floods out of all posts including link 1. Switch A receives the frame on link 1 and immediately floods out of all ports including link 2; it then receives the frame on link 2 and floods out of all ports including link 1. The frame is now circulating endlessly – unlike an IP packet, there is no time to live field in the frame, and the frame will simply circulate until one of the links is unplugged. Until this happens, the network is unusable as all bandwidth is being consumed by the endlessly circulating frame.

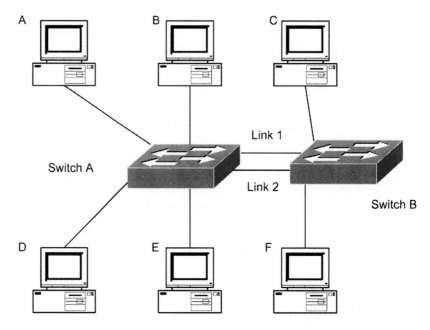

Figure 6.16: Two unmanaged switches connected together

Quick test

Briefly outline the function of a switch and compare it with a hub.

Section 7: Interconnection based on a Multistation Access Unit (MAU)

Introduction

MAUs form the centre of a Token Ring network and, essentially, have the same function as a switch. Token Ring technology is rarely installed nowadays, and it is often cheaper to replace an entire installation with 100BaseT than it is to replace a MAU. However, there may be a specific reason why Token Ring is required (e.g. it is built in to certain industrial equipment and therefore must be supported), in which case the MAU must be replaced.

MAU

As a MAU is at the centre of Token Ring network, it provides the means by which the machines can communicate. Inside the MAU the ports are connected in a ring fashion, and a Token Ring frame circulates through the ports. If a machine is active on the port, the frame is passed down to that machine. If there isn't an active machine, the frame bypasses that port. In the event that there are more machines than ports on the MAU, multiple MAUs can be connected using the RING IN and RING OUT ports on each. The only real function of a MAU is to make a complete ring from all the active ports. *Figure 6.17* shows a MAU implementation. Whilst the wiring appears as a star, the operation is, in fact, a ring.

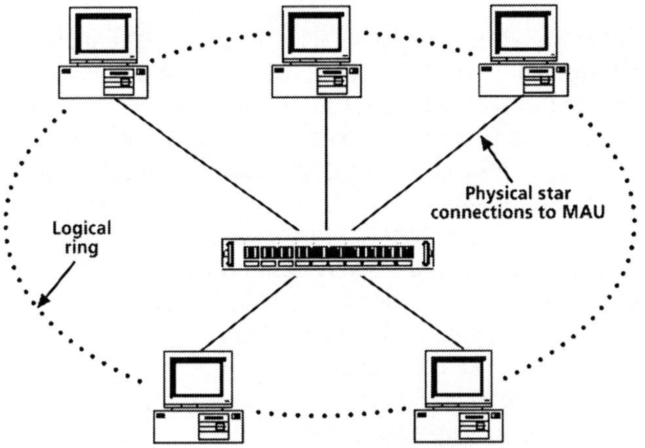

> **KEY CONCEPT**
>
> It is the method of accessing the ring in Token Ring network rather than the MAU which ensures that bandwidth isn't wasted (*see Chapter 5*).

> **REMEMBER**
>
> Token Ring network don't have collisions so collision domains aren't relevant

Figure 6.17: Implementation of a MAU

Quick test

Briefly identify the function of Token Ring MAU.

Section 8: Interconnection based on a router

Introduction

Routers are perhaps the most important networking device for medium- to large-sized networks. Along with switches, they are the main piece of equipment installed. As access to the Internet is based on routers, it is essential to understand their operation and use. Routers are also the most important traffic-regulating devices on large networks.

Routers

Routing devices operate at layer three of the OSI seven-layer model. Working at this layer, the router can make decisions based on network addresses (or logical addresses – *see Chapter 3*) as opposed to layer two (the MAC address layer – also *see Chapter 3*). Like a bridge, routers can connect different layer-two technologies, such as FDDI, Ethernet and Token Ring.

The main function of a router is to divide a network into multiple, small networks or connect a network to other networks (e.g. the Internet), which may or may not be under the same administrative control. Routing devices examine the network address (commonly the IP address) of incoming packets, to determine the best path for them through the network (path determination) and to forward them along that path (switching). Because of this capability, routers have become the backbone of the Internet (*see Chapter 11*).

Routers differ from bridges in several respects. A bridge makes forwarding decisions based upon the MAC address and is therefore only useful *within* a network, whereas routers are used for inter-network communication. As an organisation's network becomes larger, it must to be divided up if it is to retain its performance (*see Subnetting in Chapter 3*). As was seen earlier, division by a bridge or switch splits the collision domain. What neither of these devices do, however, is restrict the broadcasts. Broadcasts are a very common and a very necessary feature of a network, but need to be contained if bandwidth is not to be compromised – excessive broadcasts lead to what is known as a 'broadcast storm', which consumes large amounts of bandwidth. As there is no structure to MAC addresses, broadcast containment cannot be achieved by devices operating at layer two (the MAC address layer). Routers operate at the network layer and use the organisation's logical addressing mechanism (*see Chapter 3*) only for forwarding packets. Hence they can contain broadcasts.

Take for example, a typical IP address at the University of Sunderland. Suppose the address 157.228.1XX.XXX represents computers inside the Department of Computing and Technology and 157.228.2XX.XXX represents computers within the Business School. The 157.228 part of the address identifies the University and the XXX.XXX.1 the School of Computing and Technology and the XXX.XXX.2 the Business School. In this way a meaningful structure can be given to the network. Broadcast frames not intended for the Business School will be prevented by the router from being sent to that address because they do not contain XXX.XXX.2. Hence packets can be routed efficiently. This is the basis upon which the Internet works – 157.228. is the address for the University of Sunderland whereas 193.63.148 is the address for the University of Glamorgan. (IP addresses are ultimately controlled by the **Network Info Center** (**NIC**) in the USA. They are managed by five **Regional Information Registries** (**RIPE**, **LACNIC**, **ARIN**, **AfricNIC**, and **APNIC**).)

Routers typically are used to join LANs to the backbone of an organisation's network, thus ensuring that the backbone does not become congested with unnecessary traffic. *Figure 6.18* shows such an implementation. Notice how the routers create broadcast domains and how the switches provide collision domains.

Figure 6.19, shows a Cisco 2800 series router which is a typical small/medium enterprise router.

> **KEY CONCEPT**
>
> Routers enable separate LANs within an organisation to be connected. They provide connectivity whilst keeping the LANs separate, and they contain both broadcasts and collisions.

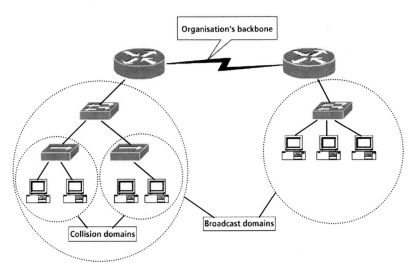

Figure 6.18: Typical implementation of a router

Figure 6.19: Cisco 2800 Series Router (front and rear views)

Quick test

Briefly describe the operation of a router and give examples of where they are commonly deployed.

Section 9: Understanding interconnection based around a Router Switch Module (RSM)/Multi-Layer Switch (MLS)/Layer 4 switching

Introduction

Whilst routers are perhaps the most important networking device, they have one major drawback – their speed. In order to route packets, routers utilise software to determine the next hop and to forward the packet. Software is many times slower than hardware, which can lead to a bottleneck in the throughput. Initially this bottleneck wasn't a problem as the majority of network traffic was kept local. In fact, there was an 80/20 design rule which said that 80% of the networked traffic should be kept local. Today, this rule no longer applies principally because of two factors:

- **the Internet** – the PC can now be a tool for accessing and publishing information anywhere in the world with users transparently hopping around the globe; and

- **server farms** – many organisations are now hosting their applications and data in one central location where it is looked after by their best staff. Users from within this location and from branch offices seamlessly access the data as though it were local.

The 80/20 rule has now been turned on its head – only 20% of the networked traffic is local. This has put increasing pressure on the routers, fuelling the development of **Multi-Layer Switching (MLS)**.

MLS

The aim of MLS is simple – to bring hardware speeds to the routing function. The way in which this problem was resolved was thinking about the routing of packets – packets usually travel in flows. *Figure 6.20* shows the flow normally taken by a data packet through two routers.

Figure 6.20: The flow normally taken by a data packet through a router

As can be seen from *Figure 6.20*, each packet will flow through the bottom three layers of the OSI 7 layer model in the router. If the device was capable of uniquely identifying each flow, a cache could then be formed meaning that the first packet to pass through the router would identify the outbound interface for that flow. Subsequent packets in that flow could then access the cache and be immediately switched to the outbound interface. This is known as 'route once, switch many times' and it is how MLS works. Of course, there is more to a destination address than simply an IP address, there is also a port number. MLS takes into account the port number when building the cache. The dotted line in *Figure 6.21* shows the path the second and subsequent packets would take through a multi-layer switch.

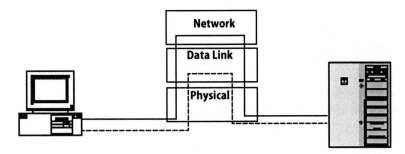

Figure 6.21: Paths taken by a packet through a MLS – 1st (solid line); 2nd and subsequent (dashed line)

Using a MLS gives a dramatic performance increase – second and subsequent packets are switched at hardware speed, minimising the router bottleneck in the network. The biggest drawback of MLS is management of the cache and caching the complex flow of traffic. Also, if networks are lost, the entire cache usually needs to be flushed and rebuilt. *Figure 6.22* shows a typical MLS device – these are enterprise level networking devices with high availability and a price tag to match.

Figure 6.22: Cisco Catalyst 4006 MLS

CEF

In early 2004, Cisco Systems Inc. introduced another variant of MLS called **Cisco Express Forwarding (CEF)**. Objectively CEF accomplishes the same as MLS, but the way in which it accomplishes fast switching of packets is different. Devices incorporating CEF are more proactive and use their built-in router to determine all possible routes through the device, i.e. identify all of the IP addresses on the ports. From this information, a switching table can be built. This table is then coded onto **Application Specific Integrated Circuits** (**ASICs**) hardware, which will actually perform the switching. When the first packet arrives, CEF already knows the target port from its switching table and can immediately switch the packet without the need for a router lookup. This further increases the performance of the device.

CEF also dramatically reduces the complexity of the cache associated with MLS devices and also simply strikes the route from its switching table should a network be lost – the rest of the switching table remaining intact.

CEF is Cisco proprietary technology and was deployed on all Cisco **Router Switch Module** (**RSM**) devices from early 2004. The entry price of a 3560 RSM was dramatically lower than its MLS counterpart, bringing multi-layer switching within reach of many organisations. *Figure 6.23* shows the 3550 family of RSMs. *Figure 6.24* shows the Cisco 6500 series of RSMs – enterprise level kit.

**Figure 6.23: Cisco 3560 family of RSMs
(picture courtesy of Cisco Systems Inc.)**

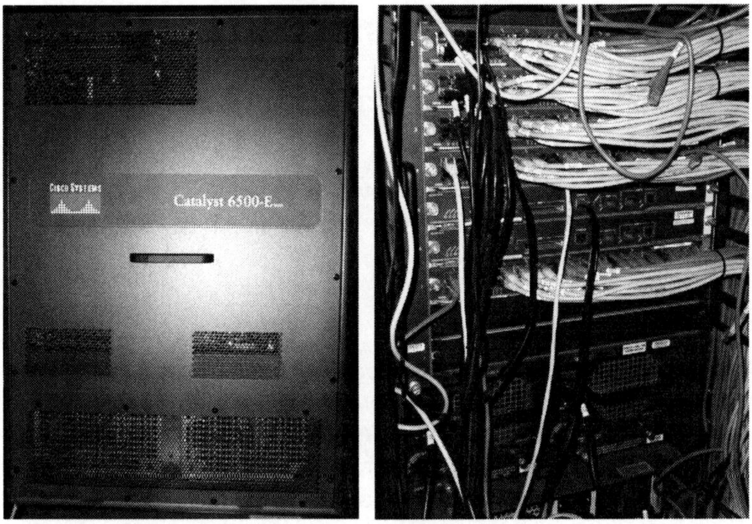

Figure 6.24: Cisco 6500 series of RSMs (front and rear views)

> **KEY CONCEPT**
>
> RSM/MLS devices are increasingly being used by more organisations as the network traffic flow moves from being predominantly local to being enterprise wide. The Internet and the growth of server farms are contributing to this new traffic pattern.

Deployment of RSM/MLS devices

RSM/MLS devices are deployed in functionally the same way as a router – in the organisational backbone. *Figure 6.25* shows typical deployment with the devices being integrated with layer 2 switches to service client PCs and servers in the server farms. It is worth noting the redundant connections – each switch is connected to two RSM/MLS devices for redundancy, load balancing and high availability. The greater number of ports on these devices make this possible at a much lower cost.

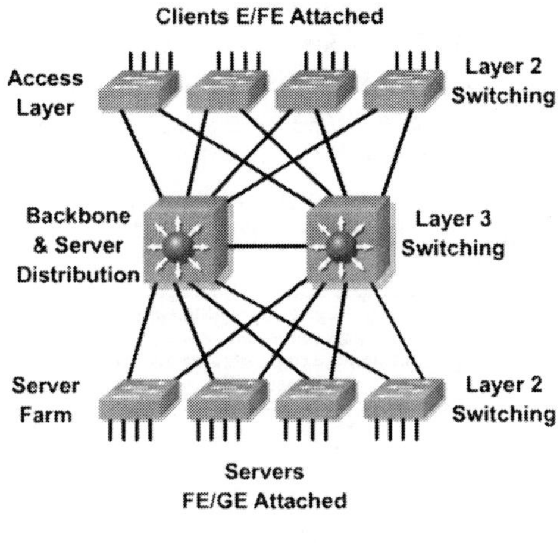

Figure 6.25: Typical deployment of RSM/MLS devices (image courtesy of Cisco Systems Inc.)

Quick test

Briefly describe the operation of a MLS device and identify why a MLS may be deployed in place of a conventional router.

Section 10: Interconnection based on a gateway

Introduction

Gateways connect two dissimilar networks together – for example, networks such as IBM's **Systems Network Architecture (SNA)** and **DECnet**.

Gateway

A gateway can be used to connect together two networks at any layer at or above the network layer. As there was often a large amount of incompatibility between networks supplied by different vendors, more translation was required than that afforded by standard networking devices. Hence gateways were used to overcome this problem. Because of the amount of translation required, gateways were often slow and more expensive than other interconnecting devices, and they were typically implemented as a software solution on a computer. With developments such as the OSI seven-layer model and schemes such as the US **Government Open Systems Integration Project (GOSIP)**, computer manufacturers have opened up their systems to allow interconnection through standard networking devices, thus negating the need for gateways.

Gateways did, however, re-emerge in **small office, home office (SOHO)** networking, where they were often used to connect the home/small office network to the Internet (*see Figure 6.26*). In this Figure, machine A is running software to act as a gateway. It has two network connections and is moving traffic between the two networks – the ADSL/cable connection and the SOHO LAN. Such gateways can be established easily using the **Internet Connection Sharing** option in Microsoft Windows (98SE onwards). In this mode, these gateways usually perform the **Network Address Translation (NAT)** function – they give multiple SOHO machines access to the Internet through the sharing of one IP address from the **Internet Service Provider (ISP)**.

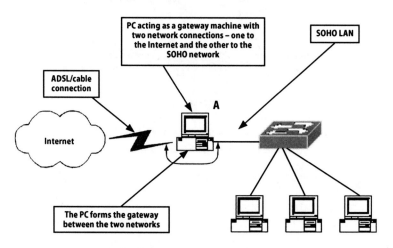

Figure 6.26: SOHO gateway

**Figure 6.27: A typical SOHO router
(image courtesy of Linksys Inc.)**

Quick test

Briefly discuss the purpose of a gateway.

Section 11: Interconnection based on Wireless Access Point/Wireless Router

Introduction

Most networks have some wireless access capability. Such is the importance of wireless networks that *Chapter 9* is dedicated to explaining them. This section presents only a very brief discussion of wireless access points and wireless routers and should be read in conjunction with *Chapter 9* for a fuller understanding.

Wireless Access Point

Just as switches typically provide the edge connection to wired networking devices, **Wireless Access Points (WAPs)** provide edge connection to a wireless network for wireless devices. Essentially the normal use for a WAP is to connect wireless devices into the organisation's wired network. *Figure 6.28* shows a typical implementation of a WAP.

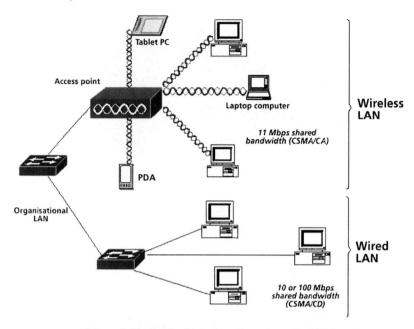

Figure 6.28: Typical implementation of a WAP

As can be seen from *Figure 6.28*, WAPs connect to a switchport in the organisation's network and allow wireless devices to communicate through it with other wireless devices or the main network.

Although WAPs may seem fairly straightforward devices, it must be remembered that these devices are often required to carry out a high workload (especially if encryption between the wireless client and the WAP is being used). Thus it is important to select WAPs which are appropriate to your use – home WAPs are usually insufficient for the needs of a large organisation. *Figure 6.29* shows a Cisco Aironet 1200 series access point, which is a typical organisation WAP, whilst *Figure 6.30* shows a Linksys WAP200 typical small business WAP.

WAPs operate at layer 2 of the OSI 7 layer model.

Figure 6.29: A Cisco Aironet 1200 series WAP

Figure 6.30: A Linksys WAP200 small business WAP

Wireless router

Wireless routers are a combination device intended for very small organisations, or the home, mainly to connect such small networks to the Internet and are designed specifically for this purpose. They combine a basic WAP and a basic router into an affordable device. *Figure 6.31* shows a typical Wireless router which also includes a 4 port Ethernet switch. It is important to realise that as these devices are mainly intended for the home and for very small organisations, their functionality and processing power is likely to be extremely limited. Often installing such devices in anything other than a very small organisation is likely to cause many problems because the router element prevents traffic from flowing around the organisation correctly. In addition, their limited functionality makes them unsuitable for connecting into an organisational LAN, whilst their limited processing power makes them unsuitable for processing organisational level encryption at volume. These problems would not occur if an appropriate WAP was deployed instead.

Wireless routers operate at both layer 2 of the OSI 7 (for communications with switched or wireless clients on the same network) or at layer 3 for communication between networks (e.g. your home network and the Internet).

TIPS & ADVICE

For anything other than a home or very small organisation, do not recommend a Wireless Router.

Figure 6.31: A Linksys WRT54GS typical home wireless router (front and rear views)

Quick test

Briefly discuss wireless access points and wireless routers.

Section 12: Routed and routing protocols

Although this is a very short section, it is important and is included to help you understand how routing devices make decisions on how to forward data across a network.

As discussed in *Section 8*, routers are used to connect together networks or perhaps even connect to the Internet. To be able to carry out this function effectively, routers need to:

- pass data between networks; and
- communicate with other routing devices regarding which networks they are connected to.

The data to be carried by the network is encapsulated into packets (*see Chapter 4*), usually IP (Internet Protocol) packets. These are then carried across the network. Such protocols are said to be routed protocols i.e. protocols which can be routed by a router.

Routers also need to be able to communicate with one another about the networks they are connected to. It is important that the routers do this so that they are able to effectively route the routed protocols to the correct network. In order for routers to communicate, there are a number of protocols which can be used such as **Router Information Protocol (RIP)**, **Open Shortest Path First (OSPF)**, both of which are open standards and proprietary protocols such as Cisco's **Enhanced Interior Gateway Protocol (EIGRP)**. These protocols are said to be routing protocols because they allow routers to share routing information. Routing protocols commonly carry information about which networks a router is connected to, the status of the link, the bandwidth of the link, any delays on the link, etc., although exact content is protocol dependent. Participating routers can then use this information to determine the best path to use when forwarding data.

It is critically important that routers are able to communicate with each other about the networks they are connected to if data is to be sent efficiently across the network.

Quick test

Briefly discuss the difference between routing and routed protocols.

TIPS & ADVICE

It is unlikely you will be given an assessment question on this subject on a module or course pitched at this level. However, you can impress the examiner with your knowledge by perhaps working this into an answer to a question on routing.

Section 13: End of chapter assessment

This chapter has discussed the major networking devices and routing/ routed protocols. Any assessment is likely to ask you either to compare and contrast networking devices or to discuss the operation/typical application of each device.

Question

Name the nine major networking devices and, for each, identify its function and typical application. If appropriate, discuss its abilities to control broadcasts and collisions.

Answer

The assessor is looking for a simple list of the major networking equipment, which is likely to be worth about one mark per item. The main marks are going to result from your discussion of each of the devices. However, nine marks are going simply for writing the list, so you may as well have them! Once you have completed your list, you can start discussing each of the major pieces of kit. For most of the equipment, you will find that a diagram will aid your discussion and also make your answer clearer. Ensure that, when you discuss each piece of kit, you identify the layer of the OSI seven-layer model in which it operates; whether it operates on bits, frames or packets; the technology in which it operates; and, if you want extra marks, what effect it has upon collisions and broadcasts. You then simply need to discuss each piece of kit and identify typical applications. Remember to plan out your answer. If you have an hour you can only really spend six minutes discussing each piece of kit if you are to cover them all within the time. However, it is more likely you will be asked to discuss three from a list within half an hour.

You may wish to embellish your answer on routers to include routing and routed protocols. This should impress the assessor.

Section 14: Further reading and research

Cisco Networking Academy Program (2004) CCNA 1 and 2 *Companion Guide* (3rd edn) Cisco Press. ISBN: 1-5871315-0-1. Chapters 1 and 4.

Network Fundamentals, CCNA Exploration Labs and Study Guide (2008). Cisco Press. 1-58713-203-6. Chapter 6.

LAN Switching and Wireless, CCNA Exploration Labs and Study Guide (2008). Cisco Press. 1-58713-207-9. Chapters 1 and 7.

Accessing the WAN, CCNA Exploration Labs and Study Guide (2008). Cisco Press. 1-58713-205-2. Chapter 1. (Also for Enterprise Architecture.)

Microsoft Windows Help – look under Internet Connection Sharing or ICS.

Chapter 7

Network design process

Chapter summary

The costs of installing a network are high – not only in terms of equipment and materials, but also in terms of installing the media and the disruption to the organisation. Most organisations are also critically dependent upon their networks, which means they can neither afford for it not to work nor to have further disruptions to repair problems. Network design is the process of analysing an organisation, its current network, its needs and its plans for the future. From this, a networking solution can be produced that will meet the organisation's current and future needs. Network design is a specialist process and so this chapter can only provide an overview of what is involved. This should be sufficient for assessment purposes at this level.

Learning outcomes

After studying this chapter you should aim to test your achievement of the following outcomes. You should be able to:

Outcome 1: Network design goals

Understand the five main requirements of network design. Question 1 at the end of this chapter will test you on this.

Outcome 2: Design components

Understand how the positioning of devices and servers can enhance network performance. Question 2 at the end of this chapter will test you on this.

Outcome 3: Methodology

Understand and be able to apply a methodology for the analysis of a network. Question 3 at the end of this chapter will test you on this.

Outcome 4: Capacity planning

Understand and be able to apply a methodology for capacity planning within a network. Question 4 at the end of this chapter will test you on this.

Outcome 5: Sample design

Apply the methodologies to a typical scenario. Question 5 at the end of this chapter will test you on this.

How will you be assessed on this?

Design is normally assessed as an assignment as it does not lend itself to being assessed through an exam. In an assignment, you will often be placed in a group where you will be given a scenario and asked to produce a solution to the problem the scenario poses. This will almost always contain some kind of capacity planning. Design questions in an exam or TCT tend to be limited to a discussion of the process; they rarely include capacity planning. However, if capacity planning is on the syllabus, it may well be tested.

Section 1: Network design goals

In any design process, it is essential to understand the goals of the design before begining.

Network design goals

Network design is a complex and challenging task. There are many elements that must be established and analysed if a network design is to be successful. A network should not be judged simply in terms of its size – a network that contains only a small number of nodes can have stringent design requirements. The goals of network design will vary according to the client organisation and the design contractors. However, the following five criteria are a good starting point

Functionality

The network must fulfil the requirements of what it is set up to do. It must do this reliably and at an appropriate speed. Issues here include performance, reliability and correct functionality. Ultimately, the users of the network must be able to carry out their tasks efficiently and effectively.

Scalability

One thing that is known for certain about today's networks is that they must change to fit tomorrow's requirements. On average, an organisation undergoes a major reorganisation every 18 months to three years, and the network must be able to adapt to such changes. The network must be able to grow incrementally, i.e. grow without the need for any major changes to the overall design.

Adaptability

Adaptability has two aspects – the network's ability to adapt to changes in the organisation and the network's ability to embrace technological change. Networking is the fastest growing area of computing and, as such, is continually developing. Any proposed networking solution should not allow anything to limit the implementation of new technologies as and when they become available.

Manageability

Networks need to be managed after their implementation. A well-designed network should facilitate ease of monitoring and management.

Availability

The network must be available for use with downtime minimised (especially unplanned downtime). Ideally, a network should be at least 99.9% available. The only way to achieve this level of reliability is to build in some redundancy to the design, for example having redundant backbone links which will automatically activate should the primary link fail.

Quick test

Briefly discuss the five basic requirements of good network design.

Section 2: Network design components

Designing a network is not just about the cabling and the network devices, but also about the positioning of servers and access to the data they hold. As was seen in *Chapter 6*, the different network devices provide a range of services, from network interconnection to collision and broadcast containment. Hence a good design will ensure the network does not suffer from excessive collisions; can contain broadcasts; and that all nodes will be able to communicate at the planned level of performance.

Network design components

As has been already noted, network performance and network technologies are constantly changing, and so designers need to ensure that the LANs they design can accommodate these changes and that performance is maximised by the careful positioning of critical components. When designing for high-speed technologies and multimedia-based applications, network designers need to address the following critical components of LAN design:

- the function and positioning of servers/broadcast control; and

- collision containment/segmentation.

Function and positioning of servers/broadcast control

Servers fall into two distinct classes:

- organisational servers (such as email servers; organisational-wide application or database or DNS); and

- workgroup servers (data and applications).

A good designer takes great care over the positioning of servers and of who will access them. *Figure 7.1* shows a well-designed network where the workgroup servers (A and B) have been placed close to where they will be used, and where the email server has been placed at an organisational level. By structuring the network in this way, the machines connected to switch A can use server A without having to use the network backbone (through the organisational-level switch), thus keeping traffic on the backbone to a minimum. If these machines need access to email, they will not cause excess traffic on the machines connected to switch B whilst accessing the organisational server (for email). Access to server B from the machines connected to switch A is possible but should not be used often. This type of design is known as a two-layer network design and is suitable for small enterprises.

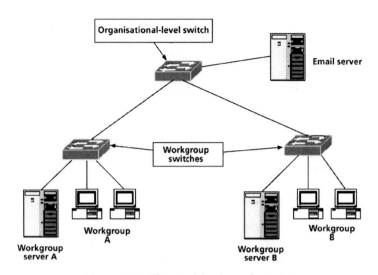

Figure 7.1: The positioning of servers

Notice there is no router in *Figure 7.1*. This could create broadcast-related problems. Because there are no routers, a broadcast by any machine will traverse the whole network, hence wasting bandwidth. The solution would be to replace the organisational-level switch with a router, which would divide the network into two broadcast domains (three if you count the email server network) (*See Figure 7.2*).

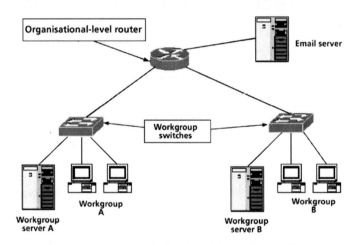

Figure 7.2: Router now divides the two networks into separate broadcast domains

Collision containment/segmentation

As was seen in *Chapter 6*, collisions can be a real problem with Ethernet networks. Indeed, during heavy loads collisions can reduce the available bandwidth. This is because the nodes contend with one another for access to the network. The designer of an Ethernet network aims to position the equipment in such a way as to reduce access contention and the number of collisions on the network. The single most important device for this purpose is the switch. In *Figure 7.1*, the switch virtually eliminates collisions on each network (A and B) and also on the organisational backbone. Hence, *Figure 7.1* shows the correct positioning of switches if they are to reduce collisions. This process is known as segmentation (micro segmentation is the term used if segmented by a switch). In a coaxial Ethernet network, bridges provide collision control.

Quick test

Explain why the positioning of servers is of critical importance in network design. Also discuss why designers should consider collision containment and segmentation when designing networks.

Section 3: Network design methodology

Network design is similar, in many ways, to systems analysis and design. The designer needs to:

- gather facts and figures about the organisation and user requirements and expectations;
- analyse the requirements of the network;
- design the structure;
- minimise the network delay in traffic traversing the network (network diameter);
- document the network.

Gathering facts and figures

This process involves finding out as much about the organisation as possible: its size, current status, plans for the building, plans for the future, number of current employees, plans for growth/downsizing, software in use, future software requirements (e.g. changing to a new computer system), management procedures, office procedures, the views of the people who will be using the network, etc.

It should also be established whether data or software are mission critical. It would likewise be necessary to determine what desktop computers are allowed on the network and if there are any protocols that need to be supported. If addresses or names are to be allocated to the machines, it has to be established who in the organisation controls such lists.

Analysing requirements

The information collected must then be analysed. Particular attention should be paid to the requirements of the network over its lifetime – for example, does the organisation plan to expand rapidly in the near future? User requirements should also be analysed carefully to ensure that the network will be able to deliver what the users want within the time frame they want it. If this is not possible, the end-users' expectations need to be managed to ensure the delivered network is not a disappointment. Perhaps the most important question to ask here

---

TIPS & ADVICE

Introducing switches into the network segments the network into multiple separate collision domains but does not contain broadcasts.

KEY CONCEPT

The correct positioning of servers is crucial to network design. If the servers are badly placed, traffic may have to traverse the entire network, hence reducing overall performance.

TIPS & ADVICE

While there are a great many things to find out about an organisation that is considering a new network design, an assessor will want to see that you appreciate the importance of facts and figures – size of data files, number of users or plans to move to a new building, etc.

is: how is a network is judged to be successful?

In analysing requirements, the network's availability should be determined. Availability is a measure of the following:

- **Throughput** – how much throughput the organisation expects from the network.

- **Response time** – the time the users expect to wait before the network provides them with the information they require.

- **Access to resources** – what resources the users expect to have access to, and what the organisational policy is on access to resources. This often has to be balanced to provide an effective network.

- **Reliability** – a realistic expectation of the network's reliability (100% reliability can be expensive to achieve!).

Organisations that demand high availability will need to carry the costs of such availability – redundant links, spare equipment, etc. However, the network's required capacity must be planned for (*see Section 4*).

Designing the structure of the network

The network structure relates to:

- the network's topology;
- the network's cabling;
- the connection of devices;
- the number of devices network traffic needs to pass through (network diameter).

The first two points are, surprisingly, quite straightforward. Current EIA/TIA recommendations state that networks should be implemented using a star topology and should have a minimum of two networking points to every desktop (not all need to be live). EIA/TIA also require that a **Wiring Closet** (**WC**) should be placed on each floor to serve no more than 1000 m². Where floor size exceeds this, two or more wiring closets should be used. EIA/TIA also specify that a wiring closet should have the following:

- Sufficient heating/cooling to maintain a temperature of 21°C when the equipment is in full operation.

- A minimum of two non-switched dedicated AC outlets (positioned every 1.8 m along the wall at a height of 150 mm above the floor).

- The floor can take the weight of networking equipment.

- Light fixtures should provide 200 lux of brightness and be at least 2.6 m above the ground. The switch should be immediately inside the door. If the light used is fluorescent, it should be clear of the cable runs (because of interference).

- A door 0.9 m wide that opens outwards with a lock to allow anyone inside the room to exit at any time (this may need to be adjusted in the light of local fire regulations).

To determine the best location for the wiring closet, a map of the building should be annotated showing the proposed layout of the computers. Using the above checklist, the potential locations of the wiring closets can be marked on the plan. Using a compass, a 50 m circle with the potential closet at its centre can be drawn to see if all the computers will fit inside this circle. If not, another location must be chosen or, alternatively, more than one closet may be needed. Even though the maximum cable length in 100BaseT is 100 m, a 50 m radius allows for awkward runs, corner turns, etc. A patch panel lead and a lead to a desktop **drop cable**, will all increase the overall length.

For the main wiring closet (the one that will provide any external connections), it is recommended that the telecomms provider's is used - where their cable enters the building (this entry point is known as the **Point of Presence (POP)**). This wiring closet is known as the **Main Distribution Facility (MDF)**; the others are known as **Intermediate Distribution Facilities (IDFs)**. EIA/TIA also recommend that the cabling is a minimum of **category 5 enhanced (cat 5e)** to the desktop and either fibre or copper between the wiring closets (vertical cabling).

'Standard' design structures

As the popularity of networks increased, a standard design structure emerged based on two or three-layer models. These design models offer a hierarchical design to networks which offers many benefits:

Scalability – Because of their design, hierarchical networks are able to be scaled easily with minimal disruption to the organisation;

Redundancy – Hierarchical networks allow redundancy to be designed and built into the network at key points further increasing the reliability of the network;

Performance – Data is moved from the access layer straight into the high speed distribution layer for forwarding. This dramatically increases performance by moving the traffic on high speed devices;

Security – Security is paramount in today's networks. The hierarchical model means devices can be identified per layer and appropriately configured for security;

Manageability – Because the network is divided into layers, the function of devices is easily discernable. Devices at each layer can usually be managed in a similar fashion;

Maintainability – The modular nature of hierarchical networks lends itself well to maintainability. Devices can easily be swapped in the unlikely event they fail or upgraded with minimal disruption to the rest of the network.

As discussed earlier, a two-layer model is suitable for small organisations. Such networks are effectively divided into two layers (*see Figure 7.3*). The bottom layer (the access layer) provides access to the network's services. In the access layer are the computers that are to use the network and their servers. These are arranged in groups so that the machines that need the services from workgroup server

A are on the same switch as the server. The bulk of the traffic in these groups should never need to leave the workgroup environment. Only email and cross-workgroup traffic needs to pass into the distribution layer. This keeps the distribution layer free from unnecessary traffic, thus helping performance. The distribution layer distributes services to the organisation – in this case, cross-workgroup connectivity and access to email. The distribution layer may well form the backbone of a university/college campus or the backbone of an entire building.

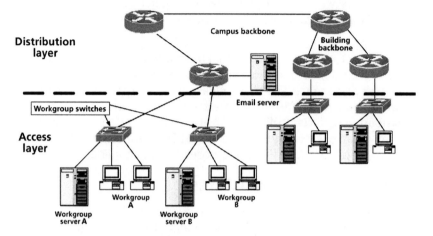

Figure 7.3: Standard two-layer network design

Often an organisation has multiple sites spread over a wide geographical area. In such cases, a further layer is added above the distribution layer. Known as the core layer, this layer provides fast, wide-area connections between geographically remote sites. For example, the University of Sunderland has two main campuses – the St Peter's Campus and the City Campus, which are about two miles apart. Using a three-layer model, there are distribution layers at both campuses (effectively acting as the campus backbone) and a core layer connecting the two campuses (see Figure 7.4).

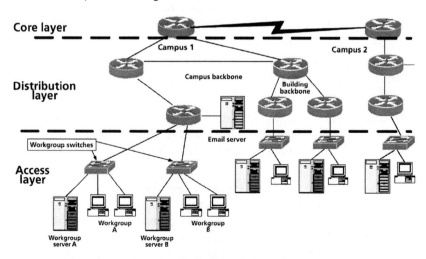

Figure 7.4: A correctly designed three-layer network

Should server farms be established, the routers in the three-layer model would be best substituted with MPLS/RSM equipment (*see Chapter 6*) and some redundant links. Cisco also recommends an Enterprise architecture for large scale deployments. This is beyond the scope of this book.

Network Diameter

As data passes through a networking device, a delay is introduced; this is known as latency and its effects are cumulative. Therefore the more devices the data has to pass through between source and destination, the greater the delay. In modern networks, particularly those supporting VoIP (*see Chapter 1*), it is good design practice to minimise latency. This can be achieved by reducing the number of devices the traffic needs to pass through.

Network diameter is a measure of the number of network devices the traffic needs to pass through between source and destination. Consider *Figure 7.5*, if PC1 wants to send data to PC3, the data needs to pass through six networking devices (a network diameter of six), which introduces six lots of latency.

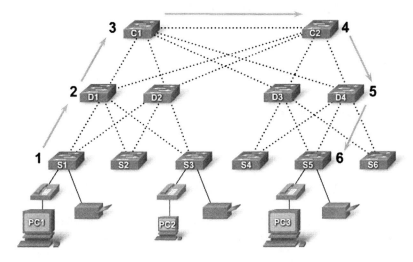

**Figure 7.5: Network diameter
(image courtesy of Cisco Systems Inc.)**

Documenting the network

The design and implementation stages of the network should be well documented. This documentation will be the starting point should there be a need for troubleshooting. Hence the documentation should provide:

- detailed maps of the wiring closets;
- details of the machines attached to these wiring closets;
- details of the type and quantity of cables used to connect to the IDFs;

- notes about any spare cables and their location;
- details about cabling between IDFs/MDFs.

Troubleshooting is a very stressful task. Therefore, the better the documentation, the faster the network is likely to be brought back up. Documentation should be as full as possible. Also, bearing in mind that 80% of networking problems are caused by layer one (cables, connectors, etc.), the cables and endpoints need to be documented very carefully.

Quick test

Briefly outline the network design methodology.

Section 4: Capacity planning

Capacity planning ensures that there will be sufficient capacity in the new network for it to be able to cope with the demands placed upon it. Measuring the capacity of the current network can help to identify performance issues and can also guide the design process.

The capacity planning process

Capacity planning has two purposes: to measure the load on the current network; and to estimate the load that might be imposed on the proposed network. Sophisticated tools are available to help with this process, but it is more likely that these loads will need to be measured mathematically. The maths involved in capacity planning is relatively straightforward. It is used to determine:

- the current load on the network;
- the proposed/additional load on the network;
- if there is enough capacity in the network to cope;
- if there are likely to be any peak-time problems (i.e. when the traffic is at its highest, will the network be able to cope?).

To do this, as much numerical information as possible is collected:

- How many computers are connected/to be connected?
- What packages do they use?
- Are the packages held centrally or locally?
- How often are they downloaded?
- What is their size?
- What sort of data is downloaded?
- How often?
- What is its size?
- How often do the users print out from the network?
- What kind of printer do they use? (Postscript printers put a

huge load on a network and should be avoided)

- What are the file sizes?
- Does a file go directly to a printer or to a computer and then to a printer (in which case it is on the network twice)?
- What about email/Internet traffic?
- How often are they used?
- What are they used for?

This should provide sufficient information about the amount of traffic moved by the network.

However, unless sophisticated software is used to carry out these measurements, the figures obtained will be an educated guess. Allowances should be made for the frame/ packet headers, which will be added to the data as it passes down the layers of the seven-layer model (*see Chapter 4*). It may be necessary to talk to suppliers about any proposed applications and, possibly, obtain copies of the software to evaluate the load before purchase. The equipment connected to the network and its operation should be checked in case it imposes a load on the network.

As much information as possible about the organisation itself must also be collected:

- How long does the organisation use its network each day (if it is open 9 – 5 then it's 8 hours)?
- What does it use its network for?
- Do the users work flexi-time or do they all have the same start and finish time?
- Are there any problems with the current network?
- If so, what weeks/days/times do these problems occur?
- Is there any other pattern to them?
- What time is lunch?
- Does everyone leave together for lunch?
- What is the pattern of the working day (is it like a school/college/university where activities change on an hourly basis)?
- Are backups of the network servers taken at night? Is this across the network?

This should provide enough information about the time period over which the traffic needs to be shipped.

Finally, the design parameters must be established:

- What is the anticipated lifespan of the network?
- Will there be any anticipated growth/decline in the organisation's activities during the network's lifespan?

- Does the building itself contain any physical constraints (e.g. solid floor or ceilings, lots of electric motors, etc.) that will cause interference?
- Should the network be a LAN only or a WAN/LAN?
- Is any existing network equipment to be retained?
- What is the available budget?
- What integration is required with other systems/networks/hardware?

Quality of service (**QoS**) also needs to be determined. QoS basically means the design parameters which were noted in *Section 3* – the responses expected by users, the network's reliability, security issues, etc.

This process should provide enough information to begin the capacity planning process. Remember, answers are needed to two questions:

- Can the network cope at present?
- Will it be able to cope with the proposed changes?

For each question, it must be determined whether the network can cope with:

- the average load (normally the answer to this is 'yes');
- peak-time load problems (usually more tricky to answer).

Peak times are when the network is under the most strain – for example, when lessons begin at college at least one class will log into the network and download software and data to begin their work. Obviously, the students and instructors wish to begin as soon as possible, but the network is probably under its heaviest load during that period – a peak-time problem. (*Section 5* gives an example capacity plan for a college and discusses the issues raised in this.)

Quick test
Briefly outline the stages involved in capacity planning.

Section 5: Sample design

Introduction

In this section the example of Irving's College of Technology (ICT) will be used to analyse the current problems it is having with its network. These problems will be discussed and some solutions proposed. ICT has an IT suite but is having problems with the performance of the network in this suite.

The 50 computers in the IT suite are networked with two servers using two segments of 10Base2 Ethernet separated by a repeater (this is old technology but it keeps the maths and the design simple to start with!). The QoS the College required was for the machines to be operational within five minutes of the class starting. Primarily, the machines run a package known as Trainoffice. Trainoffice offers a simulated office environment. In terms of network load, each machine loads the software (30 MB); uses 20 MB of data and, on average, each user prints 10 MB per session. Data is loaded from two servers (old 486 machines). Unfortunately, such are the problems with this suite that it has been closed temporarily. The Principal of ICT is very disappointed about this situation. It can be assumed that classes in the IT suite change every hour.

Process

There is lots of information contained within the previous paragraph. The first thing to note is that the IT suite has been temporarily closed because of the problems (not a good sign!) and that the classes change every hour. Thus the capacity planning involves 60 minute intervals – everything needs to be loaded, printed, saved, etc., in that time frame.

Next the figures need to be considered:

- 50 computers;
- 30 MB of software;
- 20 MB of data;
- 10 MB printed (through a server; therefore 10 MB to the server followed by 10 MB to the printer – twice the load!);
- 10 Mbps is the theoretical maximum from 10Base2 (7 Mbps actual);
- QoS of five minutes;
- 486 architecture in the servers, which means they can only ship 8 Mbps to the networking card (no PCI architecture – although old, this point demonstrates the effects architecture has!);
- software and data have to be loaded before startup.

So 50 computers x (30 MB software + 20 MB data) = 2500 MB which, when x 8 in order to convert into Mb, = 20,000 Mb of data to be loaded before startup. 10% should be added to this to allow for packet overheads (headers, CRCs, etc.). Thus the total is now 22,000 Mb. Before getting into difficulty, 10Base2 can handle 7 Mbps; after that point it is unpredictable. 22,000 Mb/7 Mbps = 3142 seconds. Thus, assuming the network can handle steadily 7 Mbps it will take 3142 seconds or (53 minutes) for all the machines in the IT suite to be ready to start a 60-minute class! Then they will need to save their data and possibly print.

There are two possibilities to overcome these problems:

- Break up the current network with bridges and additional servers to make smaller networks that will perform better.
- Install a brand-new network based on a faster technology that will also have better future proofing.

Excluding the cabling costs, the second option is likely to be cheaper than the first and also more satisfactory.

A solution would be to install a network using 100BaseT, therefore the load under 100BaseT should be examined: 22,000 Mb/100 Mbps = 220 seconds/60 = 3.66 minutes. Thus, with a 100BaseT network, the suite would be operational within about 4 minutes (subject to the server being able to handle the load). Deploying this network would require a different topology, new servers (the old cannot make use of 100 Mbps cards), new cards in the PCs and switching equipment. Switches usually come in 24 or 48 port and so at least two switches would be required. If the two-tier architecture looked at in *Section 2* was installed, three 24-port switches, and a further switch to join the three switches, would be needed. The scenario mentions servers, and the best solution would be to incorporate three workgroup servers (as shown in *Figure 7.6*, each attached to a switch, along with 17 machines (16 machines on the last switch)). The new loading would be: 17 machines x 50 MB=850 MB + 10% = 935 MB x 8 =7480 Mb / 100 Mbps = 75 seconds for the machines to become operational. This includes no margin for error but, assuming 100% was left for contingency, this is still only 150 seconds, half the QoS of 5 minutes.

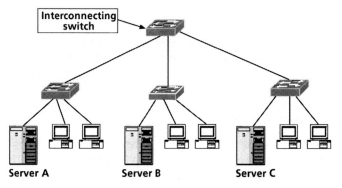

Figure 7.6: Proposed design for ICT

Printing and saving must also be accommodated – this will usually be distributed in the lesson, but may also come near the end; if it does, then it is a peak-time problem. Assume that 20 MB needs to be saved: 17 machines x 20 MB = 340 MB + 10% = 374 MB x 8 = 2992 Mb/100 = 30 seconds. The printing needs to traverse the network to the server and then from the server to the printer (it may be on the network twice so allowances must be made for this or it needs to be investigated more fully). This is ambiguous, so assume the worst-case scenario that it is on the network twice: 17 x (2 x 20 MB) = 680 MB + 10% = 748 MB x 8 = 5984 Mb/100 = 59.84 seconds. Thus the proposed network will handle the load imposed adequately. Had this been an organisation that did not change its activities every the hour, this could have been taken across the working day (8 hours?), but peak times should still be noted – arriving in the morning, lunchtime and printing late in the day.

Average load

In this scenario, everything needs to be completed within a one-hour period. To calculate the average load (which is rarely a problem) the total data is divided by the time period. In the 100BaseT final design there is: 17 machines x (30 MB applications + 20 MB load + 20 MB save + (2 x 10 MB print)) = 1530 MB; 1530 MB x 8 = 12,240 Mb. There are 60 minutes x 60 seconds in an hour = 3600. 12,240 Mb period load/3600 seconds in a period = 3.4 Mbps average load. This is well within the capacity of the network.

KEY CONCEPT

Remember, the time taken to get all the computers operational can be calculated approximately by the following formula:

$$\frac{\text{Total data and/or software to be downloaded before work can begin (in megabits)}}{\text{Maximum throughput of the technology}}$$

Remember to use megabits and to add 10% to the load to allow for packet headers, etc.

The average load on the network per day/session can be calculated approximately by the following formula:

$$\frac{\text{Total data/software/printing of entire day session}}{\text{No. of seconds in day/session}}$$

Quick test

Carefully work through the figures without looking at the calculations given here. Do you get the same answer? If not, where did you go wrong?

Section 6: End of chapter assessment

Questions

1. Outline the five design goals that must be taken into consideration when undertaking a network design.

2. Discuss how the positioning of networking devices and equipment is fundamental to good network design.

3. There are five basic steps in network design methodology. Name these five steps and discuss each one.

4. Discuss the process of capacity planning and outline how you would undertake this process for an organisation.

5. Prove that the figures shown below provide startup time of almost 21 minutes and an average hourly load of 2.5 Mbps:

    - 25 computers;

    - 30 MB software;

    - 10 MB data (both software and data must be downloaded before the machines can be used);

- 1 hour time slot;
- 10Base2 networking.

Rerun the above example to show that the same load can be handled by 100BaseT in less than two minutes.

Answers

1. To answer this question you need to name and discuss briefly the five main goals of network design: functionality, scalability, adaptability, manageability and availability. You need to demonstrate that you understand the importance of each of the terms to the process of network design.

2. This question requires you to demonstrate your knowledge about the positioning of networking devices. You should discuss why the positioning of networking devices is critical to the best performance of the network. You should also discuss what the two types of server are, and what is meant by the terms 'collision' and 'broadcast domains'. Ideally, you should illustrate your answer with diagrams that show the correct placement of both workgroup and organisational servers. You should also give examples of how the correct positioning of the various types of networking devices will create collision and broadcast domains and explain the expected benefits of this.

3. This question is in two parts. The first asks you to name the five basic steps in network design methodology. This serves as a guide to help you structure the rest of the question, but you will gain marks for simply naming them. The second part asks you to discuss each of the steps. There is plenty to discuss and so you should plan your answer carefully so you don't run out of time. You should ensure you explain that this is a sequential procedure and you should stress the importance of gathering all the facts and of correct analysis and design. Most network designers scrimp on the documentation, which is bad practice – especially when 80% of all network problems occur at layer one. You should stress the importance of good documentation and its value when something goes wrong.

4. The important thing to note about this question is that it is asking you not only to discuss the process of capacity planning, but also to embellish your answer by discussing how you would undertake capacity planning for an organisation. You need to discuss the four steps in the process of capacity planning, detailing the figures you need to calculate the current and required load. You should identify the time span under consideration – the example in the chapter had a one-hour interval. You also need to discuss how you would determine if there is enough capacity in the network to cope with both peak loads and the daily/session requirements. The assessor would not expect you to undertake the maths, but would expect an explanation of how you would determine the current and required capacity, both for peak times and for the daily load.

5.   This question is very specific. The assessor is asking you to calculate two types of capacity plan: one showing the length of time it will take for the machines to become operational (software and data to be loaded), the other showing the average load across the time period (1 hour). The formulae are given in the key concept box at the end of *Section 5*. The question also contains the answer and you are asked to prove it.

Time to start:

$$\frac{((25 \times ((10\ MB + 30\ MB) \times 8))\ 10\%) = 21\ minutes}{7\ Mbps*}$$

(*This should be replaced by 100 Mbps when re-running the calculation for 100BaseT.)

Average load:

$$\frac{((25 \times ((10\ MB + 30\ MB) \times 8))\ 10\%) = 2.5\ Mbps}{3600\ seconds}$$

The average load will be the same on 100BaseT as the network speed is not taken into account in this calculation.

Section 8: Further reading and research

Cisco Networking Academy Program (2004) *CCNA 1 and 2 Companion Guide* (3rd edn). Cisco Press. ISBN: 1-58713-150-1. Chapter 5. (Older but still useful.)

LAN Switching and Wireless, CCNA Exploration Labs and Study Guide (2008). Cisco Press. 1-58713-207-9. Chapter 1.

Accessing the WAN, CCNA Exploration Labs and Study Guide (2008). Cisco Press. 1-58713-205-2. Chapter 1. (Also for Enterprise Architecture.)

Chapter 8
Wireless Networking

Chapter summary

Although wireless networks were first proposed in 1991, it is only relatively recently that they have had wide-scale deployment. The recent take up of wireless networks has been truly phenomenal, firstly with organisations requiring roaming clients; through deployment in some coffee shops and restaurants (for a price); to wireless Internet access (often free) using wireless LANs in coffee shops, bars, restaurants, trains, etc.

Wireless LANs represent much more than you might imagine and this chapter guides you through the main areas of wireless technology.

Learning outcomes

After studying this chapter you should aim to test your achievement of the following outcomes. You should be able to:

Outcome 1: Wireless Basics

Understand basic wireless networks; their advantages, disadvantages and typical uses. Question 1 at the end of this chapter will test you on this.

Outcome 2: Wireless Connectivity

Understand wireless connectivity such as frequency, modulation, equipment, standards, etc. Question 2 at the end of this chapter will test you on this.

Outcome 3: Wireless Security

Understand the basics of wireless security. Question 3 at the end of this chapter will test you on this.

Outcome 4: Design of Wireless Networks

Understand good practice in designing wireless networks. Question 4 at the end of this chapter will test you on this.

Outcome 5: Advanced Wireless Networks

Understand advanced uses of wireless networks. Question 5 at the end of this chapter will test you on this.

How will you be assessed on this?

Assessing Wireless LANs (WLANs) is quite interesting. They are such a hot topic at the moment that you are likely to be assessed by either exam or assignment or possibly both. Clearly there are aspects of WLANs which lend themselves to being assessed by assignment. This is likely to be the design aspects and will probably require some sort of capacity planning (*see Chapter 7*). The technical aspects of WLANs, such as security issues, lend themselves well to being assessed by examination, although this will also probably be incorporated as part of the design assignment.

Section 1: Wireless basics

Wireless LANs (WLANs) were first proposed in 1991 with the formation of the **Wireless Ethernet Compatibility Alliance (WECA)** – which later changed its name to the Wi-Fi Alliance. WLANs are an alternative to conventional wired networks and were proposed in June 1997 by the **IEEE** in standard 802.11. Just as the **802.3 Ethernet standards** allow for transmission over multiple media, so does the **802.11 standard**. Specified media includes:

- infrared light;
- 2.4 GHz frequency band;
- 5 GHz frequency band.

The latter two are the preferred choice since they can give omni-directional coverage and suffer less interference (from other light sources) than infrared.

Initially uptake was slow, but in 2001 many products were developed and in 2002 acceptance of the technology in organisations, such as hotels and airports, increased. Since then the deployment of WLANs has been phenomenal and they are now commonplace – in offices, coffee shops, fast food chains, the home, railway stations and even in the trains themselves.

WLANs offer a very flexible alternative to wired networks by utilising radio waves as the medium of transmission rather than copper or fibre cabling. *Figure 8.1* shows a typical organisational WLAN deployment.

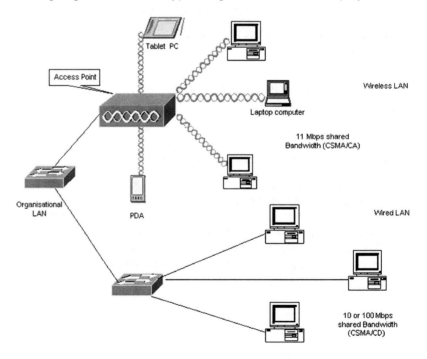

Figure 8.1: Typical WLAN implementation

802.11 WLANs operate in the unlicensed **Industrial, Scientific and Medical (ISM)** frequency bands. Effectively they are used for the physical layer and the MAC sub-layer of OSI layer 2. Although the ISM bands are unlicensed in most countries, there are still some countries in which they are not. This is particularly true for the 5 GHz band where countries, such as Russia, do not permit the use of 5 GHz WLANs.

WLAN modes

WLANs operate in one of two modes:

- ad hoc; and
- infrastructure.

Ad hoc

As the name suggests, ad hoc WLANs are those which are created on an ad hoc basis. For example, two laptops connecting together for the purposes of exchanging a file; two Nintendo DSs connecting together to play a game. An ad hoc WLAN can be thought of as a point-to-point topology (*see Chapter 3*) – just like two PCs connected together with a crossover cable to exchange data. Key features of an ad hoc WLAN are:

- no **Wireless Access Points (WAPs)**;
- independent of an infrastructure;
- based upon **Independent Basic Service Set (IBSS)** – (*see Section 2*);
- operate in a Basic Service Area (BSA) – (*see Section 2*).

Infrastructure

As the name suggests, this is the mode in which the WLANs connect to an Infrastructure via a **Wireless Access Poin**t **(WAP)**. This is the preferred mode for organisations, and usually the home, which allows clients to connect to each other and to resources such as printers and the Internet. Key features of an infrastructure WLAN are:

- one or more WAPs;
- based on **Basic Service Set (BSS)** or **Extended Service Set (ESS)** – (*see Section 2*);
- operate in a **Basic Service Area (BSA)** or an **Extended Service Area (ESA)** – (*see Section 2*);
- operates within an infrastructure.

Wireless LAN benefits and disadvantages

WLANs have enjoyed a phenomenal take up and are commonplace in social spaces, the home and in organisations. The ease of deployment and relatively low cost, together with the desire for connection to the Internet, have undoubtedly played a large part in this. In 2009, a typical 54 Mbps WAP cost £26 and a typical USB 54 Mbps wireless 'stick' about £11 – which is comparable in price terms with conventional wired LANs, but requiring fewer cables to be installed, meaning less disruption to business and also lower installation costs.

WLANs have many advantages but it is also worthwhile considering their disadvantages.

The major advantages of WLANs are:

- easy and low-cost installation;
- ability to provide connection unobtrusively, e.g. airline lounges;
- rapid deployment;
- mobility.

The major disadvantages of WLANs are:

- slow speed (compared to wired networks);
- security issues (although these are addressed, there is still a fear of 'eavesdropping');
- increased radio waves in the working environment and associated health worries;
- restricted ability to penetrate some structures;
- restricted frequency range in some countries.

Quick test

Briefly describe WLANs and give their advantages/disadvantages.

Section 2: Wireless connectivity

In essence, WLANs are networks which use radio waves instead of cables. This means that many of the principles of radio communication apply and a brief discussion of these should aid understanding. Let's consider an everyday example which can be used for comparison in this section.

Consider a national radio station, for example Radio 1 in the UK. The radio station will need to have a frequency allocated to it (for example 98.1Mhz); they will need to use a standard for putting the information onto the radio waves (modulating) – typically **Frequency Modulation (FM)** or **Amplitude Modulation (AM)**; and the authorities regulating the frequency range will need to ensure there is sufficient frequency separation from other radio stations to ensure there is no interference (called channels). Additionally, the radio station will need a transmitter and an antenna; and to receive, the user will need a radio receiver. The area the transmitter serves is known as a coverage area; and the frequency in use determines the antenna used for reception – your TV antenna is completely different to your radio antenna or your mobile phone antenna!

In the above example, Radio 1 uses Frequency Modulation (FM) and in Sunderland transmits on 98.1 MHz frequency. The further you are away from the radio transmitter (towards the edge or fringe of the coverage area), the weaker the signal (due to attenuation). There will become a point that the signal is so weak it will be unreliable (the so called 'fringe areas'). To solve this problem, radio stations use a number of transmitters and have overlapping coverage areas. This means that a roaming listener can roam throughout the country without losing the radio station (mobile phones also use this principle). However, overlapping coverage areas create another problem – that of interference in the overlapping areas (inter modulation noise). This is resolved by using different frequencies on different transmitters – thus the overlapping areas have two distinct frequencies.

Radio reception is also impeded by buildings or objects (especially metal).

Most of these principles apply to WLANs except that both the user (or the client) and the WAP transmit as well as receive, but only one at a time – like a walkie-talkie.

WLAN communication basics

As WLANs operate in many countries, a frequency range needed to be agreed. This is the so-called ISM range, and WLANs operate on either the 2.4 or 5 GHz frequency ranges and use one or both types of modulation:

- **Direct Sequence Spread Spectrum (DSSS)**; or

- **Orthogonal Frequency Division Multiplexing (OFDM)**

Figure 8.2 shows the 2.4 GHz frequency range used by the **Institute of Electrical and Electronics Engineers (IEEE) 802.11b** standard. Note that some of the channels overlap. To move from one coverage area to another without losing connection, it is necessary to have overlapping coverage areas which would need to use different channels (to prevent inter modulation noise). For example, coverage area A could use channel 1 and coverage area B channel 6 as these don't overlap.

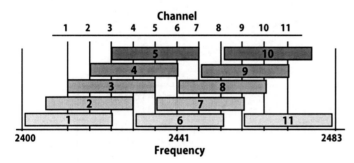

Figure 8.2: 802.11b (USA) channel mapping (image courtesy of Cisco Systems Inc.)

WAPs have a much smaller coverage area (called microcells) than a radio transmitter, which means more of them are needed to cover an area. Laying out all but the simplest of WLANs requires careful design to ensure overlap of coverage area without overlapping frequencies. *Figure 8.3* shows how to place WLAN microcells. *Section 4* gives more details on WLAN design.

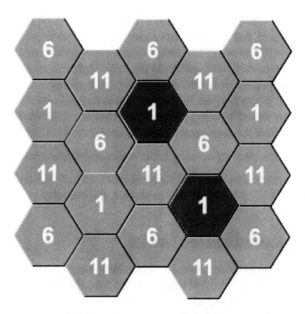

Figure 8.3: 802.11b (USA) placement of non-interrupting microcells (image courtesy of Cisco Systems Inc.)

Channels can easily be changed on the WAP and most WAPs now have the so-called 'good neighbour' feature, where they will detect other WLANs and choose the most appropriate channel for themselves. However, professionally, this is best not left to chance and so the channel can be selected manually. *Figure 8.4* shows channel selection on a Linksys WRT54GS (UK channels). Note that Mixed mode means the WAP is working on more than one standard.

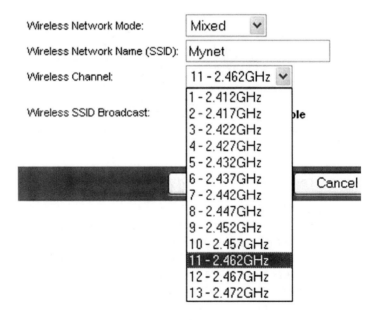

Figure 8.4: Selecting a channel for the access point on a UK Linksys WRT54GS

As with radio stations, signals from WLANs are impeded by objects such as walls. However, because transmission power is lower and frequencies are higher on WLANs, other objects, such as furniture, screens, and even people, can impede the signal. As a rule of thumb, line of sight works best for WLANs. Also, the higher the frequency, the less able it is to penetrate objects. Thus if walls and other objects have to be penetrated with a WLAN (such as in the home), it would be better to use a 2.4 GHz WAP or alternatively MIMO equipment when the standard is ratified (*see below*).

The following table summarises the various standards available in 2009.

Standard	Ratified	Network	Frequency	Speed
802.11	1997	Proprietary	2.4 GHz	1–2 Mbps
802.11a	1999	Standards based	5–7 GHz	Up to 54 Mbps
802.11b	1999	Standards based	2.4 GHz	Up to 11 Mbps,
802.11g	2003	Standards based	5 GHz	Up to 54 Mbps
Draft N	–	Standard not ratified	Possibly 2.4 and 5 GHz	Up to 248 Mbps for two MIMO* streams

*Multiple Input/Multiple Output (MIMO) technology vastly increases the data rate of WLANs. It does this by taking a higher data rate stream and splitting it into multiple lower rate streams, which are then broadcast simultaneously. MIMO also dramatically extends the range of traditional WLANs.

WLANs also require an antenna which needs to match the frequency. However, there are other considerations for **WLAN antennae**, which govern the coverage area. *Figure 8.5* shows a selection of WLAN antennae. It is important to select the correct antenna for your use. For example, dipole antennae are used for **omni-directional** coverage, whereas the flat pad type antennae are used for **uni-directional** coverage. The latter is useful to place on the outer walls of a building in order to focus the WLAN signals into the building, thereby further increasing security. **Parabolic antennae** are normally used for building to building WLANs (*see Section 5*).

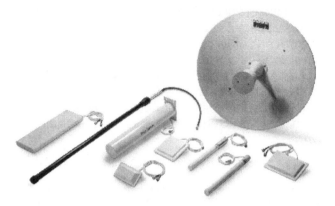

**Figure 8.5: A selection of WLAN antennae
(image courtesy of Cisco Systems Inc.)**

Setting up the basic wireless of WLANs is very simple. You need a WAP (*Figure 8.6* shows a Linksys WAP200 which is a typical small business WAP) that connects to the network (*see Figure 8.1*). This connection is usually a UTP connection and commonly supplies power to the WAP (known as **Power over Ethernet (PoE)**), as well as connection to the organisational LAN. Each wireless client (PC, laptop or PDA) connecting to the WLAN needs a wireless **Network Interface Card (WNIC)** installed for the appropriate standard (e.g. 802.11g). Providing the WAP is transmitting its **Service Set IDentifier (SSID)**, the wireless client should be able to see the network – the SSID is a unique identifier (or name) that wireless clients can use to distinguish between multiple WLANs in the same vicinity. *Figure 8.7* shows a sample of available wireless networks detected by Windows Vista (in the University of Sunderland). It probably still won't be possible to connect to any of the wireless networks, but this is a security issue, NOT a radio communication issue. Most WLANs employ security measures (notice that most networks in *Figure 8.7* are security enabled). The best analogy to this concept is encrypted channels on satellite TV. For example, if you are a Sky TV customer, you may well be able to go to Sky Movies or other premium channels, but not be able to watch them. This is because your satellite receiver isn't able to decode what it is receiving. WLANs operate in a similar fashion – security is discussed in more detail in *Section 3*.

Figure 8.6: A Linksys WAP200 – a typical small business WAP

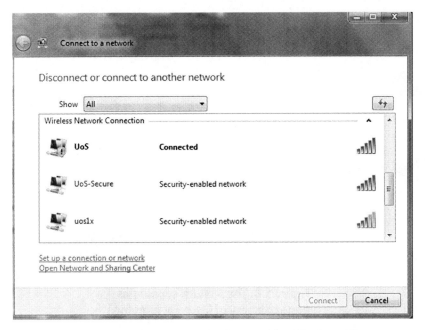

**Figure 8.7: Wireless Networks detected by Windows Vista
in the University of Sunderland**

Wireless LAN topologies

WLANs have a topology in the same way that wired networks do, however, the term used when talking about WLANs is the **Basic Service Area (BSA)** or **Extended Service Area (ESA)**. The BSA which is comprised of one microcell – the area of coverage of a WAP, whilst the ESA is comprised of two or more WAPs. WLANs with one WAP are said to have a **Basic Service Set (BSS)** and those with two or more are said to have an **Extended Service Set (ESS)**. It should also be noted that wireless clients operating without a WAP are said to have an **Independent** (of infrastructure) **Basic Service Set (IBSS)**.

A WLAN with one WAP is relatively straightforward – place the access point and/or its antenna in the centre of the area you wish to cover. For example, if you were placing an WAP in a single floor coffee shop, then the most effective situation would be to place it in the ceiling in the centre of the customer seating area using an omni-directional antenna.

A WLAN with more than one WAP requires more consideration. The first question to answer is – why is more than one WAP necessary? There are three possible reasons (*see Figure 8.8*):

- to provide a coverage area greater than can be provided by one access point;
- to provide redundancy or load balancing in a single area; and
- to extend a network, either wireless or wired by the use of wireless bridges.

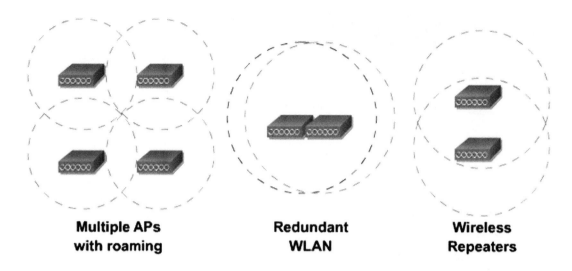

Multiple APs
with roaming

Redundant
WLAN

Wireless
Repeaters

Figure 8.8: The 3 WLAN topologies
(image courtesy of Cisco Systems Inc.)

<table>
<tr><td>

KEY CONCEPT

Remember, there is no
easy way to control the
number of users using an
access point – as a client
approaches if the access
point has an available
address (of which there
are usually 2,048), the
device can connect.
Redundant WLANs could
well be necessary to
provide bandwidth –
the connections can be
controlled by getting half
of the users to connect
to access point 1 and the
other half with access
point 2 (this is achieved
in Windows' device
configuration).

</td></tr>
</table>

Designing a multiple access point WLAN

In any multiple WAP installation, the goal is to have the coverage
areas overlap so that a client can roam without interruption. However,
too much or too little overlap can cause disruption of the wireless
connection to the client. Obviously too little overlap will mean the client
loses coverage roaming between access points, whereas too much
overlap could result in the WAPs interfering with each other. For this
reason, deployment needs to be controlled – in the same fashion as
previously discussed in the Radio 1 example. The concept is similar for
WLANs.

The 802.11b (USA) standard specifies 11 channels (*see Figure 8.2*). Thus
in the case of redundant WLAN implementations the maximum number
of WAPs that can be used concurrently is three, using channels 1, 6 and
11, which do not overlap with each other. If the density of users still
presents an issue, then a solution is to install access points operating in
another frequency range (e.g. in the 5 GHz band).

Sharing the media

WLANs operate in a similar fashion to traditional Ethernet (10Base2,
10Base5, 10BaseT) in that there is media which is shared by all
computers. You will recall *Figure 8.9* from *Chapter 5*.

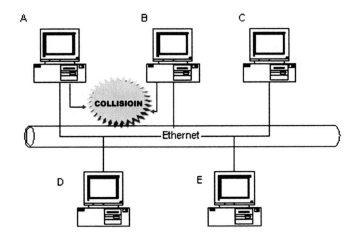

Figure 8.9: An Ethernet collision

Figure 8.9 represents **coaxial Ethernet**. Here five stations share the media and stations A and B have had a collision which destroys the data. Wired Ethernet uses **Carrier Sense Multiple Access with Collision Detection (CSMA/CD)** to share the media. WLANs defined by the 802.11 standard also share the media using CSMA techniques; however, WLANs have two additional problems preventing them from implementing **Collision Detection (CD)**:

- CSMA/CD requires full duplex transmission abilities which 802.11 WLANs don't have;

- With WLANs there is a chance that not all nodes can see each other (the hidden node problem). Consider *Figure 8.10*, where PC1 and PC2 are on opposite sides of the WAP. Both of these PCs could be close to their maximum transmission distance from the WAP and so they can detect the WAP but not each other. If they can't detect each other, then they can't detect a collision.

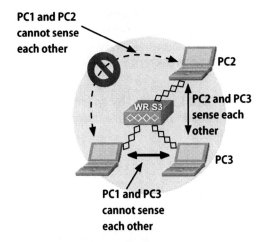

**Figure 8.10: Hidden node problem
(Image courtesy of Cisco Systems Inc.)**

To resolve these problems and ensure that the media is still shared, the 802.11 standard provides for **Carrier Sense Multiple Access with Collision Avoidance (CSMA/CA)** through a **Distributed Co-ordination Function (DCF)**. Using this method, the station wishing to transmit will 'listen' to the medium. If it is busy, then it will defer. If it is free for a specified period of time (called the **Distributed Inter Frame Space (DIFS)**), it will transmit. The WAP will check the CRC of the frame and respond with an **ACKnowledgement (ACK)** indicating that the frame was received intact. If the sender doesn't receive an ACK, then it will re-transmit.

For larger frames the standard specifies a reservation system. Here the station wishing to use the WLAN reserves bandwidth using two control packets – **Request To Send (RTS)** and **Clear To Send (CTS)**. For example, PC1 may wish to send a frame to the WAP. It will transmit a short RTS frame which will include the source, destination and the duration of the transaction (including the ACK). If the medium is free, the WAP will respond with a CTS frame containing the same information. All stations hearing these frames use the information together with the physical sense of the carrier to determine when they can transmit. Thus in the case of the hidden node problem, if PC1 reserved bandwidth, PC2 would not hear the RTS from PC1, but would hear the CTS from the WAP and so would refrain from sensing the media until the transaction duration was over. Thus collisions are avoided rather than detected.

Quick test

Briefly discuss the wireless connectivity aspects of WLANs.

Section 3: Wireless security

The previous section discussed the wireless connectivity aspects of WLANs. Although these connectivity aspects are complex they represent just that – wireless connectivity. However, there also needs to be a security aspect – we don't want any unauthorised users with the correct equipment using our WLAN. In the satellite TV example, companies, broadcasting premium channels only want their content viewed by subscribers (or authorised users). To control access, they employ encryption methods because, everyone receives the content, but only authorised users can decrypt it. Similar principles are employed with WLANs.

Let's first examine the 802.11 standard for wireless association, which is a key part of discovering and then connecting to a WLAN. It has four primary components:

- beacons;
- probes;
- authentication; and
- association.

Beacons may be broadcast regularly by WAPs and are frames used by the WLAN to advertise its presence. They will normally contain:

- SSID;
- supported rates;
- any security implementation.

Wireless clients use this information to build the list of wireless networks (*see Figure 8.7*).

Probes – these are used by wireless clients to search for a specific network (the desired or preferred network) using the SSID. Normally probes are sent out on multiple channels. WLAN clients trying to discover all WLANs probe with no SSID. It should be noted that WAPs with the broadcast SSID feature turned off will not respond (hidden WLANs).

Authentication – the original specification provided two authentication techniques:

- **Open** or **NULL** – where the client says 'authenticate me' and the WAP responds 'yes';
- **Wired Equivalent Protocol (WEP)** – the idea being to give the wireless link the equivalent privacy of a wired link. Unfortunately the original implementation of this method was flawed and it is widely recommended that it isn't used.

Association – this is the final step of wireless association. Here the security and bit rate options are finalised and the data link established. In this phase, the client learns the **Basic Service Set ID** (**BSSID**), which is the MAC address of the WAP, and the WAP assigns an **Association IDentifie**r (**AID**) to the client, which can be thought of as mapping a switchport to the client. This allows the network switches to keep track of frames destined for the WLAN client.

Security

Security is a major issue with WLANs and can be categorised into:

- security of information in transit; and
- misuse of the access point itself.

Security of information in transit

In general, most concern is for the security of information in transit; any plain text sent over the WLAN can possibly be eavesdropped. The question is whether the sender minds that information being eavesdropped. Most information of a confidential nature will be sent using a secure server and some form of encryption. For example, even sitting in a public access area, such as a coffee shop, using a WLAN to make a purchase with a reputable on-line retailer; at some point, the retailer will transfer the purchaser to a secure server and an encrypted data channel will exist between the purchaser and the on-line supplier. This encryption is instigated inside the PC in the OSI 7 layer model (layer 6 – the presentation layer). Thus the credit card information being transmitted between the purchaser and the retailer is secure, so eavesdropping the information on a WLAN will yield no useful information. In fact, it is probably far more likely to have the credit card information copied down by those sitting around (the so-called 'shoulder surfing').

As for the plain text sent during a session in a public access area (which will most probably include emails and any user IDs and passwords for non-secure servers), there is very little that can be done to safeguard this information, other than seriously considering whether or not to use the public access area.

If using a WLAN in an organisation or the home, it is more feasible to manage the WAP – *see security protocols below.*

Misuse of the WAP

Installation of a WAP without any security can lead to misuse of the WAP (and subsequently the network) by unintended users. There have been numerous reported instances of this omission – one of the better ones is the tale of a security engineer who found a neighbour in his apartment block with an unsecured wireless network. Being helpful, the security engineer used his neighbour's printer to print a document on securing a WLAN!

As there is no physical connection to a WAP, it is more difficult to monitor who is connected. It is important to remember that it is not just the bandwidth being 'stolen' that could be a problem – any material downloaded using the WAP will be logged with the **MAC address** and/ or **IP address** of the installed WAP. This may result in being liable for any charges or prosecutions arising as a result of failing to secure the WAP.

Most WAPs provide a method of regulating the users:

- through security protocols;
- MAC Address locking.

Security protocols

These are useful tools which allow a WLAN to be secured. There are many protocols and options to choose from but, not all options are supported by all equipment – especially early WNICs. The need to counteract the potential security threats has to be balanced against the need to support older WNICs. The main security protocols are:

WEP – Wired Equivalence Protocol originally used a 40 bit pre-shared key that must match on both the clients and WAPs (must be manually configured). Most vendors have now expanded this to 128 bit key. WEP protects authorised users from casual eavesdropping and is based upon **Rivest Cipher 4** (**RC4**). WEP is recognised as having security weaknesses (it is easily cracked); however, it is widely supported, although it is also widely recommended that it shouldn't be used.

WPA – Wi-Fi Protected Access. The longer-term security measure is the 802.11i standard, as WPA was introduced to address the weaknesses of WEP. WPA also works on a **Pre-Shared Key** (**PSK**) arrangement and has stronger encryption than WEP. Although supported by most modern access points, WPA doesn't have wide support on early WNICs and some consumer electronics also struggle with WPA. WPA is certified by the Wi-Fi alliance and uses **Temporal Key Integrity Protocol (TKIP)** which has two functions:

- it encrypts the layer 2 payload; and
- uses a **Message Integrity Check (MIC)** to help defend against a packet being tampered with.

Rather bizarrely, many WAPs do not always show WPA but make references to a PSK. PSK or PSK2 with TKIP are the same as WPA!

WPA2 – Wi-Fi Protected Access 2 – is the preferred encryption method because it uses **Advanced Encryption Standard (AES)**, which brings WLAN encryption standards into alignment with broader IT industry standards and 802.11i. All wireless devices manufactured after March 2006 must be able to support WPA2. AES has the same functionality as TKIP, but it adds a sequence number and uses additional data from the MAC header, allowing the receiving device to determine if the non-encrypted bits have been tampered with.

Again, devices may not show these settings – PSK or PSK2 with AES is the same as WPA2 and PSK2 without an encryption method specified is the same as WPA2.

Security is usually configured via browser access to the WAP.

When setting up WEP, WPA or WPA2 encryption, the key needs to be entered on both the access point and on the device, although some manufacturers now provide software to automate the process. It pays to be wary with this software as it probably won't run on consumer electronics such as PDAs, Nintendo Wiis and DSs, iPhones, printers, etc. Devices without the key can't access the network. As the key is entered on the device itself, the device is authorised for wireless access rather than the NIC.

MAC address locking of filtering

All WNICs have a MAC address and WAPs will usually have a security setting, which allows access to be restricted only to authorised MAC addresses and therefore WNICs. Usually there is a utility that allows you to see all of the currently connected WNICs, allowing you to select the ones that should be given access. Obviously, the control is on the WNIC – if the WNIC is placed in another machine, then an unauthorised machine could have access to the network. Not all WNICs support MAC address locking.

Advanced security

The above security measures should be enough to protect a small organisation and definitely should be enough to protect the home however; larger organisations usually wish to implement stricter security on their WLANs.

TIPS & ADVICE

Always secure a wireless LAN, ideally:
- **disable SSID broadcasts from WAPs;**
- **use MAC address filtering;**
- **use the highest common security implementation such as WPA2.**

TIPS & ADVICE

Whilst having security enabled on your WLAN is highly recommended, you should be aware that the encryption required for this security will pose a significant overhead to your WAP.

If the wireless connections slow down significantly after upgrading to or implementing higher security levels, then it may be necessary to upgrade your WAP.

Enterprise level WAPs

So far small organisation WAPs, such as the Linksys WAP200 (*see Figure 8.6*), have been discussed; however, there are other types of WAPs for larger organisations or those wanting greater security. *Figure 8.11* shows a Cisco Aironet 1200 series – a typical enterprise level WAP. A key feature of this device is the ability to provide Wireless VLANs – enabling wireless users to be integrated into existing wired VLANs. This is achieved by the WAP appearing as multiple WLANs – the user then selects the correct one and, following successful authentication, is connected. Thus the WAP can support ,for example, student and staff VLANs on the same device.

**Figure 8.11: a Cisco Aironet WAP 1200 series –
a typical enterprise level WAP**

Extensible Authentication Protocol (EAP)/Network Access Control (NAC)

EAP is really a framework for authenticating network access (*see Chapter 12*). Organisations may well want to deploy a greater level of security by authenticating users by User ID and allocating services accordingly. EAP allows this but, for deployment on WLANs, EAP requires device support. Enterprise level WAPs (such as the Cisco Aironet 1200 series) generally provide this.

EAP is commonly used for **Network Access Control** (**NAC**) by solutions such as Bradford Networks Campus Manager. Campus Manager is commonly used in Universities to control connections to the WLANs (although like most 802.1x and IBNS solutions, it can control access to wired LANs too). With such solutions, usually as the users connect to the WLAN, they are placed in a registration VLAN where they can be authenticated. As well as authenticating the users, NACs commonly installs software to scan the registry of the PC to verify it meets with organisational security and access policies. Typically this will include ensuring the **Operating System** (**OS**) is up to date and that the PC has recently been virus checked with appropriate software. Usually the NAC will be configured to switch users to a remedial VLAN should they authenticate but fail policies. For example, if the user authenticates successfully but the OS is out of date, they could be switched to a VLAN which contains updates for their OS.

Upon successful authentication and successful policy check, users are switched to the appropriate VLANs. *Figure 8.7* shows available WLANS in Windows Vista (from the University of Sunderland). You will notice from *Figure 8.12*, that the UoS WLAN appears to be open security and that the laptop can freely connect to it.

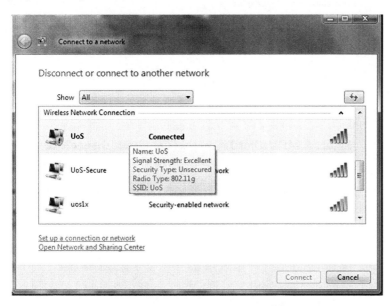

Figure 8.12: UoS WLAN is apparently unsecured

However, when a web browser is opened, the user is taken to a login page (*see Figure 8.13*).

Figure 8.13: Bradford Networks Campus Manager NAC login page

Upon successful authentication the user is given an appropriate message and has to wait while the PC is scanned and the correct VLAN determined (*see Figure 8.14*).

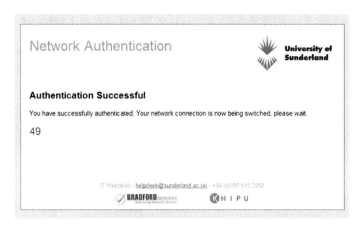

**Figure 8.14: Bradford Networks Campus Manager NAC
authentication successful page**

Figure 8.15 shows that all has been successful and that the browser needs
to be restarted.

**Figure 8.15: Bradford Networks Campus Manager NAC
restart browser page**

Finally *Figure 8.16* shows that connection has been established.

Figure 8.16: Normal connectivity after authenticating

For further information on EAP *see Chapter 12 – Identity Based Networking Services* (IBNS)/802.1x.

EAP can be used on top of the security protocols mentioned (usually you would want WPA2) to provide a greater level of access control if required. However, using just NAC servers provides a more scalable solution.

Quick test

Briefly discuss the major security mechanisms for WLANs.

Section 4: Wireless LAN design

All but the simplest, one WAP WLANs need to be designed. Indeed, even a one WAP WLAN will benefit from some thought on the placement of the WAP. The majority of issues concerning WLAN design have already been covered in this chapter, thus this section covers the WLAN design considerations and points you to the relevant parts of the chapter.

Wireless LAN design considerations

As discussed previously, WLANs utilise radio waves as their transmission medium and so the rules governing propagation of radio waves apply to WLANs. It is important to undertake a site survey (*see also Chapter 9*) as part of the design process to gather as much information about the building as possible. There are six main factors to consider when undertaking the site survey:

1. **Data rate required** – the data rate is directly related to the coverage of the WLAN, the better the coverage the higher the data rate. Rather than reduce reliability as the signal weakens between the WAP and the client (either as a result of distance or signal degrading because of obstructions), WLANs shift to a lower data rate, therefore preserving the reliability. *Figure 8.17* shows the range and typical data rates available in an unobstructed WLAN environment. It is quite common now for a minimum data rate to be specified. This is particularly so with VoIP (*see Chapter 1*) applications.

2. **Antenna type** – some access points, particularly those designed for non-domestic use, offer a range of antennae (*see Figure 8.5*). Proper antenna selection and placement is a critical factor in coverage. As a rule of thumb, the range increases with antenna height and gain.

3. **Physical environments** – an access point in an open environment (e.g. in the centre of an office ceiling) will have a better coverage than a closed or relatively closed environment (e.g. in a cupboard).

4. **Obstructions** – any obstructions between the access point and the client can affect performance.

5. **Building materials** – the type of building material used also influences range: drywalls allow radio waves to penetrate better than metal or brick walls.

6. **Line of sight** – maintaining a clear line of sight between the client and the access point will significantly increase performance. If you are using the wireless link as a bridge, this is essential as you require maximum throughput.

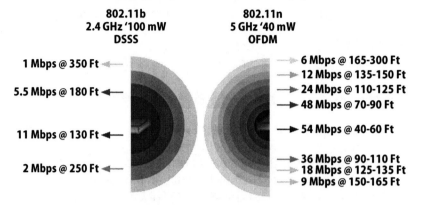

Figure 8.17: Data rates available in an unobstructed WLAN implementation (image courtesy of Cisco Systems Inc.)

Topologies

WLAN topologies are discussed in *Section 2*. Before proceeding with the design, you need to determine the topology you require.

Designing a multiple access point WLAN

Section 2 discusses the three main reasons multiple WAP WLANs are required. One of the key reasons for having multiple WAPs is for roaming. For roaming solutions, the WAPs need to be placed so that coverage is uninterrupted and so that channels do not overlap. *Figure 8.3* shows multiple microcells around WAPs with non-interrupting channels.

A multiple WAP WLAN needs to be carefully planned in order to make the best use of the resources to deliver the best service. Only proper planning can ensure that there will be sufficient wireless support for the clients. Before installation, it is recommended that a well-documented plan is in place. These areas will need to be identified:

- The number of users the WLAN can support (how many will there be? how many will fit into the space?);
- The required data rate (remember that all wireless clients share access to the medium so the maximum throughput is shared) ;
- The use of non-overlapping channels;
- Transmit power settings (which may be governed by local regulations).

The starting point is a map of the area to be covered by the WLAN. The point of the map is to ensure the correct placement of WAPs. Therefore any points where the WAPs can't be placed should be marked – this is particularly vital if they are to use existing network or electrical cabling.

Ideally at this point, possible locations can start to be identified for the WAPs and coverage circles can be drawn. The radius of the coverage circle will vary depending upon the bandwidth required. For example, if maximum signal strength is required (and therefore maximum bandwidth) from an 802.11b network, *Figure 8.17* shows that the maximum radius is 130 feet (approximately 40 metres).

Once the radius has been determined, then the coverage circles can be drawn on the map.

Figure 8.18 shows a design for a typical conference hall scenario. Although there are only three non-overlapping channels in the 802.11b (USA) standard, our requirements can still be achieved by using an 802.11a WAP for one of the areas.

54 Cubes - 4 Conference Rooms

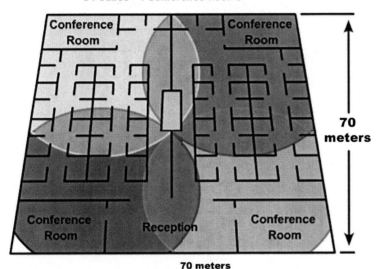

70 meters

70 meters

Figure 8.18: WLAN design in a typical conference centre (adapted from an image courtesy of Cisco Systems Inc)

SAFETY TIPS

The following safety advice should be observed (in addition to any local safety advice) when using or installing WLANs:

● Never touch or move any antenna whilst the unit is transmitting or receiving.

● Never touch, hold or locate any antenna in such a way as it is close to or touching an exposed area of skin – especially the face and eyes.

● Don't use any equipment without the antenna attached.

● Ensure the environment you are considering is suitable for WLANs and the type of wireless LAN you are deploying, e.g. hospitals.

● Ensure all antennae are at least 20 cm from all persons.

● Ensure any high gain, wall or mast mount antennae are professionally installed and at least 30 cm from all persons.

Quick test

Briefly discuss the major WLAN design considerations.

Section 5: Advanced wireless

WLANs are increasing in popularity and are being used for a variety of purposes. This section details more specialist use of WLANs.

Inter-building WLANs

As well as being deployed to service clients, WLANs are becoming a popular technology for extending networks, particularly between buildings. By using a wireless bridge and an appropriate antenna, buildings up to 32 km (20 miles) apart can be connected at speeds of up to 11 Mbps. Deployment of WLANs in such a way is very cost effective for an organisation compared to leasing a data link from a service provider. Even if it is two buildings on a site, the cost of laying a cable between them is likely to be significantly more expensive than the appropriate WLAN kit. *Figure 8.19* shows typical deployment of WLAN for inter-building communication.

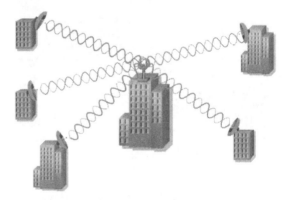

Figure 8.19: Typical deployment of a WLAN for inter-building communication (image courtesy of Cisco Systems Inc.)

Figure 8.20 shows a Cisco Aironet 1400 outdoor WLAN bridge.

Figure 8.20: Cisco Aironet 1400 outdoor WLAN bridge (image courtesy of Cisco Systems Inc.)

Creating WLANs between buildings can be a challenging task and is often governed by local planning regulations; there may also be obstacles in the line of sight between the buildings that will impair performance. Clearing these obstacles will probably require a tower for the antenna, which will itself be subject to local planning regulations.

If you are intending to use a WLAN for building-to-building communications it is advisable to contact the local planning authorities and seek specialist help at the design stage.

In general, building-to-building WLANs need specialist bridging devices and antennas.

Centralised approach to WLANs

This chapter has already shown that WLANs are extremely complex. Most organisations now deploy multi-WAP WLANs to provide an ESA. Indeed it is not unusual for larger organisations such as colleges or universities to provide a campus wide ESA. This can require a large number of WAPs and an infrastructure to suit. Management of such large WLANs is clearly a problem – 802.1x, NACs and IBNS lighten the security configurations but, the configuration of such a number of WAPs provides a real challenge to network managers. For example, if a new WLAN was added to existing enterprise level WAPs (such as the Aironet 1200 series), network managers would need to access (either physically or through the network) each WAP and make the update – a time-consuming task and prone to error. A centralised approach was desperately needed.

Many vendors are now starting to introduce such systems. An example of such a system is Cisco Systems Wireless LAN Controllers (WLCs). *Figure 8.21* shows a Cisco 2100 series WLC – a typical **Small to Medium Enterprise (SME)** WLC. This controller can support up to 6 **Light Weight Access Points (LWAPPs)** (*see Figure 8.22*).

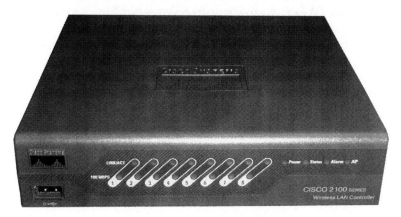

Figure 8.21: a Cisco 2100 series WLC

Figure 8.22: a Cisco 1200 series Light Weight WAP (LWAPP)

The LWAPP in *Figure 8.22* is very similar to the one in *Figure 8.11*, in fact setting aside the optional 5 GHz bolt on unit at the front, the two WAPs are physically identical. The difference is in the **Operating System (OS)** installed on the devices. The LWAPP has a minimal OS installed and relies on getting the rest of the OS from the WLC.

The LWAPPs are connected into the network infrastructure and communicate with the WLC. *Figure 8.23* shows an example of the deployment of WLCs and LWAPPs in a network. Basically LWAPPs are positioned in the user areas and they communicate over a VLAN through the network infrastructure with the WLC. The WLC sends the OS to the LWAPPs via the network together with the appropriate configuration – any changes to the configuration made on the WLC will be propagated to the LWAPPs – if the network manager designates them to receive it. Thus one change on the WLC can be propagated to all LWAPPs in seconds. The 2125 model of the WLC can support up to 25 LWAPPs, which will save a large number of individual configurations.

WLC

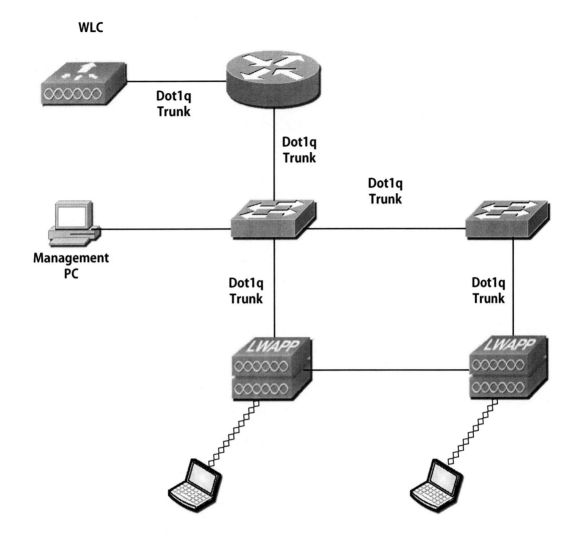

**Figure 8.23: An example WLC deployment
(Dot1q trunks are trunk links used to carry VLANs)**

There are many other configuration options for WLCs (such as groups of LWAPPs) and functionality will continue to be developed. This is definitely another area of WLANs to watch!

Quick test

Discuss both Inter-building WLANs and WLC/LWAPPs.

Section 6: End of chapter assessment

Questions

These questions relate to the assessment targets set at the beginning of this chapter. If you can answer them effectively you are in a good position to achieve good credit in assessments or examinations.

1. Discuss what is meant by the term Wireless LANs and identify their advantages and disadvantages

2. Discuss wireless connectivity. Ideally you should discuss how WLANs connect wirelessly. Note a security discussion isn't important at this stage.

3. Discuss the security options available with WLANs and identify why they are so important.

4. Discuss the major steps in designing a WLAN.

5. Discuss advanced uses of WLANs – in particular inter-building WLANs and centrally-managed WLANs

Answers

1. This is a basic question regarding WLANs. The assessor doesn't require great technical detail – you are being asked what is meant by the term WLAN. Your answer should include that it is an international standard for wireless computer networking. Ideally you should give the standard and illustrate your answer with a diagram. Don't forget you are required to give the advantages and disadvantages of a WLAN!

2. In this question the assessor is testing your knowledge of the wireless connectivity aspects of a WLAN – elements like modulation, channel allocation, antenna type, etc. The question clearly tells you not to address security but, you could mention that wireless signals can be received but that encryption can be used to protect privacy (remember the satellite TV example?).

3. Security is a great concern with WLANs. Here the assessor is asking you to discuss the security options. Ideally you should discuss each of the security options, its advantages/weaknesses and state how it applies to securing the WLAN. It is also worthwhile outlining the two reasons for security: preventing misuse of the AP (and network); and securing the information in transit.

4. This is more likely to be assessed in an assignment than as an exam question. However, if you are asked then you should discuss the major points. Ideally you should illustrate your answer with appropriate diagrams and give examples. You could also demonstrate your knowledge by discussing each of the security options and relate to an example.

5. This level of WLANs is probably outside your field of study, however, you are being asked to discuss advanced uses and so

you must. The assessor won't be wanting great technical detail but will want to know you know about advanced uses at a general level. Again, examples and diagrams will help.

Section 7: Further reading and research

www.bbc.co.uk/radio/waystolisten/analogue/

www.Wi-Fi.org (last accessed 8/7/09)

www.Cisco.com (last accessed 8/7/09)

LAN Switching and Wireless, CCNA Exploration Companion Guide (2008). Cisco Press. 1-58713207-9. Chapter 7.

www.bradfordnetworks.com/products/overview.html (last accessed 8/7/09)

Chapter 9
Networking Installation

Chapter summary

In this chapter a typical home and small organisation example will be used to show how to install a network.

Learning outcomes

After studying this chapter you should aim to test your achievement of the following outcomes. You should be able to:

Outcome 1: Scenario

Understand the typical home and small organisation example used for this chapter.

Outcome 2: Selecting the ISP

Understand appropriate methods in selecting an ISP for a simple network connection. Question 1 at the end of this chapter will test you on this.

Outcome 3: The site survey

Understand the basics of a simple site survey. Question 2 at the end of this chapter will test you on this.

Outcome 4: Design

Understand the design process for a simple network (in conjunction with *Chapters 5, 6* and *7*). Question 3 at the end of this chapter will test you on this.

Outcome 5: Installation

Understand the process of the installation of a simple network. Question 4 at the end of this chapter will test you on this.

Outcome 6: Commissioning and Testing

Understand the process of commissioning, testing and handing over a simple network. Question 5 at the end of this chapter will test you on this.

How will you be assessed on this?

Almost all networking modules contain a practical element – this may only be a design, but having an understanding of how everything links together, including understanding the application of the different cable types or being able to undertake a site survey, will dramatically increase your understanding, allowing you to undertake such assessments with a more complete understanding.

Section 1: Scenario

Irving's Estates is a small estate agency based in Sunderland. It has six full-time staff – two surveyors, three sales staff and an office manager. Mr Irving, the owner, works at the office but on some occasions will need to work from home.

Mr Irving has commissioned you to design both his office and home networks. The office is really a shop with a front office; a back office; a kitchen and toilets – *Figure 9.1* shows the layout of the office.

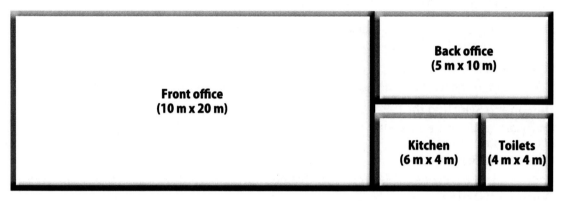

Figure 9.1: Irving's Estates office layout

In the office, Mr Irving requires:

- four staff computers.
- two computers that the clients can use to browse for properties for sale/to let.
- two printers – a colour inkjet and a laser.
- Internet connection.
- support for three laptops (for use in the back office – ideally wireless).

NOTE: Irving's Estates does not have its own website, instead it subscribes to the popular Houses4NoOne website. Irving's Estates staff will enter housing details and upload images and other data files. Thus the primary use of the Internet will be to browse and maintain its data on this website.

The office is situated in Sunderland city centre (post code SR1 1QX), and Mr Irving's home is situated in nearby Durham (postcode DH1 4AF).

Section 2: Selecting the Internet Service Provider (ISP)

Introduction

The best place to start your project is by selecting the ISP, because it is likely that the ISP will have the longest lead time for installation. You also need to determine which ISPs are available in the area and what services they offer.

Before selecting the ISP, however, it would be necessary to undertake a capacity plan (*see Chapter 7*) to determine the required upload and download speeds. We will assume for this project, that this has already been carried out and that typical ADSL speeds are acceptable. The first step then is to determine which ISPs are available in both areas. Normally there will be two types of ISP available:

- Cable based
- DSL based

Choosing the ISP

If the client is in an area that has been wired for cable TV (a cabled area), then it is likely that there will be the option of using cable broadband. If not, then the choice will probably be DSL. Whether choosing cable or DSL, the following factors should be considered:

Determine who provides broadband in the area

In areas where there are many DSL users such as a city centre, there are likely to be a number of DSL providers. This is because of **Local Loop Unbundling** (**LLU**) regulations which came into force in 2000/1 in the UK. Under LLU regulations, the major telecoms providers (British Telecom in the UK) have to allow competitors access to its exchanges and the opportunity to take over the **local loops** (the connection from the exchange to households/businesses). Under these regulations, appropriate companies are allowed to install their own equipment into exchanges and connect end user equipment. Almost certainly these companies will hire links from the telecoms providers' wholesale divisions to connect up their exchanges. In profitable areas it is common to find many operators offering this service whereas in less profitable areas, e.g. the countryside, there is likely to be little competition.

There are many websites that will help you determine who is able to provide broadband in the area. Such sites covering the UK include:

- **www.uswitchmybroadband.com**
- As well as the providers themselves, e.g. **www.viginmedia.com**

In our scenario, a quick check on the Virgin Media website (*see Figure 9.2*) shows that neither postcode is in a cabled area.

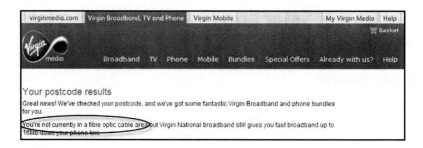

Figure 9.2: Virgin media broadband check

Using **www.uswitchmybroadband.com**, it can be seen that there are a number of DSL providers for both postcodes (*see Figure 9.3* for SQ1 1QX and *Figure 9.4* for DH1 4AF).

TIPS & ADVICE

Usually a cable broadband connection doesn't degrade with distance. Thus if you are in a cabled area and live far from a telephone exchange, cable may be a better option. Remember DSL is only available 5.5 km from the telephone exchange and speed decreases markedly with distance from the exchange.

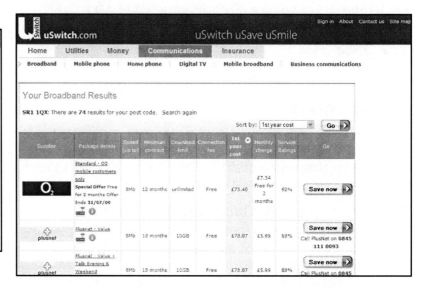

Figure 9.3: Selection of DSL providers for SR1 1QX

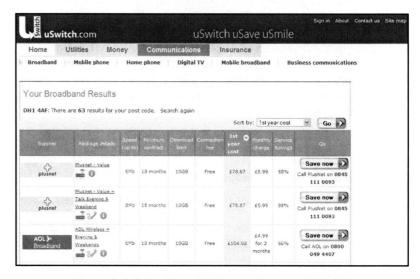

Figure 9.4: Selection of DSL providers for DH1 4AF

Speed

One of the two key factors influencing broadband choice is speed. There are two aspects to speed (*see Chapter 11*):

- upload speed
- download speed

Asymmetric Digital Subscriber Line (**ADSL**) is an imbalanced connection (*see Chapter 11*)– there is a greater capacity allocated to the download channel than the upload. Thus the upload speed is likely to be a lot less than the download speed. It is also very important to understand that the longer the telephone line from the client to the exchange, the slower the broadband. Therefore you probably won't achieve the full advertised rate and it is a good idea to check the actual speed for the location. The ISP should be able to estimate this, but there are a number of websites available to check broadband speed – the problem is, however, that you need a broadband connection to measure the broadband speed! Often it is a good idea to ask neighbours if they have broadband; what their package is (your speeds can be limited by package); which supplier they use; and whether they will let you carry out a quick speed test. *Figure 9.5* shows a broadband test of a home Virgin Media cable connection (using **www.broadbandspeedchecker.co.uk**). As you can see this connection has approximately 10 Mbps for download and about ½ Mbps for upload. This is typical for broadband.

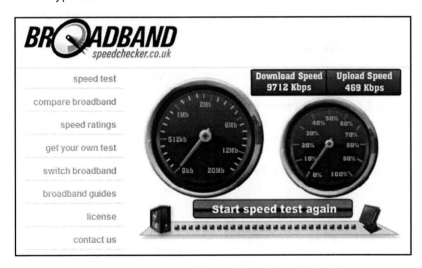

Figure 9.5: A sample broadband speed check

In our scenario, the vast majority of data will be downloaded which makes an ADSL connection suitable. In general, the higher the download speed, the higher the upload speed – but investigate! *Figure 9.6* shows further information from **www.uswitchmybroadband.com**. Regarding O2 premium broadband for the postcode SR1 1QX, you can clearly see that there is a theoretical maximum of 20 Mbps download speed and 1 Mbps upload speed. If it is possible it would be worthwhile checking to see if neighbours (a similar distance from the exchange) are getting similar speeds. Whichever the provider, all of the equipment is likely to be in the same place (possibly even the same type of equipment) in the same telephone exchange so you should get similar speeds (providing, of course, that is what is offered).

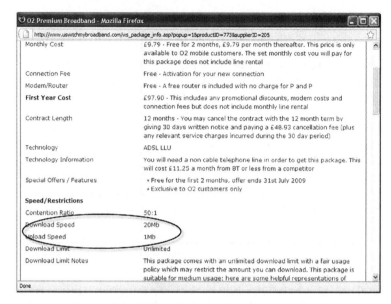

Figure 9.6: Further information from Uswitch

In our scenario, O2 are offering 20 Mbps in Sunderland, however, most providers in the Durham postcode seem to offer a maximum of 8 Mbps.

Contention ratio

ISPs have many customers and operate by effectively selling the use of its Internet connection to their users. It is highly unlikely that they will have a 1:1 ratio for Internet use. So if they have ten 20 Mbps customers, they are highly unlikely to have 10 x 20 Mbps capacity. Instead they share their capacity. For example, if XYZ ISP had a 20 Mbps connection to the Internet themselves and sold 20 Mbps access to this to their 100 clients, they would have a 100:1 contention ratio. The lower the ratio, the better.

Figure 9.7 shows that O2 premium services have a 50:1 contention ratio in the SR1 1QX area.

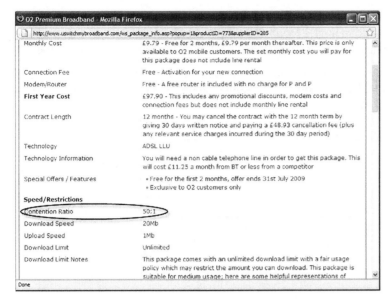

**Figure 9.7: Contention ratio for O2 premium services
in the SR1 1QX area**

In our scenario, the contention ratio appears to be 50:1 for most
providers in both areas. So this effectively has no influence on choice!

Download cap/usage limit

Many ISPs operate a download limit with some packages – particularly
those that are free or inexpensive. These limits are the maximum you
can download for the period. *Figure 9.8* shows that an AOL package for
the DH1 4AF postcode has a download limit of 10GB.

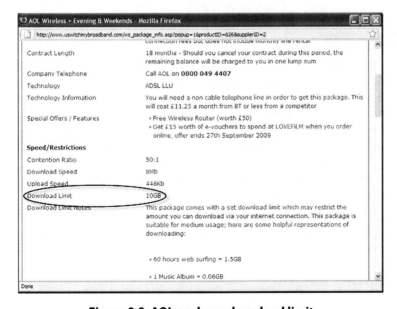

Figure 9.8: AOL package download limit

Most ISPs offer a variety of services which include those without a download limit – *Figure 9.8* simply shows an example of a download limit. It is also worthwhile investigating any **fair use** policies of the ISPs.

In our scenario, a download limit is not a good idea for the business or for Mr Irving's home. You should dismiss any packages which have one of these.

Fair Use Policies

ISPs often employ **fair use policies**. These are policy decisions that are then implemented using the ISPs network equipment (technically this is known as **traffic shaping** or **traffic engineering**). Basically, a fair use policy is a set of rules which govern the traffic that can be sent across the network. Quite often ISPs will attempt to limit the amount of a given type of data a user can download, for example bit torrents. Normally ISPs don't completely block this kind of traffic but give it low priority and little bandwidth. The result being that it takes a long time to download.

Occasionally ISPs do block critical traffic, such as VPN traffic or mail traffic, to an organisation or a home. It can be worthwhile identifying the types of traffic to be sent across the network and asking the ISP whether it will be allowed. It is also a good idea to do a search on the web to determine if there are any problems with a given ISP and given traffic types. This is particularly true in the case of a business – especially if a long contract is required.

In the case of our scenario, we are almost certainly going to want a VPN connection and to send and receive email to third parties. It is recommended, therefore, to check with the ISPs that the traffic you want to carry will be allowed by their fair use policies and to double-check by carrying out web searches.

Deals/Price

Another key factor influencing broadband choice is price and there are usually an incredible number of deals available. What you must remember is that price isn't everything – if an ISP has a low price but implements an unrealistic download limit for your client and blocks some of the traffic they wish to send; then it isn't a good deal at all. In fact the solution is likely to be unworkable. By all means use price as an influencing factor but only when you have narrowed down the list of possible ISPs to those who meet the requirements of your client – *see Making the Selection* on the following page.

Don't forget with most DSL connections you will also need to lease a suitable telephone line (usually non-cable) if one isn't already present – normally an additional cost.

Contract length

The length of the contract is probably part of the deal from the ISP but, it is worth checking on the contract length and verifying this with the plans of your client. For example, if they are planning to move office or house in the next 12 months and the contract is for 18 months, what will be the result? Will the ISP be able to connect up their new premises or will they need to pay a penalty clause?

Lead time

Lead time refers to the length of time it will take the ISP to install a connection and/or make it active. You may need to be wary of what the ISP tells you regarding this – an 'imminent' upgrade of a local exchange could be over 18 months! The bottom line is to find out if the services are available in the relevant exchange now.

Equipment needed and its suitability

You need to ensure who is going to provide any equipment needed for the connection and its suitability for your use. Most often, the ISP will provide this equipment and quite often it will be free of charge, but you need to ensure that it is suitable for your client's use.

In this scenario, if the ISP provided you with a free wireless router, you would need to determine, for example:

- the number of wired PCs that can be connected;
- wireless standards;
- ability to configure security, power output, etc.;
- antenna – what is supplied, and if it can be changed if necessary;
- power requirements (is mains power needed or is it powered some other way?).

Testimonials/references

Before making the decision, you may also want to speak to other customers of the ISP (particularly those in a similar business at the same exchange) about their experiences and whether they would recommend the ISP to you. It could be tricky to find customers of the ISP, but the ISP themselves may be able to give you the names of some clients (of course these clients may have a biased opinion!).

Making the selection

Hopefully by now, you will have appreciated that choosing an appropriate broadband connection can be quite complex and shouldn't be left to chance – especially if you are working with an organisation. It is recommended that you approach this in a professional manner in order to carefully identify the needs of your client. You can then list these requirements in a tabular format and rank ISPs against them. *Figure 9.9* shows an example.

Selection Criteria	ISPs			
	ISP1	ISP2	ISP3	ISP4
Available in the area?	N	N	Y	Y
Technology			DSL	DSL
Speed – download			8 Mbps	20 Mbps
Speed – upload			512 Kbps	1 Mbps
Contention ratio			50:1	50:1
Download limit			None	None
Fair use policies acceptable?			Y	Y
Price/deal			£15/month	£20/month
Contract length			12 months	18 months
Lead time			2 weeks	2 weeks
Suitable equipment			Equip provided but not suitable – not configurable enough	Equip provided but not suitable – not configurable enough
Testimonials			Good recommendations from: X	Good recommendations from: Y
Comments			+ telephone line rental	+ telephone line rental

Figure 9.9: Sample tabular selection criteria

Figure 9.9 provides a useful comparison of the ISPs. For this scenario, ISP4 is likely to be the best – it is the fastest. It also has the longest contract but, your client assures you that they don't intend to move. It is also the most expensive at £20 but your client is happy to pay £5 more a month for the extra speed.

Quick test

Briefly describe the major factors in selecting an appropriate broadband connection.

Section 3: The site survey

Introduction

Now that you have selected the appropriate ISP and that the necessary contracts have been signed, the next task is a site survey. In the site survey, you are determining how and where to place the network equipment. You will need to consider:

- building plans;
- the actual building(s) – a site visit;
- telecoms providers Point of Presence (PoP);
- mains electric cabling;
- the running of the cables in a suitable and safe manner;
- carrying out a wireless survey.

Building plans

If you can gain access to the building plans then it is worthwhile consulting them. You can often learn valuable information from them such as the location of electrical or data riser cupboards, wiring, the location of water pipes, etc. You should also determine whether there are any false floors or ceilings which could be used for cabling. This can make the job of installing the cabling and getting the best signal for the WAP easier. For cable installation you are looking for any suitable ducting or risers to use for cable installation. In the case of WAPs, you are looking for anything that may hinder the signal as well as electrical outlets close to your chosen WAP location.

At the very least the plans should be able to give you the location of water pipes so you avoid drilling into them!

TIPS & ADVICE

If possible, it is better to install the network cabling inside new conduit or trunking – self-adhesive trunking can be used making installation easier. *Figure 9.10* shows networking sockets installed in appropriate conduits.

Take care if you need to drill any holes and always use a pipe/wiring detector – you will be responsible for any damage you cause!

If in any doubt, call in an appropriate professional to carry out the physical installation, including such tasks as drilling holes, laying cables, mounting the WAP and conduit for you.

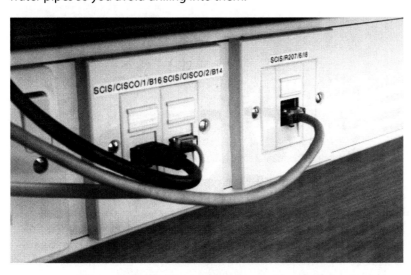

Figure 9.10: RJ-45 sockets mounted in conduit

In our scenario, we already have the building plans (*see Figure 9.1*). These actually reveal very little to us and so a site survey will be useful.

Site survey (visiting the actual buildings)

Plans of a building will only show structural features. When you arrive at a building you will be able to find out much more information such as the layout of furniture, use of room dividers, etc. You will need to use this information together with the building plans to help you decide what equipment will be necessary and how you will best install the network.

It is very useful at this stage to locate the telecoms provider's **Point of Presence (PoP)**. In a house that is to use DSL, this is usually any active external telephone socket. Cable is a little more complicated as there will usually be a special connection (*see Figure 9.11*). In an organisation, the PoP may be in a wiring closet or else terminate near specialist equipment e.g. a **Private Branch Exchange (PBX)** telephone system. Of course, if you are having a new line installed, then the telecoms provider will usually install the PoP where you require it.

Your telecoms provider's PoP is your primary connection to the Internet or other external networks, therefore you will need to connect your equipment (usually a router) to this. If you use a wireless router, then this will connect directly to your DSL/Cable outlet and probably also to any wired PCs which may result in many wires at this location – you need to check the suitability of the location to receive these wires. If you are mounting the wireless router near the ceiling you will need to consider the aesthetic aspects too – it may be better to install a separate WAP or a switch.

Figure 9.11: A typical cable outlet

In our scenario, the PoP is located on the rear wall of the office (*see Figure 9.12*); there are also several spare mains sockets next to the PoP. In the case of his house, Mr Irving has a study where all the computers to be used are located. There is a telephone socket there and several spare mains sockets.

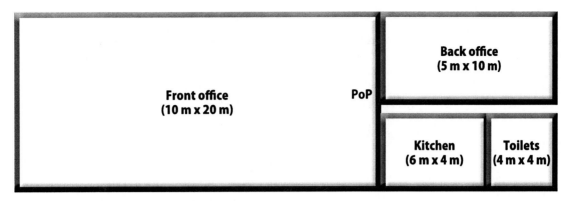

Figure 9.12: Irving's Estates layout showing PoP

Wireless survey

The purpose of a wireless survey is to determine how to get the level of wireless coverage required. There are companies that specialise in conducting wireless site surveys and it is a specialised task needing specialised equipment and software. However, in small organisations and the home with simple WLAN requirements, it is possible to carry out a reasonable WLAN survey using a WAP and a laptop or even better a **Personal Digital Assistan**t (**PDA**), for example IPAQ with site survey tools in built. There are also some devices that allow you to measure Wi-Fi signal strength. *Figure 9.13* shows such a device – but be aware that sometimes the results from these can be misleading.

Figure 9.13: A typical Wi-Fi detector – showing signal strength

> **TIPS & ADVICE**
>
> Be on the lookout for any sources of interference with the cables and the WLANs such as close proximity to fluorescent lights, microwave ovens, cordless phones, mobile phones, baby monitors, etc. These types of equipment all operate in the ISM band (*see Section 2, Chapter 8*).

You will recall from *Chapter 8* that it may be necessary to undertake some capacity planning to determine the speed required from a wireless link. At this stage you should have determined this, consulted the plans and already identified the best place for mounting the WAP (if not, you may need to do this as part of the site survey).

The wireless survey is an opportunity for you to confirm your plans. This can be achieved by mounting your WAP in the chosen place and then using a laptop or PDA to measure both signal strength and speed in key locations, i.e. where the wireless clients will reside. In Windows Vista you can use the **connect to a network** window (click the **Network** icon in the system tray and select **Connect to a network** from the menu – *Figure 9.14*).

Figure 9.14: Connect to a network menu from the system tray icon

Figure 9.15 shows this window open in the University of Sunderland. Note the signal strength meter at the right of each available network. It is a good idea to click the refresh button (highlighted in *Figure 9.15*) to ensure you are reading the correct current signal strength.

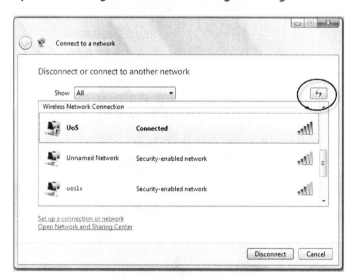

Figure 9.15: Signal strengths

Identify your network in the list and right click on it and select status (*see Figure 9.16*). This will open the WLAN status window (*see Figure 9.17*).

Figure 9.16: Selecting the status of the WLAN

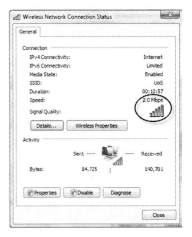

Figure 9.17: The WLAN status window

Figure 9.18: Excellent signal strength and speed

Figure 9.19: Poor signal strength and speed

Note the signal quality and the speed (both highlighted) in *Figure 9.17*. As you move around the area, changes can be detected – *Figure 9.18* shows 54 Mbps speed where *Figure 9.19* shows 2 Mbps speed. Using this tool and by moving the WAP and/or client PC, you can ensure you have the coverage you require.

In our scenario, shown in *Figure 9.20,* there is a tall wooden cabinet against the wall in the office that is close to the PoP and mains sockets. By standing the wireless router on this it was found that excellent coverage was provided all around the building (the dividing walls are made of plasterboard so the signal easily passes through them). By measuring the signal strength with the microwave oven being used, it was found that it doesn't interfere with the signal (microwave ovens operate on a very similar frequency to WLANs).

Conduit can be installed behind the cabinet to accommodate all of the cables and there is a false ceiling to pass the cables across to the client desks. In Mr Irving's home, the study is located on the first floor. A wireless survey has shown adequate coverage in the house and excellent coverage in the study.

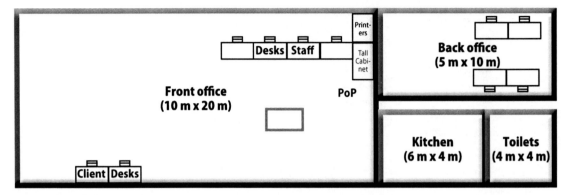

Figure 9.20: Irving's Estates office showing furniture layout

Quick test

Briefly describe the major components of a site survey.

Section 4: Design

Introduction

Now that you have selected the appropriate ISP, the necessary contracts have been signed, and you have undertaken the site and wireless survey, you should be in a position to design the network. In this design phase you will be designing the layout of the network. This involves:

- determining any equipment needed;
- determining the best location for the equipment;
- location of any required wired network sockets;
- determining any cable runs; and
- any cables needed.

Design and equipment selection are covered extensively elsewhere in this book (*see Chapters 6 and 7*) and should be read in conjunction with this chapter.

Equipment

The equipment needed will be determined by many factors, for example:

- the range of equipment to be supported;
- the number of connections required;
- the number and type of WAPs required.

Required availability/reliability

Consult *Chapters 6, 7* and *8* before making selections.

Determining the best location for the equipment

The site survey (*see Section 3*) would have helped you determine the best place for equipment.

Location of any networking sockets

Again, the site survey (*see Section 3*) should have helped you determine the number of required sockets and the required cabling runs to them.

You should also identify any cables needed such as crossover or straight through cables (*see Section 5*).

In our scenario, we require support in the office for:

- six wired computers;
- two printers (both have network sockets);
- wireless connectivity for three laptops; and
- an Internet connection.

In the home we require support for:

- two wired PCs;
- laptop wireless connection; and
- an Internet connection.

In this example a Linksys wireless router has been chosen for both the home and the office, which is an excellent wireless router for the home and a reasonable choice for a small business. The wireless router has four fast Ethernet ports on the rear; a built-in WAP; and a connection for the Internet (see *Figure 9.21*). For the home, it is all that is required. For the office, it will work, but there aren't sufficient ports at the rear to connect all six wired PCs and the two printers. For this reason you will need to supplement the wireless router with a low-cost, simple, fast Ethernet switch. *Figure 9.22* shows a D-Link 10/100 Ethernet switch. Just as with larger networking devices, it is possible to connect the switch built in to the wireless router with the D-Link switch. Switches are normally connected using crossover cables (see *Section 5*). By connecting the two switches there will be ten ports on the D-Link switch plus four ports on the wireless router giving a total of 14 ports – one on each used for inter-connection leaving 12 ports. The link between the two switches is a potential bottleneck – being 100 Mbps shared. For that reason it is recommended to connect all wired devices to the D-Link switch and then to connect this to the wireless router. The Internet is at best 20 Mbps; and the wireless at best 54 Mbps (theoretical). Therefore, the 100 Mbps link shouldn't act as a bottleneck on these links.

Figure 9.21: The Linksys wireless router (NOTE: this is an image of the cable version)

Figure 9.22: A D-Link switch

The PCs will connect to RJ-45 sockets connected in trunking to the rear of the desks (*see Figure 9.10*) and will terminate in sockets or a patch panel (*see Figure 9.26*) near the wireless router and the switch.

Quick test

Briefly describe the major aspects of network design.

Section 5: Installation

Introduction

You have now arrived at the point where you can make the installation (assuming that the telecoms provider has made active the Internet connection and that it has been tested).

In this section, it is assumed that your installation will involve:

- choosing cables;
- installing network (RJ-45) sockets and possibly patch panels;
- setting up some services such as connection to the ISP, DHCP, etc.;
- setting up wireless and, in particular, setting up security.

Choosing cables

From *Chapter 7* you know the minimum cabling to be installed is category 5e (cat. 5e) with two points to every desktop – not all need to be live but they all need to be installed. We require eight active connections.

In Ethernet networking there are basically two cable types:

- straight through cables; and
- crossover (X-over) cables.

Straight through cables, as their name suggests, are cables where both ends terminate on the same pins. *Figure 9.23* shows standards for straight through cables. T568B is the common wiring for straight through cables.

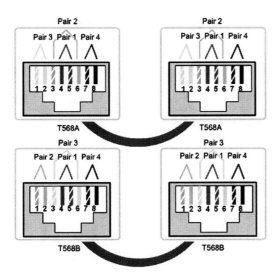

Figure 9.23: Wiring diagram for a straight through cable (image courtesy of Cisco Systems Inc.)

Straight through cables are the most common network cable and used for connecting different types of device e.g.:

- a switch to a router;
- a computer to a switch or hub;
- a computer to a wireless router or simple router.

A telephone exchange crosses over the send and receive circuits of a telephone so we hear when someone speaks into their mouthpiece through our earpiece. In a network, a switching device performs the same function. If it isn't present we need to use a crossover cable to cross over the send and receive pairs. *Figure 9.24* shows the standards for crossover cables.

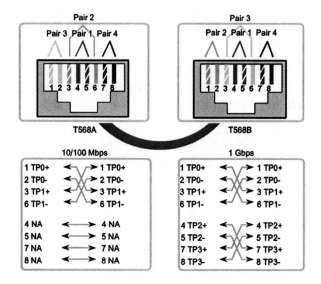

Figure 9.24: Wiring diagram for a crossover through cable (image courtesy of Cisco Systems Inc.)

Crossover cables are used for connecting similar devices such as:

- a switch to a switch;
- a switch to a hub;
- a hub to a hub;
- a router to a router;
- a computer to a computer;
- a computer to a router.

Installing network (RJ-45) sockets and possibly patch panels

Whether you are installing RJ-45 sockets (*see Figure 9.25*) or a patch panel (*see Figure 9.26*) the process is very similar.

Figure 9.25: A typical RJ-45 socket

Figure 9.26: A typical patch panel

Usually both the patch panels and the RJ-45 modules in the sockets are colour coded for the corresponding wires. All that is required is to **punch down** the connections using a **punchdown** or **krone tool**. You should keep the wires twisted as close as possible to where they are punched down.

Figure 9.27 shows a selection of tools used for the installation and testing of a network.

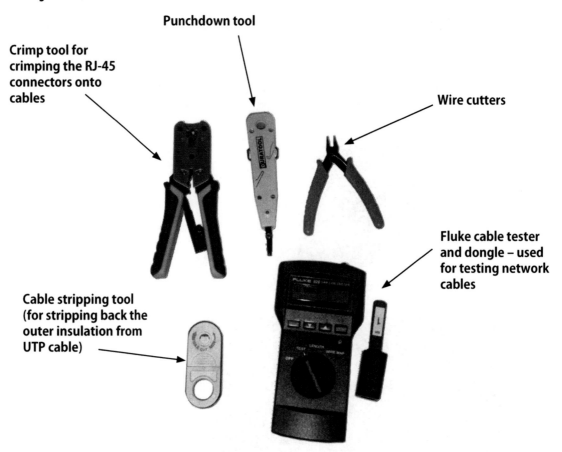

Crimp tool for crimping the RJ-45 connectors onto cables

Punchdown tool

Wire cutters

Fluke cable tester and dongle – used for testing network cables

Cable stripping tool (for stripping back the outer insulation from UTP cable)

Figure 9.27: Selection of networking tools

Figure 9.28 shows a patch being cabled using a punchdown tool whilst *Figure 9.29* shows an RJ-45 socket being cabled using a punchdown tool.

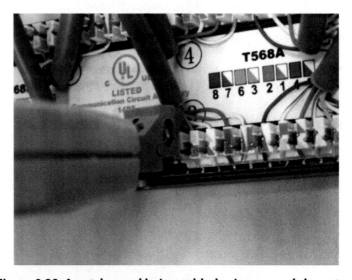

Figure 9.28: A patch panel being cabled using a punchdown tool

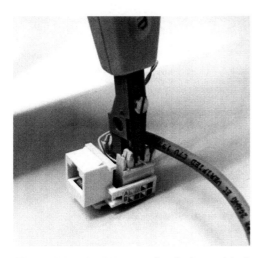

**Figure 9.29: An RJ-45 socket being cabled
using a punchdown tool**

The cables and sockets can then be tested using a network testing tool
(either a fluke tester – *see Figure 9.27*) or another similar tool.

Setting up services

There are a small number of services which your network will require in
order to be operational.

Initially you may need to make the connection to the ISP. You will
need to follow the cabling instructions from the ISP and then possibly
configure the wireless router with settings provided by the ISP, for
example a user name and password.

The only other required service is likely to be **Dynamic Host
Configuration Protocol** (**DHCP**), which will normally be turned on
by default and as such requires little or no configuration from you.
DHCP is a service that automatically configures the network settings
of appropriately configured devices (e.g. PCs). PCs need to be set
to **Obtain IP address automatically** in the **IPv4 Properties** window
(*see Figure 9.30*). The service (in this case running on the router) will
configure the IP address, default gateway, subnet mask and DNS server.
Your router will also receive its settings via DHCP from your ISP and pass
the necessary ones to the connected PCs.

Setting up wireless network and, in particular, setting up security

We now arrive at the point of setting up the wireless connection. The
examples used here are for a Linksys WAG354G ADSL wireless router.
The first step is to connect the wireless router to the PC with a straight
through cable. Ensure that the PC settings for the wired connection are
set to be obtained automatically (*see Figure 9.30*).

Figure 9.30: IP Settings for Windows Vista

Next, open a web browser and enter the IP address of the wireless router (normally 192.168.1.1). You should be presented with a login screen that will require a user name and password (*see Figure 9.31*).

Figure 9.31: Logging into the wireless router

Once logged in, the wireless section of the wireless router can be configured. Changing the name to something meaningless is recommended rather than, for example, using the clients name in the SSID as this may be broadcasted and therefore it could be a potential security weakness. *Figure 9.32* shows that the SSID name has been changed to PhilsTestWLAN.

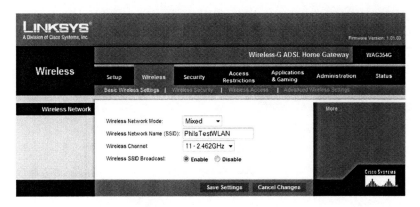

Figure 9.32: Changing the WLAN name

Once you have made the change it is important to click the **Save Settings** button and wait until you get confirmation (*see Figure 9.33*). In this case you need to click the **Continue** button.

Figure 9.33: Settings successful confirmation

Before configuring security it is good idea to try connecting first. Remove the straight through cable and then, on a wireless client, double-click the **Networking** icon in the system tray.

Then select **Connect to a network** and look for your network in the list that is displayed (note that you may well see other networks from neighbouring homes or offices that are being broadcast).

Figure 9.34: Finding your network

You can then connect to the network by selecting it and clicking the **Connect** button. You may be warned that it is insecure (*see Figure 9.35*) – but connect anyway.

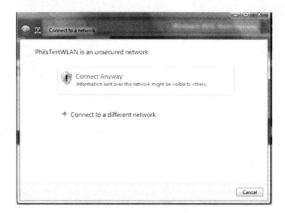

Figure 9.35: Security warning

You should then successfully connect.

Figure 9.36: Successfully connected

At this point you may wish to verify Internet connectivity by opening a web browser and viewing an external web page . Providing the connection was successful you can configure the wireless security. Remember, not all wireless devices support all wireless security levels and it is a good idea to survey the devices that will use the wireless network before configuring to ensure you configure the strongest commonly supported encryption – refer to *Chapter 8* for a list of WLAN security settings. The help section on the wireless router may also help you understand the settings.

It is useful to compile a table (*see Figure 9.37*) that details the devices and their supported level of wireless security.

Device	Encryption supported		
	WEP	**WPA**	**WPA2**
Laptop 1	Y	Y	Y
Laptop 2	Y	Y	Y
Wireless Router	Y	Y	N

Figure 9.37: Security checklist

As you can see from the security checklist in *Figure 9.37* the highest security level you can use is WPA. To do this, reconnect the straight through cable and select the **Wireless** security tab from the router (you may need to log back in) and set the setting to **Pre-shared key** (the help section of device tells us this is WPA) (*see Figure 9.38*).

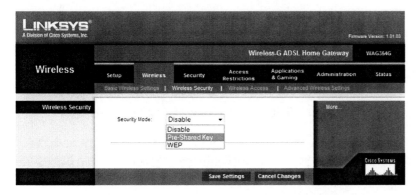

Figure 9.38: Changing the router to WPA security

The next step is to enter the key of between 8 and 128 ASCII characters. Try to select random characters especially non-alphanumerical (*see Figure 9.39*) to reduce the risk from **dictionary** attacks, and click **Save Settings**.

Figure 9.39: Entering the WPA key

TIPS & ADVICE

If you are using the laptop that will connect the wireless router, cut and paste this key into a word processor or text editor – it will make configuration a little easier. You can also copy to a memory stick to use in other computers!

Once you have had confirmation that the setting changes have been successful you can attempt to connect. First, remove the cable and then

– as you did previously, double-click the **Networking** icon in the system tray and select **Connect** or **Diagnose** from the window that is displayed. You will need to disconnect from the current WLAN, refresh the list and then reconnect to it. You should now see that it is security enabled (*see Figure 9.40*).

Figure 9.40: WLAN is now security enabled

You will then be asked to enter the WPA key (if you copied it from the previous settings, you can paste it into here to save you from having to remember the code) (*see Figure 9.41*).

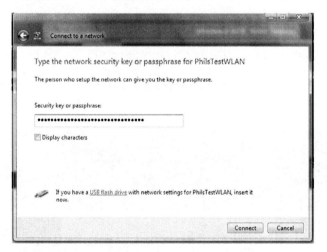

Figure 9.41: Entering the WPA key

Providing you entered the key successfully you should be connected (*see Figure 9.42*). You probably want to select both **Save this network** and **Start this connection automatically** before clicking on the **Close** button.

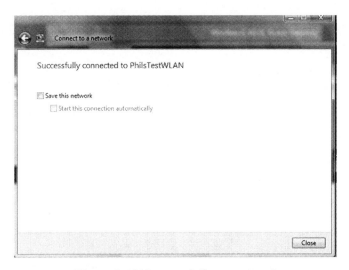

Figure 9.42: Successfully connected

You should now be able to browse wirelessly. If you can, the wireless setup is complete – unless you want to disable the SSID broadcast which will 'hide' the WLAN. To do this, simply select the **Basic Wirless Settings** tab and select the **Disable** radio button next to **Wireless SSID Broadcast** (*see Figure 9.43*) and then click on **Save Settings**.

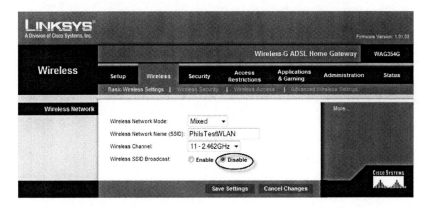

Figure 9.43: Turning off the SSID

We can now return to the wireless settings on the laptop and disconnect from the current network. When we try to connect to another network, we now see an unnamed network (*see Figure 9.44*), select this and click **Connect**.

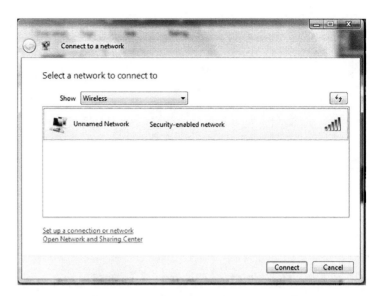

Figure 9.44: Selecting the 'hidden' WLAN – note that some networks have been omitted for clarity purposes from this image

You will then be asked for the name of the WLAN (*see Figure 9.45*); enter the name and click **Connect**.

Figure 9.45: Entering the WLAN name

Occasionally you may be asked to enter the WPA key again. You should successfully connect (*see Figure 9.46*). Again, it is wise to select **Save this network** and **Connect automatically**. You will then always see the name of the WLAN as it is saved on the computer.

Figure 9.46: Successfully connected

Quick test

Briefly describe the major stages of network installation.

Section 6: Testing, commissioning, and documenting

Introduction

Everything should now be connected and working. The last tasks are to:

- testing;
- commissioning;
- documentation;
- handing over.

You started the project with a set of objectives – what the network is expected to do. Testing is about ensuring it does them. To measure this draw up a test plan from your design objectives (*see Figure 9.47*) and carry out the tests. This test plan should include desired wireless coverage/speed if necessary.

Test	Outcome	Date of Test
Laptop 1 can:		
• access the Internet	Pass	7/7/09
• print	Pass	7/7/09
• access emails	Pass	7/7/09
• access the Houses4NoOne website	Pass	7/7/09

Figure 9.47: A sample test plan

Once you have tested the network and are sure it is fully operational, then it would be advisable to discuss your test plan with your client to determine if there are any other required tests. You should then run through the testing with the client and have them 'sign off' the network as being complete and satisfactory.

Commissioning

Computer network commissioning is the process of ensuring that all systems connected with your new network are functioning correctly and in a way intended by the designer and desired by the owner. This would include the wireless aspects, Internet connection, that speed is appropriate, that range is appropriate, that functionality is appropriate, etc. You should have drawn up the criteria using the network design goals in *Chapter 7*.

Commissioning is normally the final process before handing over to the client and, as such, will usually have input from the client. Most of the tasks of commissioning have been going on throughout this chapter, the aim being that you will arrive at this point with a network which does meet your client requirements – you now need their confirmation. Such confirmation should include reminding the client of the design goals and demonstrating how you have met or exceeded these.

It is usual in the commissioning process to have the client sign an agreement to say that the network meets their requirements and they accept it. One suggestion would be that you produce a plan similar to that in *Figure 9.48*, this would list the required criteria; have a column to show the date of the test/demonstration and a place for an acceptance signature by the client. This table relates back to *Chapter 7* (*Network design goals*) and to the beginning of this chapter where you were strongly encouraged to draft these criteria.

Requirement	Outcome	Date of Test	Client Acceptance
Functionality: • access the Internet • print • access emails • access the Houses4NoOne site	Pass Pass Pass Pass	7/7/09 7/7/09 7/7/09 7/7/09	
Scalability: • <any scalability requirements>			
Adaptability: • <any adaptability requirements>			
Manageability: • <any manageability requirements>			
Availability: • <any availability requirements>			

Figure 9.48: An example of a simple acceptance plan

Documentation

This is a critical but often overlooked part of the installation process (*see Chapter 7*). You must ensure that you leave the client with all the required documentation for the network. This should include:

- WLAN names;
- security settings;
- WLAN keys;
- passwords;
- warranties;
- contracts;
- settings (e.g. ADSL);
- copies of signal strength tests;
- copies of complete test plans (ensure that they are signed off);
- wiring plan;
- network sockets and cable documentation;
- contact telephone numbers.

TIPS & ADVICE

Often screen shots can be a good way of recording some of this information.

Handing over

This is the point the working network is given to your client. This represents the end of the installation phase of the network. You should ideally discuss with your client what is required from the handover and carry out these tasks. You should obtain written confirmation of your client's acceptance of the network, if you don't already have this.

Quick test

Briefly discuss the major steps in testing, commissioning, and documenting a network.

Section 7: End of chapter assessment

Questions

These questions relate to the assessment targets set at the beginning of this chapter. If you can answer them effectively you are in a good position to achieve good credit in assessments or examinations.

1. A client wishes to contract with a network installation company. As part of the selection criteria, the client has asked you to discuss how you would select an ISP.

2. Describe what is meant by the term 'site survey' and discuss how you would undertake a site survey.

3. Discuss how you would design a simple network layout (including wireless).

4. Discuss the process of installing a simple network.

5. Discuss the process of commissioning, testing and handing over a simple network.

Answers

1. In this question, the client is seeking reassurance that you are a professional and understand the importance of selecting an appropriate ISP for them. You are not being asked to select an ISP but rather the criteria you would use in this process. Don't just give a list but discuss each of the criteria. Ending with tabular sample selection criteria would demonstrate your professionalism.

2. Note the words! You are being asked to describe the term and discuss how you would undertake the process. The first part is a simple description (probably worth 20% of the marks for the question). The second part requires you to discuss how you would undertake the survey (this is likely to be worth the majority of the marks for the question – 80% in this case).

3. This question is asking you to discuss the design process of a simple network. You should also refer to *Chapters 6, 7* and *8* when answering to show the breadth and depth of your knowledge. Don't forget the wireless aspect – wireless is a hot

topic at the moment and the marks are likely to reflect this.

4. This question is asking you to discuss the process of installing a simple network. Note it doesn't specify whether wired, wireless and whether there is an ISP connection involved. As such, it is better to assume you need to cover all of these aspects and doing so should gain you extra marks as it demonstrates your command of the subject.

5. This question is asking you to discuss the last stage in implementing a network. Ultimately this stage is about showing your client how the network meets their objectives, having them verify the testing, etc. The examiner is not only looking for the steps but that you understand that this is the last stage of the process and that successful completion allows you to move on and the client to move forward. Emphasising getting written client acceptance and a professional commissioning process should also bolster your marks.

Section 8: Further reading and research

www.wi-fi.org (last accessed 8/7/09)

www.cisco.com (last accessed 8/7/09)

Network Fundamentals, CCNA Exploration Companion Guide (2008). Cisco Press. 1-58713208-7. Chapters 10 and 11.

www.linksys.com (last accessed 7/7/09)

www.uswitchmybroadband.com (last accessed 7/7/09)

www.virginmedia.com (last accessed 7/7/09)

www.broadbandspeedchecker.co.uk (last accessed 7/7/09)

Chapter 10

Network management

Chapter summary

Managing a network is extremely important. There is a myth that once a network is installed it will virtually run itself. For all but the very simplest of networks, this is simply not the case. Today's networks are highly complex and often mission critical to organisations: they cannot be treated in a piecemeal fashion – to perform well they must be managed and managed well. This chapter provides an introduction to network management.

Learning outcomes

After studying this chapter you should aim to test your achievement of the following outcomes. You should be able to:

Outcome 1: Users and group management

Understand basic user and group management. Question 1 at the end of this chapter will test you on this.

Outcome 2: Backup and recovery

Understand the importance and techniques available for backup and recovery. Question 2 at the end of this chapter will test you on this.

Outcome 3: Disaster recovery planning

Understand the need for disaster recovery planning, be able to assess potential risks and to test plans to ensure that an organisation can continue to operate in the event of a disaster. Question 3 at the end of this chapter will test you on this.

Outcome 4: Network maintenance

Understand the basics of network maintenance. Question 4 at the end of this chapter will test you on this.

How will you be assessed on this?

The subject matter of this chapter is a blend of both practice and theory and is likely to be assessed as such. It is likely that your assessor will ask you to write a user manual detailing how to undertake the practical aspects. Such topics as backup and security lend themselves very well to exams and TCTs.

Section 1: Users and group management

One of the most basic levels of security in a networked system is to prevent unauthorised access to the system. User accounts and group allocation are one of the most important tools in achieving this.

Creating users and groups

User accounts usually represent one of the basic levels of entry control to a network. It is critically important that only authorised personnel are given user accounts and that they are used in accordance with organisational policy.

Ideally the organisation should have user policies. These policies should contain information on:

- how the users can interact with the network (including acceptable use);

- the detailed procedure for the creation, amendment and suspension of accounts;

- what to do in the case of a breach; penalties for breach.

User policies should also contain control information such:

- as the composition of the user ID;

- length of password; acceptable password characters;

- password ageing;

- etc.

TIPS & ADVICE

Network managers should insist on written requests – should a breach of policy occur, having acted on a verbal instruction could leave the network manager in a precarious position.

It is essential to establish how to control the creation, amendment and suspension of accounts within the user policy. Account creation, deletion and suspension should only be carried out on written authorisation - normally such written authorisation comes from the human resources (HR) manager or head of the relevant department. User policy should ensure that network managers grant only the minimum privileges necessary for the users to do their job.

Additionally, careful consideration must be given to groups and their members. Most organisations have distinct groups (e.g. human resources, finance, manufacturing, etc.) that would naturally form work groups. However, the nature of the information stored on the system dictates that groups must be selected carefully. For instance, not everyone in finance should have access to the cheque printer and, if everyone has access to the purchase order system, fraudulent purchase orders or invoices could be created. Thus user needs should be discussed carefully and approved by the relevant line manager to ensure that users have only the correct privileges to do their job.

When employees leave an organisation, accounts should be suspended (on written instruction) rather than being deleted, leaving a trail for subsequent system auditing.

This type of user management varies according to the organisation. For example, universities manage huge numbers of accounts for both staff and students. At the end of each academic year, roughly one third of all student accounts will cease and, at the beginning of the academic year a new batch of accounts will be created. At the University of Sunderland there are approximately 9,000 students requiring approximately 3000 accounts to be created each September.

Different methods can be used to automate the creation of accounts, particularly in UNIX, but the accounts must still be created in a controlled way. One possible solution for a university is to create user accounts from the registration system – a file could be downloaded from the registration system and processed via scripts to create accounts. As each student in the registration system is a valid student, this process is safe. Standard student privileges would also be given, as would standard passwords – perhaps a date of birth or some other code the students choose at the time of registration.

All request documents are important and must be kept safely for audit purposes.

> **KEY CONCEPT**
> Control must be exercised over the creation of users. Creating users in an ad hoc fashion may well compromise the system.

Management of users

Once the process of creating accounts is complete, managers need to be aware that a higher workload will follow from the increased number of users. Management of users, therefore, tends to fall into one of two categories:

- normal user management; and
- exceptional user management.

Normal user tasks are the tasks network managers would expect to deal with each day – requests for help with a forgotten password, more disk storage space, printer problems, user account changes, etc. Obviously, the higher the number of users, the higher the workload and it is important to observe the organisation's user policy (particularly user account and password changes). As its name suggests, exceptional user management involves dealing with exceptional cases, and these might mean breaches of security. The network manager should be on the lookout for security breaches and should investigate accordingly. Security breaches can often be detected as long continuous logins – perhaps the user doesn't log out when leaving for lunch or in the evening. Logins after hours or from strange or unknown computers often indicate a security breach. Ideally, of course, this should be blocked by the organisation's security policy (*see Chapter 12*). Most operating systems have extensive facilities for monitoring security and for tracking users.

> **KEY CONCEPT**
> Users must be managed to keep the system healthy. Security is dependent upon good user management.

The management of workgroups also tends to be exceptional. Occasionally, a user will be assigned to another workgroup. Network Managers need to ensure users are allocated to the correct groups in accordance with the organisation's user policy.

Quick test

Briefly discuss the issues involved in user management.

Section 2: Backups and recovery

Perhaps the single most important task in managing any computer system is providing for its continuity. This involves protecting the organisation's data – most organisations cannot survive without access to it, and the following five ways of protecting data are frequently recommended:

- backup;
- backup;
- backup;
- backup;
- backup.

This is not a misprint – it is intentional. Users and network managers must realise that the only way an organisation can retrieve lost data is if it was backed up in the first place. Without a backup there is little chance of an organisation being able to retrieve its data. When this is possible, it is often very expensive and can take a long time. Data is the lifeblood of an organisation and, if unavailable, it is unlikely the organisation will be able to function properly. If the data loss was complete, some organisations may not survive. Consider a credit card company that lost all its customers' balances – it would probably never be able to recoup all the money it was owed. If a bank had major problems and lost the balance of its customers' accounts, how would its customers react?

It should also be understood that most systems change on a frequent basis – especially the data. As such, regular backups should be taken and the organisation should be prepared to lose any data that isn't backed up. The organisation should ask itself how much data it is prepared to lose – if the answer is 'very little', regular backups must be taken.

Backups cannot be undertaken piecemeal: they are essential to the well-being of the organisation. As such it should be made someone's responsibility (on his or her job description) to make regular backups, and someone else's responsibility to ensure they are taking place. If not, they may not happen, which could result in catastrophe. Backups must be planned and a set of instructions written in a way that ensures that even the least technical members of staff will understand how to make one.

Testing the backup

It is no good simply backing up a computer and trusting that the backup has worked. The backup needs to be tested to ensure that the data has been copied. The backup media's test needs to be thorough – a backup is only as good as its test. The only way a backup can be truly tested is to restore all the files.

Unless the organisation has a separate computer with the same version of the operating system installed, this is usually not possible and an alternative must be found. **However, the files should never be restored on to the same computer – if the backup has failed the original files will be corrupted.**

If the organisation does not have a 'spare' computer, it is best to write a script or utility that places a copy of a master text file around the filing system in predetermined locations (usually around mission critical data – both before and after it). The backup should then be taken and these text files removed from the computer. An attempt should then be made to restore the files from the backup and compare them to the master. If verification of the copies is successful, then there is a high probability that the backup would also be successful if it were to be restored on to the original computer. If not, another backup should be made immediately on another media set.

Types of backup

There are three main backup techniques, and the selection of the most appropriate technique is just as important as selecting the right backup device.

Full

Performing a full backup on a frequent basis is usually the best way of protecting the system. This involves taking a copy of all the data, applications and systems files (including the operating system) and storing these to media. Everything on the system is copied to the media, which requires a backup device with a large storage capacity, usually tape. Because of the volume of information being stored, this type of backup takes the longest to perform. Should the organisation need 24-hour access to its data, this kind of backup can be disruptive. However, because all the information is on one backup set, this type of backup is the quickest way of restoring the system.

Incremental

Incremental backups are used to cut down the time taken for a full backup. Using this method, a full backup is taken and then the first incremental backup copies only the files modified (whether they are system or data files) since the full backup. The second incremental backup copies only those files (system or data) modified since the first incremental backup, and so on. This drastically cuts down the time taken to back up, but can lead to a complex chain of media sets as each media set contains only files modified since the last backup. This means it would take a lot longer to restore the files and that the backup is dependent upon more media, which increases the probability of failure when restoring.

Differential

Differential backup is really a compromise between the previous two backup techniques. With differential backup, a full backup is taken and then subsequent differential backups. Each differential backup copies all files modified since the **last full backup**. This affords a higher level of protection than incremental backups, but not as high as a full backup. It

The time taken to restore is of the utmost importance – this is the time when you need the greatest speed. Fast backups are also important – normal business should not be interfered with. Therefore full backups are always recommended unless there are compelling reasons not to do so.

In modern systems it is likely that full backups will be of data only. Perhaps a separate backup will be kept of applications and the operating system.

also takes longer to back up than an incremental backup, but less time than a full backup. Finally, it takes longer to restore than a full backup but not as long as an incremental backup.

Backup cycles

Introduction

Media must be used in accordance with the manufacturer's guidelines (in terms of heat, humidity, acclimatisation, etc.) and should also be cycled. The manufacturers issue instructions with the media detailing constraints on their use, which must be adhered to. The cycling of rewriteable media, particularly tapes, is of the utmost importance – each tape should be used frequently and to a similar extent. Tapes stretch as they are used, especially at first. If they are underused, reliability may be impaired in the same way as if they are overused. Network managers should ensure each piece of rewriteable media is used a similar number of times. This cannot be achieved by random selection. Therefore two cycling techniques are discussed below that allow for the efficient cycling of rewriteable media, which is particularly relevant for tapes (the second technique affords a high level of protection, assuming a full backup is taken every night).

Grandfather/father/son

This is perhaps one of the simplest backup cycles and originally came from the experience of using tape. The first tape created becomes the son and is kept. The second tape created becomes the new son, the older one becoming the father. When the third tape is created, this becomes the son, the oldest tape becomes the grandfather and the previous son becomes the father.

Thus a whole generation of backup tapes is created and it is possible to recover back to the third backup. In a daily cycle, this means that files lost up to three days ago can be recovered. However, as computer systems become larger with more users, lost files are often not noticed in three days. For example, consider a part-time class at a university – they may only be in university once a week. If they discover a lost file, it is too late to recover it using this method of cycling. Thus organisations have adopted more complex strategies for cycling.

Four-week cycle

This method preserves each week's backups for four weeks. Full backups are taken on separate tape sets every business day. The last working day's tape is kept and the remainder are reused. This pattern is repeated for week two to week four. In week five, the first weekly backup tape is brought back into service. Assuming all data can be fitted on to one tape cartridge and assuming five working days, this requires 24 cartridges. However, the weekly tapes should not be used solely for weekly backups – this would under use them and so they could fail.

Backups should be kept for a 'reasonable' time. The definition of reasonable will depend upon the organisation.

Sometimes organisations keep weekly or monthly backups indefinitely.

Additional considerations

The following should also be considered when undertaking backups:

- Replace rewriteable media (particularly tapes) regularly (the purchase date should be written on the media, together with a tally of the number of times used).

- Upon receiving any errors, the media should be replaced immediately.

- Clean drives regularly, following the manufacturer's instructions.

- Always store backup media off-site in a fireproof safe.

Quick test

Discuss the major backup techniques and give an overview of backup cycling.

Section 3: Disaster recovery planning

Introduction

Almost all organisations are critically dependent upon access to their data and are usually unable to function without access to it. For such organisations, the use of IT systems for data storage can be both a lifeline and a threat. Consider a credit card company whose premises have burned to the ground. With copies of their data stored off-site and access to a similar IT system, the company would be able to operate as normal within a very short space of time. However, if the reverse were true – the company had access to its premises but had lost access to its data, they would be highly unlikely to survive.

Almost all organisations will have insurance policies and hardware maintenance contracts, but what neither usually provide is a solution from the equipment being lost until the replacement arrives or repair is undertaken – that is the role of Disaster Recovery Planning.

Backups

Disaster recovery planning is crucially dependent upon backups – if you don't have up-to-date backups, then there will be nothing to restore on the replacement computers or in the alternate premises. You must make sure that:

1. you have current backups;

2. they are stored securely off-site, preferably in a fireproof safe;

3. the backups have been thoroughly tested;

4. software disks/licences are also stored securely off-site.

Disasters

Disasters in this context means anything that prevents the organisation from being able to access its data and can include security breaches, **Denial of Service (DoS)** attacks as well as the usual fire, theft, flood and natural disaster. *Figure 10.1* summarises the leading causes of data loss.

Hardware or System Malfunction	44%
Human Error	32%
Software Corruption or Program Malfunction	14%
Computer Viruses	7%
Natural Disasters	3%

**Figure 10.1: Leading causes of data loss
(source: Ontrack Data Recovery)**

You cannot prevent disasters from happening, but you can carry out risk assessment; minimise the risks and adequately plan for disaster recovery.

Risk assessment

Risk assessment is the process of identifying risks that your organisation faces. There are generally two methods of risk assessment, which are complementary:

1. An objective survey of the organisation to identify any risks.

2. A brainstorming session with key individuals.

When carrying out risk assessment it is important to identify as many risks as you can, by encouraging 'thinking outside the box' when brainstorming. Don't forget to think of internal risks as well as external – most computer fraud (around 2/3) is committed by employees. Once the risks have been identified, they need to be prioritised. This is known as exposure and is obtained by multiplying the value of a risk by its likelihood of occurrence. By minimising the risk you reduce your exposure. *Figure 10.2* shows an example of risk assessment.

Example of risk assessment/minimisation

You have an expensive mountain bike and decide to leave it unlocked in a particularly nasty neighbourhood, where it is almost certain to be stolen. The bike is worth £1,000 and you are 99% (.99 probability) certain it will be stolen. Your exposure is £1,000 x .99 = £990. Suppose you add a very expensive lock that will protect the whole bike, you estimate that this will reduce the risk of theft to 50% (.5 probability). You have reduced your exposure to £500. By not leaving the bike in that neighbourhood and using the lock you reduce the chance of theft to 10% (.1 probability). Your exposure is now £100. You could of course insure your bike and pass on the risk (risk mitigation), but what would you do in between your bike being stolen and it being replaced?

Figure 10.2: An example of risk assessment

Planning

Disaster recovery planning is about planning for business continuity in the event of a disaster, whilst hoping that it never happens. Most auditors now like to see that the organisation has considered disaster recovery planning and will often ask to see the disaster recovery plan.

The essence of disaster recovery planning is to identify whether disasters will:

- stop you using your premises;
- stop you accessing your data; or
- stop you using your hardware.

For example, the car bomb that struck Commercial Union London in 1992 blew out all of the windows in their tower block. This rendered the building unusable but, because they had multiple data links, they were still able to access data remotely and, using a register of unused space in branch offices, were able to open for business as usual on the Monday following the blast the previous Friday.

In order to effectively plan for disasters you need to identify what you would do in such situations. There are a number of options, which are briefly described below:

Self-protection

Large organisations with multiple premises may be able to protect themselves. Consider a university, which uses PCs and UNIX machines in a number of different buildings spread across a city. If disaster struck one of the key business units, for example finance, providing the data was intact, the finance department could relocate into one of the other buildings, perhaps a teaching building. Assume it took over a PC lab and had the phones re-routed. Providing the department had made arrangements to take over a server machine and the lab in times of disaster, it could move into the classroom, load the data, organise the telephones and be 'open for business' relatively quickly. Disruption to classes could be handled either by using spare capacity in other labs, or at worst, altering the working hours of finance to work when the class was empty.

Smaller organisations may well be able to achieve this too – a small accountancy or law practice may be able to easily work from a home.

In the case of network self-protection, you may wish to keep spare kit or spread connections so that if, for example, a switch fails, all of the connections can be moved to spare capacity on other switches. Some spare wireless kit could prove very useful in recovering from a network disaster.

> **KEY CONCEPT**
>
> Whilst self-protection seems relatively straightforward, you must plan for it. You must also make sure that you have the expertise available to make it possible – if your support team isn't available, how will you make the transfer?

Mutual protection

Mutual protection is where two or more organisations enter into an agreement to offer space and services to each other should disaster strike. These types of plans tend to be more suitable for organisations that aren't in competition with each other, for example schools and colleges – if School A is unable to access its administrative data, it could move to School B with its data and carry out its business.

If you think this type of plan may be suitable, you should carefully draft a legal agreement. All parties should also monitor relevant changes, for example, changes of equipment, available space, changes of management, etc. Overall, the parties should ask themselves: 'Am I prepared to stake my organisation on this?'.

Commercial plans

There are a number of companies who offer commercial plans for disaster recovery. These plans range from sending your data to the company who will load it onto their machine and provide you with remote access, up to a 'white room' service. A white room is an unused room complete with all computer equipment, desks, chairs, telephones – everything an organisation would need to carry on business should disaster strike. Some companies have mobile offices that can be towed by truck and set up in the casualty organisation's car park.

Obviously, the price varies according to the service you want, which might include companies offering the loan of a machine (for a specified time) or perhaps even sending a technical team to help you get up and running again (with the loan equipment).

Factors that should be considered when entering in to a commercial agreement are:

- Types of computers the company use – are they compatible with your own and will you be able to simply use them without any specialist training?
- The ratio of computers kept to the number of clients the company has – a company keeping 1 computer for every 10 clients is likely to be a safer option than a company keeping 1 computer for every 100 clients.
- Ability to upgrade the plan in times of disaster – if disaster strikes and your technical team aren't available will you be able to upgrade to get the contractors technical team?
- The length of time of the loan of equipment – will it be long enough for you to process the insurance claim and to cover the lead times with your kit?
- The expertise available in the company – will it meet your needs?
- Testimonials from those who have suffered disaster and used the companies service.
- Financial stability of the company.
- Lead time before the company will have you up and running again.
- Clauses allowing you to test their services.

Testing your disaster recovery plan

Auditors may be happy that you have a disaster recovery plan in place, but will it actually work if disaster strikes? Having spent time and resources on a disaster recovery plan, most organisations also want assurances that it will work. The only way to convince yourself of this is to simulate a disaster and try out your plan. For example, pretend that your system has gone down or that disaster has struck and try moving to your white room and recover the operation. Most disaster recovery companies will allow you to test out their services, but there may be a charge for this.

KEY CONCEPT

All disaster recovery plans are critically dependent upon planning, backups and keeping the plans up-to-date. Make sure that you plan everything:

- Keeping an up-to-date telephone directory (and a copy off-site!), which includes a means of contacting your key members of staff wherever they are.
- Taking regular backups and keeping them off-site preferably in a fire-proof safe).
- Monitoring your disaster recovery plans and keeping them in contract and up to date.
- Monitoring the health of your disaster recovery provider.
- Regularly testing your backups.
- Testing your disaster recovery plans.

Quick test

Briefly name and discuss the various types of disaster recovery plans available.

Section 4: Network maintenance

The successful maintenance of a network is paramount if it is to be a valuable asset to an organisation. In this section, the term network maintenance relates to activities to keep the network operating effectively. This can obviously mean maintenance as in troubleshooting and repairing, but it also means other aspects such as:

- estimating resources usage;
- server administration;
- network monitoring;
- virus protection.

Estimating resource usage

Estimating resource usage is an important part of network management. The goals of this aspect of management are to detect trends arising from the use of the network and to use these trends to plan future upgrades. To identify trends accurately, and to provide a benchmark for resolving problems, it is important to measure the network and its performance immediately after installation. Known as baselining, this process ideally measures the load on the network and the network's response time at each user's machine. Only when this information has been collected can meaningful comparisons be made.

Estimating resource usage is an all-encompassing term and can include:

- measuring the performance of the network;
- monitoring disc space on the server (if this is part of the network manager's role);
- monitoring the bandwidth usage of the network or parts of it.

Ultimately the process of measuring resource usage is to ensure that the network is meeting the requirements of the organisation and that it can continue to do so in the future. In the process of estimating the resource usage, the network manager will often use sophisticated software to ensure that there is sufficient capacity within the network, particularly at key points such as servers or Internet access.

When monitoring, the network manager will build up a pattern of growth (or possibly decline) which will allow an estimate as to when an upgrade will be necessary. It is very important to make this estimate so that sufficient funds and planning can be given to any upgrade before it becomes a problem to the organisation.

Server administration

Sometimes it is the responsibility of the network manager to administer the servers. Server administration is really beyond the scope of this book as there are many types of server in operation – primarily Windows-based servers and Unix-based servers.

However, network managers need to ensure that they are confident with managing the servers they are charged with and understand what maintenance is required. Such maintenance may include:

- estimating resource usage;
- updating the operating system;
- virus checks;

Network monitoring

Network monitoring and estimating resource usage often go hand in hand. Normally, there are two main reasons for network monitoring:

- to ensure the network is running effectively and;
- to plan for the future.

Ensuring that the network is running effectively involves monitoring the network for irregular activity. This could include an abnormal increase in traffic; an abnormal increase in a type of traffic – many viruses create broadcasts which contribute to an abnormally high number of broadcasts; network links going on- and off-line (flapping) – which could indicate a link problem; the failure of routers or other devices in the network.

Planning for the future can be extremely complex. In this process, network managers are using information gathered from monitoring the network, its devices and individual links in order to plan for the coming years. Such planning could involve diverse aspects such as the upgrading of an Internet connection or upgrading network equipment which is near the end of its life or which does not have sufficient processing power or even the right features.

Virus protection

Computer viruses are yet another threat to networks and systems. Unfortunately, the development of networks and emails means that viruses can be spread more quickly. The security policy must deal with the threat of computer viruses, which can lead either to a denial of service or can be used to open a 'back door' into the system. With viruses, prevention is definitely better than cure. Protecting the system from viruses involves educating the end-users of the necessity to be aware of the risks of computer viruses and the way in which they are spread. The organisation's policy must aim to minimise the threat of viruses, and the users must adhere to this policy, either by choice or by coercion – but the former is more acceptable! Such a policy must:

- regulate the use of portable media such as floppy disks, memory sticks, CDs and DVDs in the organisation;
- control the sending and receiving of email attachments;
- control downloads from the web;
- control the installation of software;
- ensure that every machine has an up-to-date virus checker installed;
- ensure that each machine is regularly updated with the latest version of the anti-virus software.

Users should be discouraged from using portable media unless they can demonstrate a need and the media have been virus checked. Some organisations make unauthorised use a disciplinary offence. Sending and, particularly, receiving email attachments should be discouraged unless absolutely necessary. Even when necessary, these attachments should be in a zipped form rather than executable. This facilitates easier virus checking on the receiving machine. Remember, plain ASCII text is always safe – it is the attachments, etc., that cause the problems. Downloads from the web are extremely dangerous and users should be discouraged from downloading (and certainly installing) software and files. Indeed, the only software that can be safely installed is shrink-wrapped software from a trusted manufacturer or supplier. Each machine should have a reputable, up-to-date virus checker installed, and this must be kept up to date with the latest releases from the manufacturer.

The network operating system also needs to be chosen carefully. A system that offers a high degree of security (with separate logins for each user) and administration rights to the manager solely, will go a long way to protecting itself. Should a virus somehow sneak in to the system, under such conditions it should not be able to infect easily either other users' files or the operating system itself. Regular system backups must be taken and several generations should be kept – restoring yesterday's infected file is of little use, but last week's out-of-date uninfected file is of use. These backups should be on external media that can be removed from the system and stored safely. Again, the anti-virus policy must be continuously monitored and updated if it is to remain effective.

> **KEY CONCEPT**
>
> Viruses are a real threat to organisations. Good administration is essential to minimise this threat.

Quick test

Briefly outline the main tasks of network maintenance.

Section 5: End of chapter assessment

Questions

1. Discuss the major steps involved in creating users and groups; and the management of users.

2. Discuss the various backup techniques and give the advantages/disadvantages of each. Also discuss media cycling.

3. Briefly discuss the process of risk assessment and disaster recovery planning, stating why it is a necessary practice for most organisations.

4. Briefly discuss the major aspects of network maintenance.

Answers

1. This question is in two parts. The first asks you to discuss the process of creating users and groups. Ideally you should discuss control, security and the need for user policy. The second part is asking you to discuss the management of users. Here you should discuss both routine and exceptional management giving examples of each.

2. To answer this question, you need to discuss each of the backup techniques. Ideally you should discuss the technique

and how it operates. The question asks you specifically to give the advantages and disadvantages for each. Failing to do so will cost you marks.

Secondly you are asked to discuss media cycling. Ideally you should describe what is meant by the term and discuss the two examples given in *Section 2.*

3.	To answer this question, you should identify the stages of disaster recovery planning: risk assessment, planning, and the variety of disaster recovery options available. Ideally, you should discuss briefly each option and identify the advantages and disadvantages. A good idea would be to remind the assessor of the need to keep regular backups and to test them – it shows a greater understanding of the problem.

4.	To answer this question, you need to identify the major tasks of network maintenance. The assessor is looking for evidence that you understand that once the network is installed, maintenance is necessary. They are seeking evidence from you detailing the major tasks of network maintenance and ideally, you should supplement your answers with examples.

Section 6: Further reading and research

Cisco Networking Academy Program (2004) *CCNA 1 and 2 Companion Guide*, (3rd edn). Cisco Press. ISBN: 1-58713-150-1. Chapters 8 and 28. (Old but still useful)

Cisco Networking Academy Programme (2004) CCNA 3 and 4 Companion Guide, (3rd edn). Cisco Press. ISBN: 1-58713-113-7. Chapter 18.

Chapter 11
Connecting to the outside world

Chapter summary

This chapter provides an overview of networking by illustrating how all the equipment works together in order to provide connectivity. Since the Internet is currently a hot topic, it discusses the various Internet connection options and outlines how a request for a web page is generated on a PC and handled by the network.

Learning outcomes

After studying this chapter you should aim to test your achievement of the following outcomes. You should be able to:

Outcome 1: Types of Internet connections

Understand the differences between the main types of Internet connections and be able to select the most appropriate for a particular situation. Question 1 at the end of this chapter will test you on this.

Outcome 2: The Internet (TCP/IP) case study

Understand how the Internet operates when requesting and receiving web pages. Question 2 at the end of this chapter will test you on this.

How will you be assessed on this?

Knowing how a connection to the Internet is made, and how data travels in the form of packets and frames (crossing internal networks and the Internet) will give you the 'big picture' of how networks operate. Even if this is not assessed directly, it will deepen your understanding, which will come through in any assessment you undertake. In a practical assessment, you could be asked to recommend an Internet connection for a given company. You could also be asked in an exam to discuss how connection to the Internet can be achieved and how data is exchanged. You can, of course, weave the content of this chapter into most of your answers for extra marks.

Section 1: Types of Internet connections

There are many ways to connect to the Internet: dialup; DSL; cable; etc. This section discusses the major current ways of connecting.

Dial-up connection

Most people are familiar with this method of connecting to the Internet and it is still a common connection. Dial-up connection involves the use of a pair of modems and a telephone line. The modems convert the digital computer signals into analogue signals that are suitable for transmission over the telephone network. Another modem at the other end converts them back. This is known as a point-to-point (PPP) serial link and is available through virtually all ISPs. Once at the ISP's premises, the data is transferred on to its LAN and begins its journey to the Internet. Dial-up connection is also known as plain old telephone service or POTS for short. Typically, modems provide 33.6 K upload speed and 56.6 K download speed.

Digital Subscriber Line (DSL)

DSL is a method by which a permanent connection to the Internet can be provided to an end-subscriber using existing telephone lines. Quite simply, this is achieved by dividing the bandwidth of the conventional telephone line into channels, in a similar way that the bandwidth of TV/radio broadcasts is divided into channels (BBC1, BBC2, ITV1, etc.) (*see Figure 11.1*). Technically, this is known as **Frequency Division Multiplexing** (**FDM**). Frequency ranges are allocated to particular services.

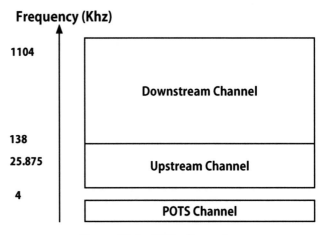

Figure 11.1: ADSL channels

There are generally two groups of DSL available:

- **ADSL** – Asymmetric DSL; and
- **SDSL** – Symmetric DSL.

'Asymmetric' means the line is imbalanced in favour of receiving data. In the case of ADSL, a small frequency range is allocated to the telephone service, a second, larger frequency range to the upstream connection to the Internet and the third and largest channel to the downstream connection to the Internet.

With ADSL it is possible to receive at up to 8 Mbps, but outbound transmission is limited to around 512 Kbps. As most home connections surf the web and download files, video and music, ADSL is ideally suited for this purpose. However, if a web server was connected or an organisation made large and frequent transmissions, ADSL would not be so suitable. There would be a considerable difference in speed when downloading a file compared to uploading.

In 2008, ADSL2 (known as ITU G.992.3) was launched in the UK. This is basically an improved version of ADSL providing up to 12 Mbps. ADSL2+ was also launched providing a theoretical 24 Mbps and over 2 Mbps upload speed. In 2009, ISPs were beginning to offer 20 Mbps download and up to 2.5 Mbps upload.

'Symmetric' means the line is balanced being able to send and receive data at the same rate. In the case of SDSL, a small frequency range is allocated to the telephone service, and two larger equal-sized frequencies are allocated to the upstream and downstream connections to the Internet.

With SDSL it is possible to send and receive at up to 2 Mbps making it ideal for small businesses who upload as much data as they receive. As SDSL is a business solution, it is more expensive than ADSL (£170 per month at 2009 prices) but comes with guaranteed service and a lower contention ratio than standard broadband (*see Chapter 9*).

Whichever type of DSL is deployed, connection requires a device to split the channels (often called a **microfilter** – *see Figure 11.2*) and a broadband modem or ASDL router. The computer is attached to the modem or router which, in turn, connects with the telephone to the microfilter.

Figure 11.2: A typical ADSL microfilter

Although the theory sounds straightforward, the cable and legacy telephony equipment that carry ADSL were never meant for this purpose, and so the technology that makes this possible is nothing short of a miracle!

DSL technology has been a godsend to the telephone companies. It has allowed them to provide high bandwidth data rates to dispersed locations with relatively small changes to the existing telephone infrastructure.

The two main disadvantages to DSL are that it is only available up to 5.5 km from the telephone exchange and not all exchanges are outfitted to support it. Range may increase as technology develops.

Cable modems

Some parts of the UK have now been provided with Internet access through cable TV systems. In most of the parts of the country, the cable systems that have been installed have been designed to transfer data, and it is common to find integrated cable modems inside cable TV boxes. Again, using **Frequency Division Multiplexing (FDM)**, data is effectively added to the cable system using a separate, dedicated frequency. However, because the cable is under the control of the cable company and has a much greater bandwidth than the twisted pairused in traditional telephony, cable companies are able to tailor their service and to offer higher data rates than ADSL. For example, most cable companies can offer at least a 20 Mbps connection and some have been trialling 100 Mbps to the home. The cable companies can tailor its direction – a residential customer is more likely to download information than to upload and so the cable company will provide a faster downstream connection than upstream. A web-hosting company would probably want the connection the other way around.

Like DSL, cable modems (*see Figure 11.3*) provide a permanent connection to the Internet: they are always on, and when the computer is on, they can represent a security hazard. Usually, the frequency used by the cable companies is employed to provide an extended Ethernet network over a WAN, with a geographical reach of up to 100 miles. It is therefore not unusual to see a cable box with a dedicated Ethernet port at the rear.

Figure 11.3: A typical cable modem

ISDN

Integrated Services Digital Network (ISDN) was, and still is, very popular in the USA, but it has never really caught on in the UK, largely due to price. With ISDN, a telephone subscriber is provided with two digital telephone lines. If they are used for voice, they require special telephones to be connected to them. The most common ISDN connection is **ISDN2**, which provides two bearer (or B) channels, each of which can carry 64 Kbps, and one **Delta** (or D) channel that establishes and manages the session. Thus ISDN provides a maximum of 128 Kbps in either direction. The subscriber pays call costs for ISDN and also for the line rental for each of the lines. Thus a one hour session will cost twice as much as a one hour phone call plus the rental for the two lines; this makes it very expensive when compared to ADSL.

ISDN is now mainly used for video conferencing; for large organisations that require an infrequently used backup line for WAN connections; and for dial-in remote management of network equipment. ISDN is usually available as ISDN2, ISDN6 and ISDN30. The number represents the number of lines and hence the bearer channels (there is still a Delta channel). Thus for ISDN30 there are 30 lines, 30 channels of 64 Kbps, 30 line rental charges to pay and 30 times the call costs. ISDN in the USA and Japan is slightly different from that in the UK and most of Europe. More importantly, ISDN equipment sold in the USA/Japan is usually incompatible in Europe and vice versa.

Satellite

Since 2003, companies have been offering broadband connection speeds through a combination of satellite and telephone technology (*see Figure 11.4*). Although this method has been available for some time, it is the use of the Sky Digital satellite system that makes this an affordable option – previously it was via a dedicated satellite.

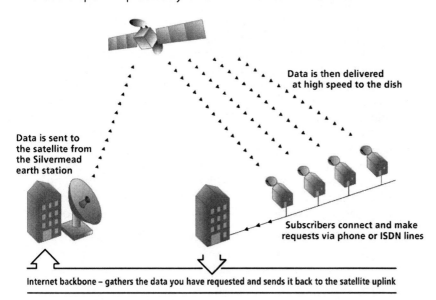

Figure 11.4: Broadband via satellite (courtesy of Silvermead)

This type of technology is probably most suitable for those who can't receive broadband services because of their location – remember ADSL requires technology to be added to telephone exchanges, which may still not be present in some rural areas. Also, some subscribers are too far from their exchange to have DSL. As shown in *Figure 11.4*, this technology uses the existing telephone line to send a request, for example, for a web page to the ISP. The ISP then retrieves the page from the Internet at high speed and returns it via the satellite to the user. This should happen as quickly as conventional broadband services. The technology requires a satellite modem and a modification to a conventional satellite receiver. The main disadvantage of this technology is that it ties up a conventional telephone line. Other than that, as a service it is virtually identical to broadband – although speeds may be slower.

Private wire

Organisations such as web-hosting companies, large institutions, e-commerce sites and universities that require very high-speed connection to the Internet can connect using private wires. These are private dedicated connections from the organisation to its ISP, usually using fibre optic cabling. Using technologies such as ATM or Ethernet type circuits (*see Chapter 5*), this link can be as high as 40 Gbps but it is very expensive.

Such links are also known as **Ethernet Extension Services (EES)**, **Ethernet Private Circuit (EPC)** and **LAN Extension Circuits (LES)**. Many organisations also use such connections between sites.

Mobile connections

Mobile connections provide a means of connecting to the Internet using the mobile phone network. Although this has been possible for a number of years, the connection speeds were initially very slow (around 9.6 Kbps). **Third generation (3G)** mobile networks changed that by providing a connection speed of up to 384 Kbps inbound (almost 7 times faster than standard dial up – remember early broadband was 128 Kbps) and 64 Kbps outbound. In 2009, the current standard is commonly referred to as 3.5G. Technically the standard is **High Speed Packet Access (HSPA)** of which there are two types: **High Speed Download Packet Access (HSDPA)** which supports download speeds of up to 14.4 Mbps and **High Speed Upload Packet Access (HSUPA)** which provides upload speeds of up to 5.76 Mbps. These speeds compare very favourably to fixed (wired) broadband services such as ADSL and cable. The next generation of mobile broadband 4G is known as the **Long Term Evolution (LTE)** project and allows for 326 Mbps download and 86 Mbps upload which will equal or surpass current wired technologies.

It is worth noting that these speeds are all theoretical maximums and you are unlikely to achieve them in practice. Connection to mobile networks is typically achieved using USB dongles (*see Figure 11.5*).

Figure 11.5: A 3.5G USB Dongle

If the costs are competitive and coverage can be widened, use of this technology is certain to grow.

WiMax

WiMax is an acronym for **Worldwide Interoperability for Microwave Access**. Although it was proposed some time ago, it only began to come into use around 2008. WiMax is described in IEEE 802.16 and aims to provide a high-speed broadband service. It provides wireless access with broad 'mobile phone type' coverage. WiMax operates in a similar fashion to wireless networks but at a higher speed and across greater distances.

Essentially all that is needed for WiMax is a WiMax USB style dongle and an account with a WiMax provider. The WiMax provider needs to have a WiMax mast within 10 miles of your location and provide you with the encryption code to access the mast.

As DSL reaches its limits on speed, it is possible that WiMax will take over as it provides a cost-effective means of providing high-speed broadband into the home without laying new cables. WiMax also provide the possibility of connecting remote rural users who currently can't access broadband (*see Figure 11.6*).

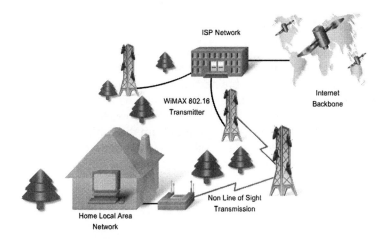

**Figure 11.6: WiMax typical deployment
(image courtesy of Cisco Systems Inc.)**

In 2009, WiMax deployments in the UK were extremely limited and along with 4G and LTE, it is a technology to watch.

TIPS & ADVICE

It is important you understand the various connections to the Internet and their characteristics. You will almost certainly be asked about this in an assessment.

KEY CONCEPT

Different types of Internet connections have different attributes. When deciding on a connection, the one that best matches the client's requirements should be chosen. Of course, it is important to make sure their ISP can handle it.

KEY CONCEPT

It is important to note that WiMax is not based on the same technology as 3G; 3.5G; 4G and LTE. It is based on similar technology to conventional Wireless LANs and may well offer an alternative to these mobile technologies in the future.

WANs across the Internet using VPNs

Traditionally organisations had their own WAN links for speed and security. As connections to the Internet become faster, connections between an organisation's sites across the Internet could make a viable alternative to lower speed WAN connections – if they were secure. As we saw in *Chapter 1*, **Virtual Private Networks (VPNs)** provide a means of securing transmissions across the Internet using encryption technologies.

Using such technologies, it is possible for organisations to make dramatic cost savings by replacing their non mission critical WAN links with VPN tunnels across the Internet (*see Chapter 1*). The 2009 economic climate is seeing many organisations realise these savings.

Quick test

Briefly discuss the major ways of connecting to the Internet.

Section 2: The Internet (TCP/IP) case study

Throughout this book, standards, equipment, topologies and technologies have been discussed. Whilst understanding all this is of crucial importance, we still have not considered the 'big picture' – i.e. how does it all work? If, for example, an Ethernet or cable modem was chosen, how would the web browser download the information from the Internet? How does it find the information?

This section intends to answer these questions by outlining the process of connecting to the Internet and retrieving a web page. This section assumes an Ethernet network connection is being used. Quite often now, PCs connect to DSL links via Ethernet (wired or wireless).

Internet settings

Every computer connected to the Internet needs a minimum of four settings: an IP address, a subnet mask, a default gateway and a DNS server. These can be obtained either by going into the network settings from the control panel or by running the **winipcfg** command (Windows 98) or the **ipconfig** command (Windows NT, 2000, XP and Vista). *Figure 11.7* shows sample output from the **winipcfg** command. If set to automatic, the computer will obtain these settings from a **DHCP (Dynamic Host Configuration Protocol)** server.

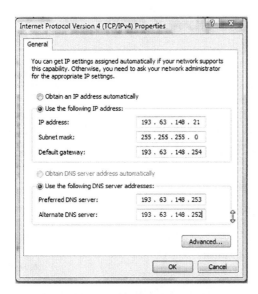

**Figure 11.7: Ethernet settings
(networking option from control panel in Windows Vista)**

Looking at each of the settings in turn, the IP address is the computer's logical address on the Internet (*see Chapter 3*) and the subnet mask is a binary pattern used to locate the network (*see Chapter 3*). The default gateway is the place to which the computer sends the packet if it has no idea what else to do with it. The **Domain Name Server** (**DNS**) provides a means of looking up the domain part of a URL and determining its IP address. The adapter address (not shown) is the MAC address of the Ethernet NIC (*see Chapter 6*).

In the IP address, the first byte tells us that this is a class C address (because it is in the class C address range – *see Chapter 3*). Thus the first three bytes are used to specify the network address (in this case 193.63.148). The subnet mask (*see Chapter 3*) 255.255.255.0 tells us to compare the first three bytes to determine the subnetwork. Thus we can see that the default gateway is on the same subnetwork as the machine itself (because the first three bytes are identical). An address of 157.228.102.1 would be on a different subnet.

However, how does this relate to a web page? A URL is essentially a text representation of an IP address. When we enter a URL (e.g. **osiris. sunderland.ac.uk**) into a web browser, the web browser communicates with a domain name server (DNS) and retrieves the IP address but it doesn't display it. So if 157.228.102.1 is keyed into your browser, it will retrieve the same page as if **osiris.sunderland.ac.uk** had been keyed in.

TIPS & ADVICE

Examine the settings on your PC and then try keying 157.228.102.1 into your browser.

Beginning the journey

Figure 11.8 represents an Internet connection.

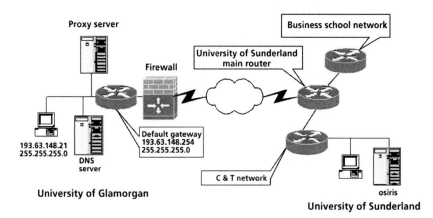

Figure 11.8: An Internet connection

A PC at the University of Glamorgan is being used to view the home page of the Department of Computing and Technology at the University of Sunderland (**osiris.sunderland.ac.uk**). Both networks are Ethernet. The URL is entered into the browser, which immediately queries the DNS server and retrieves the IP address of 157.228.102.1. It does this by broadcasting an Ethernet frame to the DNS server which then responds with a unicast frame (to one machine only) containing the IP address. For our purposes it does not matter how the DNS server knows the address – very crudely, all DNSs across the world talk to one another to update their tables.

The machine at Glamorgan now knows the address of **osiris. sunderland.ac.uk** as 157.228.102.1. It uses its subnet mask to identify the parts of the address that give the network address (*see Chapter 3*). It does this by logic: by ANDing the address and the subnet mask together. In binary 255 is 11111111 – all bits are 1 in the byte. A bit set to 1 means compare. Thus 255.255.255.0 means compare all parts of the first three bytes. The network portion of the IP address is therefore 193.63.148 (the last byte is the host ID – the Glamorgan PC in this case). As 193.63.148 and 157.228.102 are not identical, the PC knows the machine it is looking for is not on the same network as itself.

The Glamorgan machine does not know what to do with the packet. However, it has been configured to send such packets to the default gateway. Although the PC knows the IP address of the default gateway, it has no idea of the MAC address of the default gateway – necessary for communication with it over Ethernet. To find the MAC address, it needs to resolve the IP address. It does this through a process known as Address Resolution Protocol (ARP). The machine broadcasts an Ethernet frame which asks the machine that has the IP address of 193.63.148.254 to respond with its MAC address. The default gateway router receives this broadcast and realises the IP address is its own. It then responds with a unicast frame to the Glamorgan PC. It can unicast because it knows the Glamorgan PC's MAC address – it was in its frame

– and, obviously, it knows its own address. Unicasts are preferable to broadcasts as they do not consume as much network bandwidth (they go to one machine only, not all the machines).

The Glamorgan PC now knows the MAC address of the default gateway, and it encapsulates the IP packet requesting the web page into an Ethernet frame addressed to the default gateway. This frame is placed on to the Ethernet network where it begins its journey to the default gateway.

TIPS & ADVICE

Access a web page, then open a DOS command prompt window (**Run > cmd**) and type in **arp -a** and press enter. You will see the ARP cache -a map of IP and MAC addresses.

Notice the mapping of an IP address to a MAC Address (see *Figure 11.8*).

```
cv Command Prompt                                              - □
C:\Documents and Settings\Phil>arp -a

Interface: 192.168.1.104 --- 0x2
  Internet Address      Physical Address      Type
  192.168.1.1           00-16-b6-1e-b5-b6     dynamic
  192.168.1.109         00-1c-bf-13-80-80     dynamic
```

Figure 11.8: A DOS command prompt window

The proxy server

In the event the University of Glamorgan uses a proxy server, the browser will itself request that the IP address of the requested web page is sent to the proxy. It does this for two reasons. The first is to establish if the proxy already holds a copy of that web page. It if does, it can retrieve it more quickly and less expensively than if it went to the Internet (ISPs and directly connected companies may be charged for the use of certain links, e.g. transatlantic). Secondly, it checks the organisation's security policy – is this URL allowed? The proxy server then handles the retrieval of the web page itself, sending it to the default gateway.

The default gateway

If the proxy server and/or the PC don't know the whereabouts of a web page, the request lands at the default gateway. The default gateway is usually a router and it may have a number of routes connected to it. As was seen in *Chapter 6*, routers have two purposes – to determine the best path and to switch the packet. In this case, the router needs to determine which of the paths it is directly connected to will lead to the required IP address. It isn't feasible for a router to know every IP address on the Internet and so it, too, has a default gateway: if it doesn't know what to do with a packet it forwards it to its default gateway.

In our example, the University of Glamorgan router is connected only to the Internet and the Glamorgan network. As a 157.228.102 address clearly doesn't belong to the University of Glamorgan, the router has no idea what to do with it and so sends it to its default gateway – in this case, on to the Internet.

Firewall

Before passing on to the Internet, the packet may be subjected to a firewall. A firewall is either a piece of software or more likely a hardware device whose purpose is to provide greater network security (*see Chapter 12*). A firewall can be thought of as a collection of numbered and guarded exit doors to an organisation: employees have to leave by certain numbered doors and, if the doors are locked (perhaps it's not time for them to leave), they can't get out. If the door is unlocked, they can leave but they may be subjected to a search to determine if they are carrying any secrets.

A firewall does exactly the same thing with data. Data exiting from an organisation does so via port numbers (the door numbers in the analogy), which can be open or closed.

Commonly used port numbers are:

Port	Application
21	FTP
23	Telnet
25	SMTP
80	Web.

Packets passing through the firewall may also be subjected to a search to see if they contain any data that isn't allowed under the organisation's security policy. If they do, they are dealt with severely – they are destroyed!

On to the Internet

If packets pass successfully through the firewall, they are ready to be placed on to the Internet. Almost certainly, the bandwidth of the organisation's Internet connection will be smaller than that of its LAN. Not all packets will be able to fit on to such a limited bandwidth and so some will be lost. TCP (Transmission Control Protocol – *see Chapter 4*) waits for an acknowledgement from the recipient of the packets transmitted. In the event it does not receive one, it simply sends a replacement packet. Once on the Internet, the packets head toward huge routers with huge routing tables. When they arrive at these routers, their destination IP address is examined and, if the router knows the route the packet should take, it is switched to that route. If not, it is forwarded to that router's default gateway.

Often represented as a cloud (as in *Figure 11.8*), the Internet is a complex web of connections and routers. However, one thing that should be noted about the Internet is that it operates on TCP that is inherently reliable. As the Internet is such a mass of connections, each has several backups. For example, there are satellite connections between the UK and the USA, but there are also trans-oceanic cables and satellite connections to and from Europe to the USA. Thus a transmission will almost always get through even if links are down – the Internet will route around the downed links. The reliability of the Internet was harrowingly demonstrated on 11 September 2001. After the aircraft hit the World Trade Center, its conventional telephone services were lost. However, IP telephones were able to route around the downed links.

KEY CONCEPT

Firewalls are an important part of an organisation's security, but they do not meet all an organisation's needs – they should be part of a policy that includes routers and proxy servers. The policy should also recognise network users. Without such an integrated policy, firewalls are of little use (*see Chapter 12*).

Arriving at the destination

Eventually the packet will approach the University of Sunderland and will arrive at its router. When it arrives, it will be immediately subjected to a firewall. If it is bound for an open door, it will be allowed. If not, it will simply be destroyed. Once through the door, it will be inspected by the firewall to determine if it is the sort of packet that should be allowed through. Providing it is, it is passed on to the University LAN (encapsulated in an Ethernet frame). After the firewall, a router will examine the network element of the IP address and forward the packet to the appropriate network. Once it arrives on the appropriate network, the router on that network will either know the MAC address of osiris or it will ARP to get it. Once it has the MAC address of osiris, it will forward the IP packet (encapsulated inside an Ethernet frame) to osiris. Osiris will open the packet and examine the contents – a request for a web page. Osiris will then recycle the packet, replacing the destination address with the source address (i.e. putting the address of the Glamorgan machine as the destination and its own address as the source).

The return journey

If the contents of the web page are too large to fit into one packet, the server will replicate the packet structure. It will then fill the packet with the required contents and send the packet back: to the default gateway, to the University proxy server, through the firewall and on to the Internet. Once it arrives at the University of Glamorgan, it will be subjected to the firewall and will then be placed on to the University LAN. It will pass on to the proxy server (inside an Ethernet frame because it's on a LAN), which will check its contents. If the proxy allows the packet through, it will take a copy of it so that further requests for that web page can be satisfied from it rather than having to go on to the Internet. It will then be passed to the router to be delivered to the machine.

As the router knows the MAC address of this machine, it encapsulates the packet inside a frame and sends it to the machine. The machine strips off the Ethernet and IP headers, extracts the data and displays it. All this happens in the 'blink of an eye'.

Summary

In this discussion of the Internet and of how networks (in this case Ethernet) facilitate the movement of traffic to and from the Internet, only the most important networking device – the router – has been highlighted. Typically, however, Ethernet frames would pass through a host of Ethernet networking devices, including switches.

Quick test

Briefly outline how a request for a web page generates both Ethernet frames and IP packets and how these result in the web page being retrieved and displayed.

> **KEY CONCEPT**
>
> Packets containing web page requests travel far – across Ethernet networks and the Internet and through many, varied devices.

Section 3: End of chapter assessment

Questions

1.   Identify the most common ways of connecting a home PC to the Internet. Briefly discuss each option, highlighting its advantages and disadvantages.

2.   Briefly outline how a request for a web page makes its way to the Internet.

Answers

1.   To answer this question, you need to list the most popular connections from the home to the Internet (i.e. modem access; DSL; cable; and possibly ISDN and mobile connections). For each of these connections, you need to discuss the features of the connection type – for example, always on, the equipment needed for the connection and the advantages and disadvantages. For instance, ADSL is asymmetric, which makes it ideal for connecting from the home: it has a faster downstream connection than upstream; there are no call costs; and it is faster than a conventional (modem) connection. You should also discuss the disadvantages – for example, it has a slower upload speed than download and, although still faster than a modem connection, it may not be suitable for all teleworking.

2.   As you couldn't possibly discuss all that is covered in this chapter in an exam question, this question is only concerned with how a request for a web page makes its way from the PC to the Internet. In practice, networks are most likely to be Ethernet, and so you should state this before you start. The best place to start is a discussion of the network settings on a PC and what they mean and do. From that you can expand your answer to discuss how the PC decides whether or not the web server is on the same network as the PC. Assuming it is, it will cut out most of the answer to the question and a good part of your marks! Therefore assume it isn't and show the role of the default gateway; default gateways set on the router; the proxy server; and the firewall.

Section 4: Further reading and research

Cisco Networking Academy Program (2001) *First Year Companion Guide* (2nd edn). Cisco Press. ISBN: 1-58713-025-4. Chapter 30. (Older but still useful.)

Dick, D. (2008) *PC Support Handbook.* Dumbreck Publishing. ISBN: 978-0-9541711-3-1. Data communications chapter.

Accessing the WAN, CCNA Exploration Labs and Study Guide (2008). Cisco Press. 1-58713-205-2. Chapters 1 and 6.

www.warriorsofthe.net/movie.html (last accessed 14/5/09)

www.wimax.co.uk (last accessed 11/6/09).

Chapter 12
Network security

Chapter summary

Information security is often as paramount for organisations as it is for the military. Companies have commercially-sensitive information as well as having obligations under legislation such as the Data Protection Act and the European Data Directive. Before the widespread use of computers, information security was provided by robust filing cabinets, perhaps a security guard and usually a personnel screening system. The aim was simple – to limit access to sensitive information.

It was also relatively easy to spot someone stealing information – long periods spent at the photocopier and carrying large boxes of paper out of the building!

With the widespread use of computers it is much easier to steal sensitive information – by using a DAT cartridge, for example, it is possible to steal 160 GB of data on a cartridge small enough to fit into a shirt pocket. To put 160 GB in context – the entire *Encyclopaedia Britannica* is around 1 GB! With networking you don't even need physical access!

This chapter guides you through the basics of network security, identifying the tools available, likely sources of attack and the need for a co-ordinated plan. You must remember that network security is a huge subject and only a basic guide can be given – if in doubt seek specialist help.

Learning outcomes

After studying this chapter you should aim to test your achievement of the following outcomes. You should be able to:

Outcome 1: Security

Understand the need for network and system security and be able to evaluate security, devise, implement and monitor security policies. Question 1 at the end of this chapter will test your ability to do this.

Outcome 2: Security technologies

Understand the security technologies available and their place in a secure system. Question 2 at the end of this chapter will test your ability to do this.

How will you be assessed on this?

This chapter is mainly theory and it is highly unlikely that your academic institution will have the time or the skills to have you implement security. As such, it is likely to be assessed as theory, perhaps asking you to draft a security policy as part of an assignment or discuss security technologies in an exam.

Section 1: Security

To be effective security must be a planned and co-ordinated effort based upon risk assessment (*see Chapter 10*) with various security tools and techniques being brought together in a co-ordinated fashion to help secure the organisation.

It is very important to realise that threats change on an almost daily basis and that you must constantly monitor your security policy and devices; make improvements; and test those improvements to ensure the best possible protection.

Introduction

Network security is a major topic in computing and not without reason. Most organisations are critically dependent upon their information, of which the only copy is almost certainly held on computer. Theft or fraud involving that information is serious but even more serious is the organisation being denied access to its own information. Known as a **denial of service attack**, this may be as simple as someone accessing their computer system and changing all of the passwords.

The main threats to a computer system are:

- misuse of the computer system;
- attacks on the network;
- computer viruses (*see Chapter 10*);
- disaster (*see Chapter 10*);
- data loss;
- theft of hardware.

To be effective, security must be a policy-based approach. The policy can then be implemented using a variety of techniques such as manual procedures, limiting end-user access, firewalls, routers and leased communication lines. This section briefly explores the main issues of network security and provides suggestions on countering any threats.

The most important piece of advice that can be given to protect the organisation is to take regular backups of the system, to try out these backups, ensuring that they work, and to store the backup tapes securely off-site in a fireproof safe. Whilst this will in no way help prevent attacks on the computer system, it will provide the organisation with a way to recover if anything should happen (*see Chapter 10*). In the case of the last three items on the list, if you don't have backups you will probably never recover and the chances of your organisation continuing (let alone continuing unharmed) are not in your favour.

Misuse of the computer system

The problem of computer security is hard to quantify through concrete examples as many organisations that have fallen victim prefer to cover up the problem, as public exposure will cause even more damage.

Consider a bank losing £2 million through poor computer security – would you be happy banking with them?

Various surveys have indicated that as much as 2/3 of all computer misuse is actually committed by employees of the organisation. Common sources of misuse include creating (and paying) bogus employees, creating dummy purchase orders and paying invoices, etc. These examples of employee misuse require little technical ingenuity but confirm that within most organisations there is plenty of scope for fraud. Policies need to be in place which make it more difficult for such activities to take place. Physical separation of duties make it more difficult. For example, the same person shouldn't pay the invoices as created the purchase order, similarly before creating an employee on the payroll system, a request must be received from the HR Dept.

Employees need to be educated not to share their user IDs and passwords. Someone using your ID or password is effectively taking on your persona to all audit trails on the system. Should a fraud take place, it is you that will be held accountable.

Employees exceeding their level of authority can also be a problem. Assuming passwords are not shared, then the best way to tackle this possibility is to configure the user interface. For example, if the user's duties are only paying invoices, then menu systems should be created that only offers this option. In this way, it becomes very difficult for the user to exceed their level of authority.

Attacks on the network

Various surveys by the **Computer Security Institute** (**CSI**) found that 70% of organisations said their network security defences had been breached. Sixty percent of the incidents came from within the organisation, confirming again that the internal threat is greater than the external threat.

Four types of network threat can be identified:

- unstructured threats;
- structured threats;
- external threats;
- internal threats.

Unstructured threats are mainly from inexperienced individuals using tools they downloaded from the Internet. Whilst they aren't particularly technically competent, they have some sort of intent or wouldn't be 'having a go'. The fact that they are is a problem.

Structured threats are from seasoned hackers who are competent and motivated. They have an understanding of networking and more sophisticated tools.

External threats are as you would expect – from outside the organisation securing access through dial-up connections or the Internet.

Internal threats are when someone has authorised access to the network or physical access to the networking devices.

Physical security of devices and major cabling is paramount – if someone can physically access your devices, then they can probably defeat the passwords (most equipment provides for password recovery from physical access). Similarly, if they have access to major cabling, simply cutting this will cause a great deal of harm.

Types of attack

Network attacks can be broadly categorised into three:

- **reconnaissance attacks**;
- **access attacks**;
- **Denial of Service (DoS) attacks**.

Reconnaissance attacks

Reconnaissance attacks are akin to a burglar checking out a neighbourhood – looking for unlocked doors, half-open windows, etc. They don't intend to carry out a burglary immediately, but are looking for weaknesses. Networks have similar weaknesses – such as folders you may have made sharable in windows and forgotten to close, exposed server directories, etc. Hackers will make a note of these weaknesses and come back to exploit them when fewer people are looking.

Access attacks

Access is a broad term referring to unauthorised data manipulation, systems access or privilege escalation. Data manipulation is viewing information that the intruder wasn't meant to have access to (this could include copying or moving the information). In order to carry this out, the intruder needs to gain access and, quite often, seasoned hackers will use tools to achieve access. In the same way as a burglar uses lock picks, hackers use either password crackers or other utilities, which either exploit a weakness in the system, or simply brute force (tirade of passwords) to gain access.

Access attacks that involve privilege escalation are ones in which legitimate users (or hackers who have succeeded in getting low-level access to the system) attempt to gain higher-level access. This can involve running some kind of software – perhaps a password-sniffing tool to identify passwords being sent across the network. Shared machines at universities and colleges are particularly prone to this kind of attack, so beware!

Denial of Service (DoS)

Denial of Service (DoS) attacks are one of the most feared forms of attack. Here the intruder wants to deny an organisation access to its own network or services. In doing so, that organisation is prevented from functioning – the longer it can be prevented from functioning, the less likely it is that the organisation will recover.

Elements of good practice

It is important that network security is viewed as a continuous process – new threats emerge daily and you must test to determine the effectiveness of your security. It should be based around a security policy. *Figure 12.1* shows the four essential steps in network security.

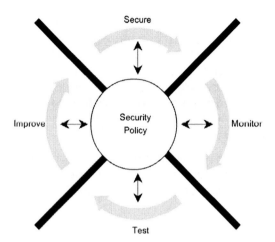

Figure 12.1: Major processes in network security (the security wheel) (Image Courtesy of Cisco systems Inc.)

Before embarking on the security wheel, a security policy needs to be devised by the organisation. Key to this policy are:

- identifying the assets to be protected (these can be computer systems, network connections, data, documents, etc.);
- define the organisation's security objectives;
- identify the current network infrastructure (usually using network maps).

Once the above information has been gathered, the organisation is in a position to draft its security policy. It cannot be emphasised enough how important this document is and developing it can be a daunting task. ISO/IEC have produced a code of practice (ISO/IEC 27002) to assist with Information Security Management and drafting policies. This document has 12 sections:

1. Risk assessment
2. Security policy
3. Organisation of Information Security
4. Asset Management
5. Human Resources study
6. Physical and environmental security
7. Communications and operations management
8. Access control

9. Information systems acquisition, development, and maintenance
10. Information security incident management
11. Business continuity management
12. Compliance

Security Level

It is worthwhile examining the organisation's security objectives. In general, the tighter the organisation's security, the more difficult it is for genuine users to access the system. Consider a college or university. You can probably walk into any college building without challenge – a fairly open level of security. Now consider a prison; to visit someone in prison you may need an pass, will probably have to arrive at a given time, will need some form of ID and possibly be subject to a search – a much more closed level of security.

Ideally the organisation will set an appropriate level of security for the assets to be protected – balancing the need for security against the need for access. There are essentially three models of security:

- Open;
- Restrictive;
- Closed.

Open networks

In the open network model (*see Figure 12.2*) security is balanced in favour of ease of access for the users. This model is usually insecure and organisations using this model wouldn't usually be connected to the Internet. The following characteristics typify the open model:

- assumes assets to be protected are minimal;
- assumes all users are trustworthy;
- easy to implement;
- few or no security measures implemented;
- free access to all areas;
- should a breach occur, damage and loss are likely to be great;
- network managers not usually held responsible for breaches.

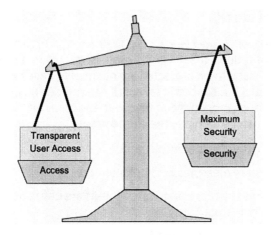

**Figure 12.2: Open Network model
(image courtesy of Cisco Systems Inc.)**

Restrictive networks

The restrictive network model (*see Figure 12.3*) is usually the minimum an organisation should deploy (especially if they are connected to the Internet). The model equally balances the need for security with the need of users to access the system. The following characteristics typify the restrictive model:

- harder to implement;

- assumes that assets are substantial;

- assumes that not all users are trustworthy and that threats are likely;

- many security measures implemented;

- user ease of use is diminished as security is tightened.

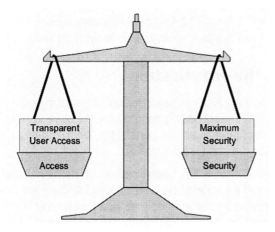

**Figure 12.3: Restrictive Network model
(image courtesy of Cisco Systems Inc.)**

Closed networks

The closed network model (*see Figure 12.4*) would normally be found in financial institutions, the military, hospitals, etc. where the assets (especially the data) to be protected are deemed to have great value. The closed model is balanced in favour of network security and access is likely to be much more difficult than with the other two models. The following characteristics typify the closed model:

- the most difficult to implement;
- all security measures are implemented;
- assumes assets are premium, all users are untrustworthy and threats are frequent;
- user access is difficult and cumbersome (perhaps using biometrics);
- network managers' skill set need to be high; they are held responsible for security and will usually not be liked by the user base.

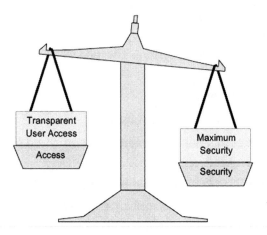

**Figure 12.4: Closed Network model
(image courtesy of Cisco systems Inc.)**

Securing the organisation

Once the security policy has been drafted the security wheel can begin. The policy is implemented (the secure part of *Figure 12.1*) using security devices such as firewalls, access control lists on a router, encryption and authentication devices (*see Section 2*).

Once the security policy has been implemented, the network needs to be monitored for access breaches or attacks. There are commercial pieces of software available to help you do this such as the Cisco Secure Intrusion Detection System. Such software will help you determine whether the network devices have been configured properly.

You will need to test the effectiveness of the safeguards you have put in place, against the security procedures that you devised. You may have developed the best security policy in the world but, unless you test it, you will never know whether it is working. Again software is available to help you do this.

Finally, you will need to continually improve the security. You can only do this by collecting and analysing information that has been gathered from the monitoring and testing phases. Don't forget, new vulnerabilities appear everyday.

You should regard security as a continuous process with all four steps of the security wheel being repeated continually and, where necessary, triggering amendments to the security policy.

> **KEY CONCEPT**
> Computer security is a continuous process of secure-monitor-test-improve and cannot be viewed as a single operation.

Quick test

Give a brief introduction to network security, identifying the major problems and models of network security.

Section 2: Security technologies

The secure part of the security wheel requires the use of various technologies to help secure the organisation. There is not one single technology that will secure an organisation and it is important that you understand the range of technologies available so that you can best decide how to deploy them as part of the overall security strategy.

Introduction

Computer security is a major topic in computing and many millions of pounds are being spent by organisations in an attempt to keep their systems secure; and by security technology developers in order to improve their products and secure their customers.

This chapter briefly discusses the major technologies available to help make organisations more secure. These are:

- physical disconnection;
- user accounts;
- NAT/PAT;
- firewalls;
- access control lists on a router;
- AAA security;
- Identity Based Networking Services (IBNS) such as 802.1x

Physical disconnection

It is often said that the most secure computer system is one that has no network, is switched off and which is locked away securely, perhaps in a safe. Whilst this is true, such a computer system isn't particularly useful to an organisation. What is needed is an acceptable balance between this extreme security and the need for the organisation to access and use its data.

Such extreme security does provide a useful starting point for evaluating what access to what data with which machine is actually needed. Useful questions can be asked such as:

- Does this machine need to be connected to the network? (Perhaps a PC running software such as pcAnywhere Access Server shouldn't be connected to the corporate network – as it is a potential security risk.)

- Does this machine need access to the whole network? For example should a student's PC in a college have access to the finance network.

- Do all employees need access to all data or can it be limited?

- Does an organisation need to host its own web pages? If they are only static, the risks can be reduced by holding them on a third party server.

- Does everyone need access to the Internet or can they be given access to a restricted set of websites/web pages?

By answering these and similar questions you are able to determine more about the security requirements of the organisation (*see also Chapter 10, Risk assessment*).

User accounts

User accounts are sometimes overlooked as a security technology, but they form an essential part of your overall security policy. If two users share an account and fraud is detected from that account, how do you know who committed the fraud?

User accounts depend on education. You need to make sure that everyone understands the need to have and use their own account and to keep their user ID and password secure.

Accounts also provide the ability to tailor access to information. For example, a clerical assistant in a hospital may be allowed to see names and addresses of patients, but should they be allowed to see detailed medical records for each patient? Only by having everyone use their own accounts can the level of access be controlled.

Access Control Lists on a router

Access Control Lists (**ACLs**) on a router are a means by which traffic can be controlled based upon IP addresses. Traffic can be filtered on source address, destination address and port, giving network managers the ability to prevent unauthorised traffic from reaching a network. *Figure 12.5* shows a college whose student machines have the IP address range 192.168.1.x and whose finance machines have the IP address range 192.168.2.x. Normally traffic from the 192.168.1.x network will be allowed to flow through the router and to reach the 192.168.2.x network which contains the finance server. Placing a correctly configured ACL on router A preventing access to the 192.18.2.x network from the 192.168.1.x will prevent the students from ever being able to reach the finance network. Better still would be to prevent all other networks from accessing the 192.168.2.x network.

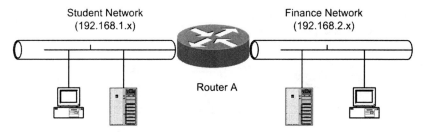

Figure 12.5: A sample college LAN

An ACL is usually placed on an interface. It is preferable to place ACLs as close to the source as possible to prevent traffic traversing the network backbone only to be dropped when it reaches the destination. It is important to realise that an ACL drops the packet; there is simply no reply which gives an element of stealth to the protected network.

VLANs

Whilst the ACL example above prevents unauthorised access to the finance network, it relies on the entire finance department being located in one physical space with only one network serving it. Most modern organisations don't work on this model and instead have functions such as finance distributed across the entire organisation. For example, at the University of Sunderland, finance staff work in each faculty and most buildings. The above example wouldn't support this operation. Instead, a VLAN model is required (*see Chapter 1*), which supports Virtual Local Area Networks across an organisation. *Figure 12.6* shows the same college whose personnel, finance and student groups are spread across many buildings but in this example using VLANs to keep the networks private. The router provides the ability for the VLANs to communicate with each other, but should have ACLs configured to prevent unauthorised access.

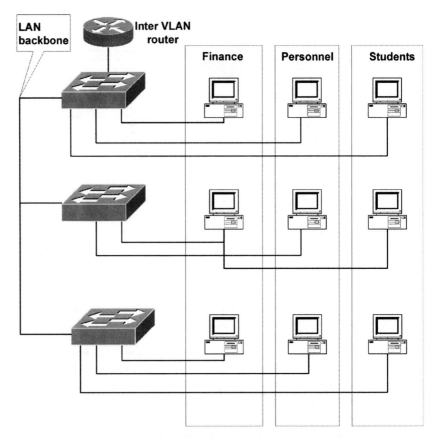

Figure 12.6: Using VLANs and Inter VLAN routing to secure functional areas distributed across an organisation

Network Address Translation (NAT)/Port Address Translation (PAT)

NAT and **PAT** (*see Chapter 3*) are key elements in network security and are used to separate internal and external addressing schemes making it very difficult for a hacker on the outside to gain access to a computer on the inside. *Figure 12.7* shows a typical deployment of NAT. The router sits between the organisation's internal network and the ISP. Computers on the inside of the network are using a private IP address range (as defined by **RFC 1918**). When a computer on the inside network wishes to communicate over the Internet, the router translates the internal private network IP address (192.168.1.1) to the external IP network address (157.228.1.1) – hence the term **network address translation**. The packet originating from 192.168.1.1 cannot be routed over the Internet (as it is a private IP address) and has its source address replaced by that of the router before being placed on the Internet. More importantly for security, this computer cannot be contacted across the Internet. Even if an intruder knew the IP address of the computer, the routers in the Internet are configured not to route private IP addresses. Thus any attempt to contact the computer would not even reach the organisation.

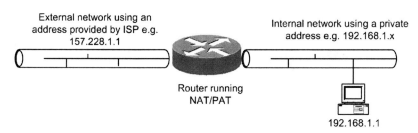

External network using an
address provided by ISP e.g.
157.228.1.1

Internal network using a private
address e.g. 192.168.1.x

Router running
NAT/PAT

192.168.1.1

**Figure 12.7: A router using NAT/PAT connecting
an internal and external network**

Firewall

There are generally three types of firewall available:

- hardware;
- software;
- specialist security appliance.

They are generally placed at the network entrance to an organisation
and are often either built into the border router itself (the so-called
'hardened router'); or are a specialist security appliance (e.g. Cisco
Adaptive Security appliance (**ASA**) range – their predecessors were
called the PIX range (a term still used)), which connects the internal and
the external networks; or are software on a computer. The function of a
firewall is to examine packets (both sourced from internal and external
addresses) and to apply pre-configured security policies to them.
Usually the main function is to prevent hackers and harmful data from
entering the organisation, although they can be configured to examine
packet contents and prevent sensitive data leaving an organisation or
prevent access to websites/traffic that don't meet the organisation's
policy.

Of the three categories, software firewalls are generally considered to
be the weakest. This is because they run upon an operating system that
itself could be compromised. Thus if you had the best software firewall
in the world, it could be defeated by attacking the operating system it
runs on.

Hardware firewalls are much harder to defeat and are usually a router
with an enhanced version of the router operating system. Whilst
such devices are many more times harder to defeat than a software-
based operating system, they are not as tough as a specialist security
appliance.

Specialist security appliances, such as the Cisco ASA range, are designed
from the outset for security with a secure operating system. Unlike
a router that will allow traffic to flow unless configured not to, such
devices usually deny traffic unless configured to allow it, making them
the most secure type of firewall available. *Figure 12.8* shows a properly-
secured organisational network.

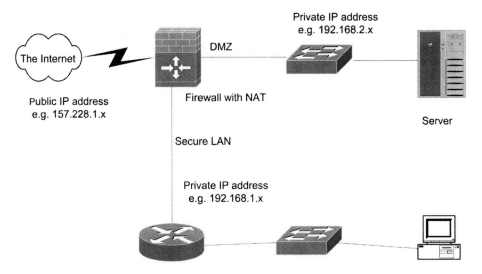

Figure 12.8: A properly-secured organisational LAN

AAA, authentication and syslog servers

Obviously, security can be compromised if intruders manage to obtain access to key networking devices. First and foremost, key networking devices should be physically secure – most can have their passwords reset if you have physical access to them!

Authentication, Authorisation and Accounting (AAA) servers provide security to key networking devices. Using AAA servers, anyone wanting to log into a key networking device must be authenticated by a secure server.

The authentication part of AAA is relatively straightforward – is the user allowed access to this device? Then authorisation determines the level of access the user has to that device, for example whether they are allowed to view or change the configuration. Finally the accounting part writes a secure audit trail of every entry and change that has been made. Often the audit trail has to be written before the change can be made.

There are three types of AAA server:

- **Kerberos**;
- **RADIUS**;
- **TACACS**+.

RADIUS and TACACS+ are the two predominant AAA servers. TACACS+ is Cisco proprietary where RADIUS is open standard.

Syslog servers hold another form of audit trail – normally a key networking device displays a message of every change made on the computer being used to make the change. This information can form a crucial audit trail and so can be copied to a syslog server to give a more permanent record. A syslog server can be nothing more than a piece of software running on a PC (e.g. Kiwi Syslog).

Network Time Servers

In a secure network it is important that the clocks on all network devices are kept synchronised. Any audit trails written to logging devices are much more useful if the time stamp is accurate, providing a means by which the network manager can correlate the audit trail to specific events. **Network Time Servers (NTSs)** use the **Network Time Protocol (NTP)** and are used to synchronise the times on all network devices; the synchronisation usually comes from a satellite using an atomic clock (*see Figure 12.9*).

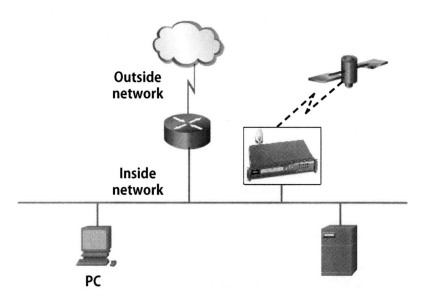

Figure 12.9: Typical NTS usage (image courtesy of Cisco Systems Inc.)

Identity Based Networking Services (IBNS) – 802.1X

It can't be repeated too many times that security is of paramount importance to organisations, and in response to this importance, an IEEE standardised framework has been developed (**IEEE 802.1x**), This really represents an extension to VLAN configuration – you will note from previous discussions of VLAN technology that a port on a switch is assigned to a VLAN either by being configured on that switch or alternatively from looking up the MAC address of the attached PC on a server. Both of these represent a possible security weakness – MAC addresses can now easily be cloned on a PC. Cloning a MAC address of, for example, a finance machine and plugging a laptop into a finance switchport is relatively straightforward and would give an intruder access to the finance network. Although there would be a high degree of physical access required and possibly further authentication, it still does represent a weakness.

802.1X addresses this issue by dynamically allocating the VLAN port based upon the authentication credentials of the user. Thus the user is challenged for authentication – something that only they would know or have (perhaps a username and password) by the network. Following successful authentication the port on the switch (the switchport) the PC is connected to is placed in the correct VLAN for that user. 802.1x is also known as port level authentication. Figure 12.10 shows a typical 802.1x deployment.

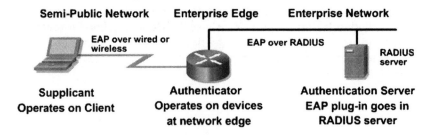

Figure 12.10: Typical 802.1x deployment (image courtesy of Cisco Systems Inc.)

802.1x uses the **Extensible Authentication Protocol (EAP)** to send messages between the PC wanting access to the network (known as the supplicant) through the Authenticator to the Authentication Server. In an 802.1x enabled network the Authenticator (usually a switch) is the point of enforcement for network security. Usually all ports on the Authenticator are placed into an unauthorised mode by default. A user connects or switches on a PC. The Authenticator then challenges the user for authentication using EAP. The Authenticator acts transparently relaying the EAP messages between the Supplicant and the Authentication Server. Following successful authentication, the Authenticator may be given a configuration to enforce policy for that Supplicant. For example, if the user successfully authenticates as a finance user the Authenticator would be configured to allow that Supplicant access to the finance network. If the Supplicant successfully authenticated as a student then the Authenticator would be configured to switch the supplicant to the student network.

Should the supplicant be switched off, the Authenticator will detect this and switch the port into its unauthorised mode. This will also happen if the user logs off sending an EAPOL-logoff message.

802.1x is a widely accepted standard and implementations are available from many vendors.

802.1x can also be used with wireless networks but there can be issues with this. Consider *Figure 12.11*, where two wireless clients are connected to a Wireless Access Point (WAP). If one of the two clients (the Supplicant) successfully authenticates with the Authentication server, then the port on the Authenticator (the Catalyst 2950 switch in *Figure 12.11*) will configured to allow access. Any client then connected to the WAP will also have access. In this model, the WAP is responsible for authenticating clients connected to it. Furthermore, the port will stay authorised until either the authenticating Supplicant logs off or a re-authentication request fails. The solution is to use advanced wireless technology (*see Chapter 8*).

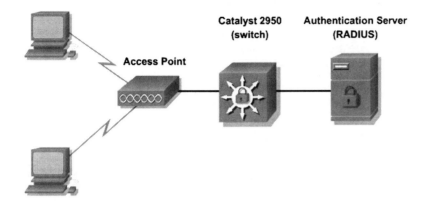

**Figure 12.11: 802.1x operating wirelessly
(image courtesy of Cisco Systems Inc.)**

See also Chapter 8 – Wireless Security.

Quick test

Briefly discuss the major security technologies.

Section 3: End of chapter assessment

Questions

These questions relate to the assessment targets set at the beginning of this chapter. If you can answer them effectively you are in a good position to achieve good credit in assessments or examinations.

1. Outline the need for network security and discuss elements of good practice.

2. Name the major security technologies and for each briefly discuss its operation and detail how it increases security.

Answers

1. As you are aware, computer security is of paramount importance and is cause for concern for most organisations. In answering this question, you need to highlight the critical importance of computer security, which may be helped by making comparisons to a paper-based method.

   You should briefly mention the possible threats to a computer-based system before going on to outline the elements of good practice. I would recommend that you draw the 'security wheel' outlined in *Figure 12.1* and discuss each of the steps. It is important that you highlight that computer security is a continuous process and must be treated as such – don't forget that new threats appear almost daily. Ideally you should also discuss the models for network security.

2.   For each technology you should discuss how the technology operates and how it provides network security. To gain extra marks, highlight any advantages/disadvantages to using the technology and give examples of where the technology could be used and where it should be placed in the network for maximum effect.

You can also impress the assessor by highlighting that the security technologies should be used as part of a co-ordinated security strategy and that by using them piecemeal it is likely to compromise their effect.

Section 4: Further reading and research

Cisco Networking Academy Program (2003), CCNA 3 and 4 *Companion Guide*, (3rd edn). Cisco Press. ISBN: 1-58713-113-7. Chapters 11 and 16 (older but still useful).

Accessing the WAN, CCNA Exploration Labs and Study Guide (2008). Cisco Press. 1-587131-625. Most chapters but especially Chapter 4.

Network Security 1 and 2 Companion Guide (2006). Cisco Press. 1-58713-205-2. Chapter 4.

www.iso.org/iso/home.htm (last accessed 22/6/09).

www.freeradius.org (last accessed 23/6/09)

www.gnu.org/software/radius/radius.html (last accessed 23/6/09).

Glossary

10GE 10 Gigabit Ethernet.

802.1x Network security standard.

ACL Access Control List.

Ad-hoc Wireless infrastructure Wireless network term given to a WLAN which has no access point – just an ad-hoc relationship.

ADSL Asymmetric Digital Subscriber Line.

AES Advanced Encryption Standard – an encryption standard adopted by the US government.

AP Access Point (wireless).

ARP Address Resolution Protocol.

ASCII American Standard Code for Information Interchange.

backbone (cabling) This is the cabling that connects the main network components – for example, switches, routers, etc. It forms the backbone of the network. Sometimes called vertical cabling.

Baseband signalling Signalling which occupies the entire frequency range, e.g. Ethernet.

Baselining Process of determining the level of performance of a network at installation/ following change.

baud The measure of the number of times a signal varies per second. Often confused with bits per second as early systems encoded one bit per signal variation. Modern systems encode multiple bits on a signal variation.

bit Binary digit, a 1 or a 0 – the basic level at which computers operate.

bps Bits per second – a measure of throughput usually related to networks. The number of bits per second that can be/are transferred.

Broadband Term often used to describe high-speed Internet connection.

Broadcast domain Area in which broadcasts can occur on an network.

Broadband signalling Signalling where the frequency range is divided into channels – like radio stations.

Broadcast storm This is an excessive transmission of broadcast packets in a network which can cause serious network performance issues.

BSA Basic Service Area – WLAN term.

BSS Basic Service Set – WLAN term.

BSSID Basic Service Set Identifier – WLAN term.

Cable broadband Broadband supplied through a cable television provider.

Cable modem Device used to connect to a cable broadband connection.

Cat 3 Telephone cable that cannot handle high-speed data. Techniques can be used to improve performance, such as ADSL.

Cat 5 This is the most common form of cabling in networking. Most new buildings are wired using this cable. It is capable of handling data transmission at 100 Mbps.

Cat 5e Category 5 enhanced cable – the current (2009) minimum cable standard for wiring a building.

CIDR	Classless Inter-Domain Routing.
Classful subnetting	Dividing networks into subnetworks at the classful boundary.
Classless subnetting	Dividing networks into subnetworks other than at the classful boundary.
Collision domain	Area in which collision can occur on an Ethernet network.
Contention ratio	Level of over-subscription of a connection (typically broadband).
CRC	Cyclic Redundancy Check – an error-detection mechanism.
Cross over cable	An RJ-45 cable used to connect like devices, e.g. a PC to a PC.
CSMA/CA	Carrier Sense Multiple Access with Collision Avoidance – the protocol used on WLANs.
CSMA/CD	Carrier Sense Multiple Access with Collision Detection – the protocol used on wired Ethernet.
Dictionary attack	Using a dictionary to 'guess' passwords.
DMZ	De-Militarised Zone. Typically a medium level security zone where and organisation would place its web server.
DNS	Domain Name Server – this is the network server that converts the domain part of a URL into an IP address.
Download cap	The maximum amount you are allowed to download.
DSL	Digital Subscriber Line – using telephone cable to send broadband signals.
DSSS	Direct Sequence Spread Spectrum – WLAN modulation technique.
EES	Ethernet Extension Services – extending your Ethernet network across a telecoms provider's network.
EISA	Extended Industry Standard Architecture – a popular architecture used in computers since the 1990s.
EPC	Ethernet Private Circuit – extending your Ethernet network across a telecoms provider's network.
ESA	Extended Service Area – WLAN term.
ESS	Extended Service Set – WLAN term.
Fair use policies	Policy of an ISP regarding what can be downloaded.
flow control	The ability to restrict the flow of information to accommodate slower devices on the network.
FTP	File Transfer Protocol – used to send files across a computer network.
Gbps	Gigabits per second (1000 Mbps).
GE	Gigabit Ethernet.
Horizontal cabling	Cabling from IDF/MDF to desktop.
HSDPA	High Speed Download Packet Access – mobile broadband term.
HSPA	High Speed Packet Access – mobile broadband term.
HSUPA	High Speed Upload Packet Access – mobile broadband term.
HTTP	HyperText Transfer Protocol – used to transfer web pages across a network.
IBNS	Identity Based Networking Services – network security based upon user authentication.
IBSS	Independent Basic Service Set – a WLAN term.

IDF	Intermediate Distribution Facility – a wiring closet where network equipment and wiring is located.
IP	Internet Protocol – the networking protocol that is used on the Internet.
IP number	In version 4 (IPv4), a 4-byte dotted decimal number, e.g. 157.228.102.1, which represents the logical address of a computer on the Internet.
ISA	Industry Standard Architecture – the first internal PC architecture used by IBM-compatible PCs.
ISM	Industrial Scientific Medical frequency bands – used by WLANs.
LES	LAN ExtenSion circuit extending your network across a telecoms provider's network.
LLU	Local Loop Unbundling.
LWAPPs	Lightweight Wireless Access Points.
Mb	Megabits.
MB	Megabytes – different from megabits.
Mbps	Megabits per second – also written as Mbit/s.
MCA	Micro Channel Architecture – an internal PC architecture developed by IBM for its PS/2 and RS6000 range of computers.
MDF	Main Distribution Facility – the first distribution facility in a building where networking equipment is located and wiring terminates. Usually houses POP.
MLS	Multi Layer Switching.
Modular switches	Switches which have a chassis able to accept plug in modules.
NAT	Network Address Translation.
Network diameter	Number of devices a frame must pass through from source to destination.
NTS	Network time server – Device providing the time for NTP.
NIC	Network Interface Card.
NOS	Networked Operating System.
NTP	Network Time Protocol – protocol for synchronising the time on network devices across a network.
OFDM	Orthogonal Frequency Division Multiplexing – WLAN modulation technique.
Parity	An error-detection mechanism – a bit is added to the end of a series of bits (usually a byte) to permit an error in the transmission to be detected.
PAT	Port Address Translation.
PCI	Peripheral Component Interconnect – an Intel-devised internal computer architecture that provides much greater speeds than either ISA or EISA.
PCMCIA	The architecture used by laptops and other small devices – credit card-sized interface cards.
POP	Point-of-Presence – the telephone provider's connection in a building – houses telecommunication and possibly networking equipment.
RSM	Router Switch Module.
SDSL	Symmetric DSL.
Server farm	Centralised location of all an organisation's servers.
SMTP	Simple Mail Transfer Protocol – used by mail servers to exchange email.

SSID	An ID or a name wireless clients can use to distinguish between multiple WLANs in an area.
Stackable switches	Switches which can be interconnected using a special cable giving a higher speed.
STP	Shielded twisted pair cabling – more immune to interference than UTP.
Straight through cable	RJ-45 cable used to connect differing devices, e.g. a PC to a switch.
Subnetting	Process of breaking a network into smaller networks.
TCP	Transmission Control Protocol – the transmission control method used by the Internet.
TFTP	Trivial File Transfer Protocol – used for small files. Less reliable than FTP.
TKIP	Temporal Key Integrity Protocol – a security algorithm (used on WLANs).
URL	Uniform Resource Locator – a web address, e.g. cisco.sunderland.ac.uk.
USB	Universal Serial Bus – a high-speed serial interface.
USB2	A faster version of USB.
UTP	Unshielded Twisted Pair cabling – widely used in modern installations.
Vertical cabling	See *backbone (cabling)*
VLAN	Virtual LAN – a protocol enabling a LAN to be divided into several virtual LANs.
VLANs	Virtual LANs.
VLSM	Variable Length Subnet Masking.
VoIP	Voice over Internet Protocol.
VPN	Virtual Private Network – a protocol for establishing (virtual) private networks over an insecure network, e.g. the Internet.
WAP	Wireless Access Point.
WECA	Wireless Ethernet Compatibility Alliance – later became Wi-Fi Alliance.
WEP	Wired Equivalence Protocol – weak WLAN security standard.
Wi-Fi	Wi-Fi Alliance – a organisation controlling the development and compatibility of wireless Ethernet.
WiMax	A standard for wireless broadband.
Wireless bridge	Using a wireless LAN to bridge two other LANs.
Wireless router	A device combining a router and a wireless access point.
Wiring closet	Closet (at least one per floor) where all the horizontal cables for the floor terminate and connect to network equipment.
WLAN	Wireless Local Area Network – a wire-free networking solution.
WLC	Wireless LAN Controller – device used to control many LWAPPS.
WNIC	Wireless Network Interface Card.
WPA	Wi-Fi Protected Access – a security protocol for WLANs.
WPA2	Wi-Fi Protected Access 2 – a higher security protocol for WLANs.

Index

Lightning Source UK Ltd.
Milton Keynes UK
172262UK00005B/40/P